'There is no wine that is itself alone, for all wine, like all human character (of which wine is the reflection and the symbol) is conditioned by circumstances.'

Hilaire Belloc

# NIGEL BUXTON

# WALKING IN
# WINE
# COUNTRY

*PHOTOGRAPHY BY GLYN WILLIAMS*

WEIDENFELD AND NICOLSON LONDON

# ACKNOWLEDGEMENTS

My thanks are sincerely due in the first instance to France and the French, and especially to the people of rural France. As I hope my readers will readily understand, I have received kindness and help from many more organizations and individuals in the wine business in France than I can now conceivably name. In those circumstances, to select even a few for particular mention here would be invidious, and I can only hope that all those whose cooperation has meant so much to me will regard this book as proof of my appreciation of everything that they have done.

Their number being smaller, I am fortunately able to name at least some of my benefactors in the wine trade in England. More than a few good vintage years ago, David Gilbertson (then of Gonzalez-Byass), Patrick Forbes of Moët et Chandon, Anthony Leschallas of Mentzendorff and Company and John Surtees of Percy Fox and Company gave me a number of introductions that led not only to the first of my walks in viticultural France, but also to connections and friendships which have greatly enriched both my professional and my private life. I shall always be grateful. In more modern times, Nancy Jarratt, Catherine Manac'h (of Food and Wine from France in London), Michael Druitt, Jeremy Roberts, Alan Cheesman and Simon Blower have from time to time set me upon especially rewarding paths. I thank all of them.

In the world of professional travel and tourism my debts of gratitude are again, in general, too many for individual acknowledgement. But again, also, certain sources of help in particular must not go without recognition: first, the French Government Tourist Office and all its staff; second, French Railways, who have unstintingly contributed to the success of numerous journeys; third, Air France and its associated companies in London; and last, but of never-failing professional help and personal friendship, British Airways, whose fine French wines, selected by the likes of Hugh Johnson and Michael Broadbent, have enhanced so many of my travels by air, and who have carried me so often to and from the wine country of France; last, Citroën UK, who – recognizing that for my many reconnaissances in wine country a good set of wheels was often of no less importance than a willing pair of feet – have more than once entrusted me with one of their thoroughly admirable cars. It is no more than the truth to say that without the help of such well-wishers *Walking in Wine Country* would not have been feasible.

Then there are my close publishing colleagues. For the author of a book of this kind a certain embarrassment of attribution is inescapable; he sees his by-line and hears the whole work referred to almost as if it were his alone, yet he knows very well that without the skills and in some instances exceptionally hard labour of a number of other people his own contribution would be worthless. Common decency, therefore, not to dwell on any more personal motivations, requires my thanks to Emma Way of Weidenfeld and Nicolson, who took it upon herself not only to embrace the idea but to work on almost every detail of its realization, and to Barbara Mellor, my editor, whose professionalism has been an instructive and salutary pleasure to experience. The appearance of the book speaks for itself, and to have had the opportunity of working with Glyn Williams, who took the pictures, and Kenneth Carroll, who designed the *tout ensemble*, is something of which any writer might be proud. Steven Spurrier very kindly made time to look over the proofs with his wine consultant's eye, and saved me as far as

possible from gross idiocies on the subject in which he is so expert; any errors that persist are mine alone.

Finally, thanks are due to my friend and sometime Fleet Street colleague Andrew Duncan, who at a crucial moment gave me invaluable advice and encouragement, and to my wife, who long before the walking was done and the micro-chips took over typed many thousands of words on the sort of machine that the museums are now scrambling for. Her rewards have never been the equal of her labours.

**Editorial note** Most of the people who feature in one way or another in this work do so under their proper names. When I have quoted anything they may have said I have been as faithful as possible to the reality, but I have not sought their permission for such quotations and they themselves are not in any way responsible for them. In cases where I have judged that identification of individuals might entail even the slightest risk of embarrassment for them, I have given such persons fictional names and may possibly have modified certain other details that could conceivably lead to recognition.

Copyright text © Nigel Buxton 1993
Copyright photographs © Glyn Williams 1993
Copyright maps © George Weidenfeld and Nicolson Ltd 1993
Copyright photographs © Nigel Buxton 1993 on pages 50, 80, 88, 95, 98, 99, 101, 139, 160, 170, 188, 196, 198, 206, 232.

First published in 1993 by George Weidenfeld and Nicolson Ltd, Orion House, 5 Upper St Martin's Lane, London WC2H 9EA

British Library Cataloguing-in-Publication Data. A catalogue record for this book is available from the British Library.

Edited by Barbara Mellor
Maps by Line + Line
Designed by Carroll Associates

Typeset in Great Britain by Keyspools Ltd.
Printed and bound in Italy by L.E.G.O. Vicenza

# CONTENTS

# AUTHOR'S NOTE

This book is about two of my greatest sources of pleasure, walking and wine, and the special way in which the one hugely enhances enjoyment of the other. The main part of the text consists of narrative descriptions of walks I have made over a number of years in all the major wine-making areas of France; this is supplemented by more factual information about the walking and the wine in the various regions, including actual itineraries and brief notes about the wines themselves.

There is no end to publications about wine: some very good, some rather bad, some indifferent. What any serious author on the subject soon discovers and will readily acknowledge is the virtual impossibility at any given time of knowing or writing about – or having the time or the space to publish – all there is to know about this or that particular kind of wine, let alone about wine in general. As a result, wine *country* is seldom written about at all, and for most people wine itself has become almost entirely divorced from its essential territorial origins. *Walking in Wine Country* has no pretensions to being another treatise on wine *per se*, but simply and less ambitiously an attempt to put wine – French wine – into a practical, revealing and rewarding perspective.

The sections entitled 'The lie of the land' attempt to give a useful idea of the general topography of each area. The notes about specific walks, either experienced by me or suggested as being feasible, should additionally help the reader in making a choice of itinerary among the many possibilities for walks that most regions offer.

There are important qualifications, however. These notes are intended only as a practical addition to the narrative description of my own experiences, or as ideas for the sort of walks that might seem worth investigating in greater detail. The route directions derive from notes made 'in the field' and from memory in conjunction with a study of the appropriate maps, which except in one or two rare instances have been the 1:25,000 sheets published by the IGN. But no matter how specific such directions appear to be, they have no claims to infallibility, and are in no case a substitute for the would-be walker's own sensible planning. The maps indicate vineyard areas, principal towns and villages and approximate routes of walks taken. There are also references to the appropriate 1:25,000 IGN sheets.

As the notes on individual walks are intended as accessories to the larger business of planning walking itineraries in the wine regions, so the sections concerning the wines themselves are offered as helpful glances at a subject which to be usefully understood requires a far closer study, and which is well served by a large and specific body of wine literature. At the back of the book, I list and comment upon a selection of what seem to me some of the best wine books in print, or worth trying to find. In addition, I give likely sources of information about French wine and visiting the wine regions.

# INTRODUCTION

One evening, dining with friends in London, I was invited by my host (who shares my view that such guessing games, if not taken too seriously, can be both instructive and fun) to identify the red wine that we were drinking. I pretended to give the matter careful thought: holding the glass up to the light, swirling and inhaling and 'chewing' as advised by the experts, making thoughtful noises, and so on and so (as I hoped) intelligently and impressively forth. In fact, I had known the answer quite quickly; not through skill or cleverness, but largely because I had bought a few bottles of the same wine some months before at the domaine in Languedoc where it had been made.

I had arrived at the domaine in the course of a walk in spring in one of the most attractive parts of the Minervois. The owner and his wife – he the wine-maker, she the business manager – had been surprised and pleased that a visitor should have arrived on foot at their somewhat remote property and had received me very kindly. We had tasted in the cellars and talked a lot, and after a while I had gone on my way a good deal more knowledgeable about the wines of the Minervois than I had been before, and with my rucksack heavier by a bottle of cold rosé that I was looking forward to drinking with a picnic. Next day I returned by car and bought some of the domaine's red to take home.

Now, with the wine from that same domaine in my glass at my friends' dinner table in London, recollections of France crowded in on me: the sun on my face in the early morning; the scents of wild thyme and sage and acacia; the cistus and honeysuckle in the *garrigue*; the cuckoo calling. I recalled the sun-crisped bread (the *baguette* had been travelling on top of my pack) and the pâté and the cheese for lunch in the foothills of the Montagne Noire. The wine was nowhere near being 'great', but it was a good, honest one of individual character; drinking it again, I thought of the wine-maker and his wife, both of whom had been individuals of marked and agreeable personality. I saw their centuries-old château and the yellow broom on the borders of the vineyard, and remembered how beautifully cold had been the water with which I had replenished my flask.

That wine had meant something else to me, too: the walk that day in the Minervois, though by no means the first of its kind, had been the first that I had undertaken with the purpose of what was to become *Walking in Wine Country* specifically in mind. Alone up there in the *garrigue* I had unstintingly celebrated the fact with the cold rosé, looking out across the vines and thinking that, for a writer by trade, the road to a purposeful use of something I liked so much had been a curiously long one.

The walking had come before the wine. A romantic idea of walking almost certainly began with my mother's stories of her solitary adventures as a small girl in the Welsh hills, and with imagery such as that of Robert Louis Stevenson's 'The Vagabond':

*Give to me the life I love,*        *Bed in the bush with stars to see,*
*Let the lave go by me,*              *Bread I dip in the river –*
*Give the jolly heaven above*        *There's the life for a man like me,*
*And the byway nigh me.*             *There's the life for ever.*

For a country child who liked to be out in all weathers it was powerful stuff.

In my schooldays the infant romantic fancy was nurtured by superior tales of high adventure: James Fenimore Cooper, whose characters went fleet of foot through the forests or trekked across the great prairies of America; Walter Scott and John Buchan, both of whom brought the drove roads and heather-covered moors of the Scottish borders and highlands into a south-of-England bedroom. Later there came Bunyan, Borrow, Wordsworth, Keats and Coleridge; Rousseau, Balzac and Ruskin: romantics and walkers all.

What contribution, if any, this unscholarly mishmash of influences made to the predilections of adult life it is hard to say, but walking became something like a passion. Year after year, season in and season out, I walked the South Downs of my native Sussex. I walked on the Great Ridgeway and in the Scottish borders and highlands and Welsh Marches. I walked the coastal paths of Wales and Devon and Cornwall and on long trails in western Canada and America. I walked in the foothills of the Drakensberg in South Africa and through the Kalinkandaki valley in Nepal. Then one spring came the coincidence of circumstances that led straight to the wine country of France.

I was going walking again on the Sussex Downs. The post came as I was leaving the house and I put several letters in my pocket to open on the train. One of them was an invitation to spend a weekend at a château belonging to one of the big champagne houses not far from Epernay. That day, too, and not for the first time by any means, I had a paperback edition of Hilaire Belloc's classic *The Path to Rome* in my pack and was reading it as I lunched in a little sheltered hollow overlooking the Weald. Early in his walk, passing through Belfort at the foot of the Vosges, Belloc comes across a ramshackle house offering 'open' wine for sale:

*'Choosing the middle price, at fourpence a quart, I said, "Pray give me a hap'orth in a mug." This the woman at once did, and when I came to drink it, it was delicious . . . lifting the heart, satisfying, and full of all those things wine merchants talk of, bouquet, and body, and flavour. . . . So I bought a quart of it, corked it up very tight, put it in my sack, and held it in store against the wineless places . . .'*

France, wine and walking! There on the Sussex chalk

with a breeze off the Channel and the sun and the sound of larks and the scent of the turf, how I fancied myself suddenly on the long byways of France with all that I needed in a pack on my back, sleeping out as the occasion warranted, buying my wine when opportunity offered, as Belloc had done. Instead of being met by car at the airport in Paris (the big champagne firms tend to do things in style), why not take the train from Paris to Epernay, and by a circuitous route walk to a weekend of good food, good wine and good company that would be even more enjoyable for the exercise? I had already acquired a considerable taste for the wines of Champagne; now I improved it hugely by a down-to-earth acquaintance with the chalk hills, woods, valleys and villages of the Marne. It was the first step in what was to be a whole new experience of walking and wine and France, the beginning of a relationship from which *Walking in Wine Country* was to be born.

Other walks in other wine-making regions of France soon followed; not at this time with any notions of a systematic association of subjects in mind, but because more and more I derived great personal satisfaction – physical, emotional, intellectual – from them. Most of the vineyards of France are in some of the most obviously beautiful parts of the whole incomparably beautiful land: Alsace, Savoy and the Jura, the Loire, Burgundy, the Rhône valley, Provence, Languedoc, Gascony and Aquitaine. Wine country means the foothills of the mountains: the Vosges, the Alps, the Massif Central, the Pyrenees. It means great rivers and their scores of tributaries. It is thousands of square miles of accessible, topographically varied terrain, with roads if one needs them, but also with an infinity of traffic-free byways and paths if one does not. It means a wealth of still-beguiling, very ancient towns and villages and some of the most impressive cities in Europe. Moved by a love of walking and wine and all the other civilized things of life, a person could live as long as Methuselah and still not exhaust the pleasures of France.

'The more I have learned about wine in the course of a quarter of a century of enjoyment, the more I have realized that it weaves in with human history from its very beginnings as few, if any, other products do,' says Hugh Johnson in his masterly and enthralling *The Story of Wine*. If there is romance in walking, there is even more in wine. It is older than European civilization itself. It is history. It is art. It is literature from the Bible to Belloc. In France it is abbeys and monasteries and churches and castles. It is great châteaux and fine mansions and sturdy farmhouses and not a few even humbler dwellings that look as if they have changed little since the time of Charlemagne. Romance? Wine – good wine – may involve mechanical harvesters and computers and stainless steel and factory-like *cuveries*; but

good wine – individual wine worth tasting with interest and talking about – in France is more likely still to mean pickers in colourful variety hard at work by hand and eagerly sitting down to hearty harvest luncheons and dinners. In countless domaines from the Vosges to Mont Ventoux, from Bordeaux to Bandol, it still means very old timber presses (and even grapes being trodden barefoot) as well as state-of-the-art hydraulic contrivances. There is stainless steel in plenty, of course, but there is still oak enough in the form of vats and casks, often in medieval cellars, to satisfy the most starry-eyed romantic.

No less, and perhaps above all, wine is people: people and their good husbandry; people and their labour and skill and love and traditions and respect and ambition and imagination and pride. More and more I seriously doubt if dull or fundamentally disagreeable people are capable of making interesting, thoroughly enjoyable wine. So from one appellation to another, from Ammerschwihr to Aguilar, from the Médoc to Mont-Ste Victoire, I walked my way to new experiences and pleasures of wine. The more I walked in wine country, the more I saw that although I had supposed myself to be fairly knowledgeable on the subject, almost all wines, even very famous ones, had until recently been little more to me than beverages in bottles, distinguishable – the best-known ones – by reputation, but very largely only by their intrinsic qualities, and by price. Rarely was I able to put a landscape, let alone any other detail of origin, to a label, no matter how illustrious the name on it. In this, like most people, I had been ignoring an enormous potential of pleasure.

Now things were different. Now Fleurie, for example, once merely one of the better wines of the Beaujolais as far as I was concerned, was a village I had looked down over from a long, lazy hillside picnic. Gigondas was no longer just a name among what were said to be good-value wines from the Rhône (whatever *that* really signified), but another village, this time at the feet of the pre-Alps, where on a hot September day I drank gratefully from a communal fountain before visiting a wine-maker who sent me on my way with a bottle of his '85 to drink with lunch high among the Dentelles de Montmirail. Good wine is good wine, but it is even better when the name on the bottle becomes also hawthorn in bloom on the hills of Sancerre, or the blessing of shade at high summer in the vineyards of Bandol, or the wild beauty of the high Corbières.

Famous names are few and far between in the wine racks of my one-time coal cellar, but to such as there are I am now able to put pictures far more informative and evocative than the labels; and no matter how the wines themselves may age, they constitute a treasury of souvenirs that will become more valuable as time goes by.

# ALSACE

## INTRODUCTION

Hidden away in the extreme north-west corner of the country, off the main routes between the English Channel and the most popular holiday areas of the Continent, Alsace is far from being one of the better known names among the wine-making regions of France. All too many people, indeed, think it is in Germany. Strasbourg, Colmar and Mulhouse are the cities to look for on the map, the first and last, 110 kilometres (70 miles) apart, roughly marking the northern and southern ends respectively of the island of mountainous country that is the Vosges. The great plains of northern France, including Champagne, are to the west. The Rhine and Germany are to the east.

The viticultural region lies partly in the department of the Bas-Rhin ('Bas' because it is lower down the river) and partly in the Haut-Rhin. The area highlighted here is that which is generally regarded as the heart of the whole Alsace vineyard, and lies in the Haut-Rhin. It is doubtful if anywhere more closely resembles the popular idea and the romantic ideal of wine country.

Colmar is the wine capital for which the somewhat surprising claim is officially made of being the driest place in France after Perpignan. The high Vosges, it seems, collect most of the moisture carried by west winds. Summers are usually very warm; autumns blessed with long, sunny days; winters healthily cold, but seldom severe. Micro-climates – so significant to the vigneron, so mysterious to the rest of us – abound.

---

*A vineyard of Riesling outside the village of Rodern. Many of the grapes of the commune are vinified in nearby Ribeauvillé, at the oldest coopérative in France.*

---

# BRIEFING

## THE LIE OF THE LAND

Occupying a narrow band of territory seldom more than two or three kilometres (a mile or two) wide along the eastern slopes of the Vosges; overlooked by forests and castles on the modest yet imposing heights; looking to the neighbouring Rhine, and beyond that great river to the western slopes of the Black Forest, the gently rolling acres of the vineyards of Alsace are interspersed with villages and small towns unsurpassed for picturesqueness by any in viticultural Europe.

Closely populated and intensively cultivated for centuries, this land between the Vosges and the Rhine has nothing of the wildness of the Corbières, the topographical tedium of so much of the region of Bordeaux, the intricacy of Provence. Rather, it is like some great, well-managed public park: neatly tended, but not over-ornamented; well-ordered, but not over-organized. Unlike – say – the northern Rhône, its vineyard paths are physically undemanding: there is no need here for the agility of a mountain goat.

## WALKS

It is the wine villages, with their great and particular charm, which make the experience of walking in the Alsace wine country unique. Moreover there are never more than three kilometres (just under two miles), and usually not more than two (just over one mile), between one wine village and the next. And the going is all open, with not a single forest or extensive wood to be negotiated and no need to have recourse to busy hard-top roads.

**Kintzheim to Turckheim:** 24 kilometres/15 miles; allow 7 hours.
So many are the paths between one village and the next that detailed direction-finding information is unnecessary, it is perhaps most helpful to list the villages on the itinerary in the order in which they are encountered, since except between Riquewihr and Kientzheim (note the spelling) it would be almost perverse to seek to avoid them. They are, from north to south: Kintzheim (*sic*), Orschwiller, St Hippolyte, Rodern, Rorschwihr, Bergheim, Ribeauvillé, Hunawihr, Riquewihr, Kientzheim (Kaysersberg), Ammerschwihr, Katzenthal, Niedermorschwihr and Turckheim. By taking the most direct route between Riquewihr and Kientzheim one is denying oneself the pleasure of visiting Beblenheim, Mittelwihr, Bennwihr and Sigolsheim (where there is a sanctuary for storks).

**Maps**

| | | | |
|---|---|---|---|
| 1:25,000 | 3717 ouest | Sélestat | includes Haut Koenigsbourg |
| | 3717 est | Sélestat | includes Kintzheim |
| | 3718 ouest | Colmar | includes St Hippolyte and Turckheim |
| | 3719 ouest | Guebwiller | includes Eguisheim |
| 1:50,000 | 3717 | Sélestat | includes Haut Koenigsbourg |
| | 3718 | Colmar | |
| | IGN Carte des Vosges: Colmar – Munster – Gerardmer – St Dié; published by Le Club Vosgien. Covers main wine area and most of Vosges. | | |
| 1:100,000 | 31 | | |

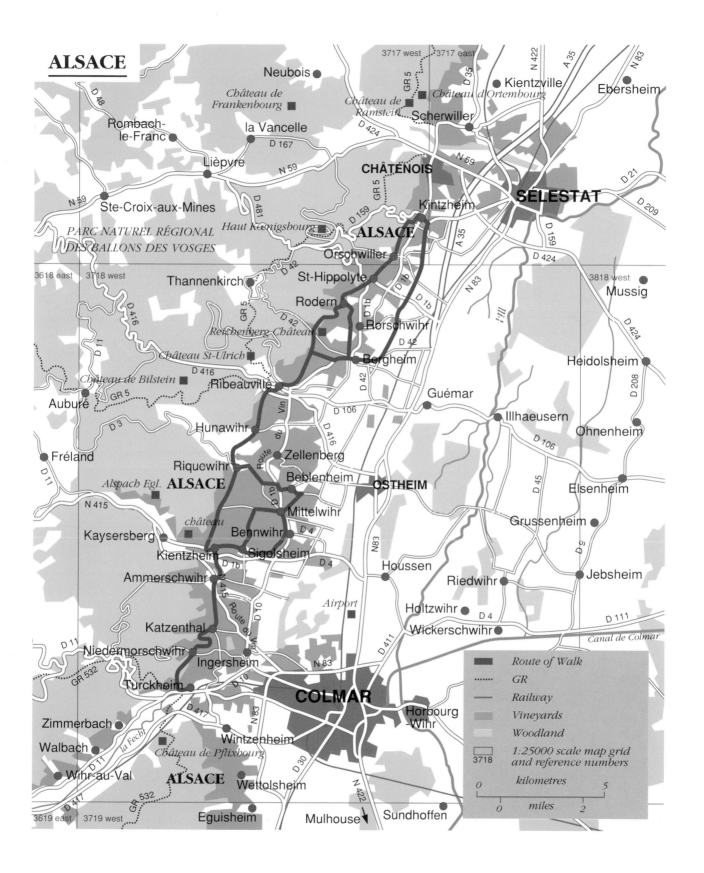

# ALSACE

Neubois

Château de Frankenbourg

la Vancelle

Rombach-le-Franc

D 167

Lièpvre

N 59

CHÂTÉNOIS

Ste-Croix-aux-Mines

N 59

PARC NATUREL RÉGIONAL DES BALLONS DES VOSGES

Haut Koenigsbourg

ALSACE

Orschwiller

Thannenkirch

St-Hippolyte

Rodern

Reichenberg-Château

Château St-Ulrich

Bergheim

Château de Bilstein

Ribeauvillé

Aubure

Hunawihr

Fréland

Zellenberg

Riquewihr

Beblenheim

ALSACE

Alspach Egl.

Mittelwihr

N 415

château

Bennwihr

Kaysersberg

Sigolsheim

Kientzheim

D 4

Ammerschwihr

Katzenthal

Niedermorschwihr

Ingersheim

Turckheim

Zimmerbach

Walbach

Wintzenheim

Château de Pflixbourg

Wihr-au-Val

ALSACE

Wettolsheim

Eguisheim

Neubois

3717 west  3717 east

GR 5

Château de Ramstein

Château d'Ortembourg

Scherwiller

Kientzville

Ebersheim

N 422  A 35  N 83

D 35

SÉLESTAT

D 21

D 209

D 159

D 424

Mussig

3818 west

Borschwihr

D 1b

D 42

Heidolsheim

D 208

Guémar

Illhaeusern

Ohnenheim

D 106

D 45

Elsenheim

OSTHEIM

Grussenheim

D 9

Houssen

Riedwihr

Jebsheim

Holtzwihr

D 4

Wickerschwihr

D 111

Canal de Colmar

COLMAR

Horbourg-Wihr

Sundhoffen

Mulhouse

| | Route of Walk |
| --- | --- |
| | GR |
| | Railway |
| | Vineyards |
| | Woodland |
| 3718 | 1:25000 scale map grid and reference numbers |

kilometres
0 — 5

miles
0 — 2

17

# AUTUMN AMONG
# THE WINE VILLAGES

*As is commonplace in Alsace, though rare elsewhere in France, the vines in this Hunawihr vineyard are trained to over a metre and a half (five feet) high. The harvest usually begins about the middle of October, but may continue into November. For maximum sugar and flavour, the later the picking the better.*

Ribeauvillé at half past ten on a so-far-unpromising October morning: 'Entry to the vineyards is forbidden on pain of prosecution' warned a notice; but I confidently took this to refer to wheeled vehicles, not pedestrians, and went on up into the vines. The sun appeared briefly and I paused to admire the exceptionally attractive medieval town with its backdrop of vine-covered slopes and the wooded heights where the silhouette of Haut Koenigsbourg dominated the horizon, then quickened my step. Though I had risen very early in the Tour Hôtel with the intention of making my way to Haut Koenigsbourg, no more than two hours' walk to the north, the weather had been awful and I knew that my calculations of time and distance would have to be revised. I had waited an hour or more for the rain to stop, then gloomily set out, hoping for the best, but knowing that I would simply have to take things as they came.

Of all the wine regions of France, none receives more published praise for the quality of its food than Alsace, and though breakfast was past, and neither the weather forecast nor the sky offered much hope of an enjoyable out-of-doors picnic, I was still devilishly tempted by the food shops of Ribeauvillé. '*Hubert Siedel: Boucherie, Charcuterie Fine, Fromage . . .*' promised the sign above a shop in the Grande Rue, and within were sumptuous dis-

plays of hams and sausages of noble proportions and rich complexions, cheeses in astonishing variety of size, colour and texture, pyramids of 'home-bottled' fruits, and walls of wine. Outside a nearby greengrocer's, half a dozen species of mushroom, evidently freshly gathered from the forests of the Vosges, clamoured for the sort of cookery that according to the guidebooks is one of the glories of the region, but which in my own experience remains elusive. A few paces further on a shop window was entirely filled with a display of bottles labelled *framboise* and *fraise* and *mirabelle* and *poire Williams*: Alsace's famous *alcools blancs*.

The vines press close against the walls of Ribeauvillé, as of most other places in the wine country of Alsace, and within a few minutes I was among them, looking down and back on the town. Some four kilometres (two and a half miles) south of Ribeauvillé, home to the celebrated wine firm of Trimbach, was Riquewihr, and the no-less-famous firm of Dopff-au-Moulin, whom I already knew. Double that modest distance would bring me to Kaysersberg, Domaine Weinbach, and Colette Faller – yet another renowned wine-maker on whom I intended calling. Barely three hours' easy going further south still, past Colmar, would see me in Eguisheim, where I wanted to meet the very highly regarded family firm of Léon Beyer. Making some 24 kilometres (15 miles) in all, this had seemed a not-unreasonable plan for what I had hoped might be a fine early autumn day. But now? Suddenly, as if in answer to my unspoken prayer, the sun came out again. It was only a week from harvest time and I strode on down the firm track with high hopes for the grape-pickers and for finding somewhere in Hunawihr where I would be able to have a glass of wine.

I did not notice the name of the *caveau*, if it had one, but I did make a record of the wines I tasted: a Sylvaner ('not wild about it'); a Riesling ('good, very dry') and a Gewürztraminer ('delicious'). The effect of the wine was to remind me that I had breakfasted very lightly, and when the amiable *patronne* suggested that I ought to try a little Munster cheese ('*C'est de la région et se comporte très bien avec le Gewürz*') I made no resistance. She was right. The spicy (*Gewürz* is German for spice), aromatic, intensely fruity Gewürztraminer and the powerful, creamy cheese went marvellously well together. The postman arrived on his rounds and was given a glass of wine, apparently as a matter of course. I ought, he said, to go up into the mountains some day to see where the best farmhouse Munster was made.

Finishing my wine, I walked up to Hunawihr's famous fortified church, passing on the way a little courtyard where the open door, with the date 1576 carved on its lintel in eroded antique figures, revealed a copper still with its fire burning brightly. A heady scent of pear brandy filled the air. I paused for a while, hoping that someone would appear who might talk to me about distillation, but – characteristic of rural France at one o'clock in the afternoon – the impression it gave of a place deserted was undisturbed.

The church cemetery gives direct access to the slopes, appositely named Hinter Kirch. After about a kilometre and a half (one mile) I was walking on sand and sea pebbles, almost like a beach. For anyone versed in the

*The wine villages of Alsace are invariably bright with geraniums, and the shops, such as this* boucherie-charcuterie *in St Hippolyte, are full of tempting displays of local produce – perfect for picnic lunches.*

wines of Alsace this was not far short of hallowed ground: the Schoenen-bourg slope, planted exclusively with Riesling, and no less illustrious in Alsace than the Johannisberg hillside in the Rheingau or the Clos de Bèze in Burgundy. Dopff-au-Moulin and Hügel both own holdings here. And at the foot of the slope, astride the Sembach stream where it emerges from the confines of the Grosstal, is one of the prettiest wine towns in the world.

At weekends and for all but a few months of the year, Riquewihr is invaded by tourists, yet still it inspires affection. That a certain amount of less than lovable wine flows in its most popular places of refreshment and entertainment I do not doubt, but a lot of fun seems to flow with it; a lot of *Gemütlichkeit*. That it has survived at all is wondrous. Century after century, no part of the great battlefield that is northern France has known more destructive wars than Alsace: yet more than half of the present town was built before the beginning of the seventeenth century and the appalling Thirty Years War that engulfed Europe in savagery.

For more than seven centuries, from the dissolution of Charlemagne's empire in 870 until the end of the Thirty Years War in 1648, Alsace was German. Ceded then to France, it was annexed by Prussia in 1871 after the Franco-Prussian War and not repossessed by France until 1918. Seven centuries of possession or influence have left their mark, and in architecture (most obviously and overwhelmingly, with its half-timbering, Renaissance ornamentation, and sensual extravagance), art, and virtually every other aspect of cultural life, the Germanic past of the region is inescapable. Take a traveller familiar with Germany but never before in France, put him to sleep and wake him in Riquewihr, and it is all of a case of Louis Roederer to a litre of Liebfraumilch that he will at first suppose himself to be still on the eastern side of the great river frontier.

On this autumn day I came steeply down the hillside where men were clipping foliage from the vines in preparation for the *vendange* (to make the grapes more accessible), and so through the north gate of Riquewihr and into a throng of tourists and a scent of vanilla from the pastry shops, and of

*Like all the vineyards of Alsace, Rodern benefits from long, sunny autumns. The later the harvest the greater the concentration of natural sugar in the grapes: hence Alsace's famous Vendange Tardive wines.*

grilled sausage. Many of the tourists were German women of a certain age with bare legs and business-like walking boots and bright socks and smart knee-breeches. All carried small rucksacks with anoraks neatly rolled on top. Once or twice, one of them gave me a comradely '*Guten Tag*'.

I did not linger in busy Riquewihr. Hardly 500 metres from the very heart of the town, up in the vines again, the peace and quiet were profound and the views superb. To south and west lay the grand, rolling vistas of the vineyard slopes and the wooded foothills and valleys and the far-off heights of the Vosges: the Hohneck and the Grand Ballon, I supposed. Eastwards, 50 or 60 kilometres (say 30 or 40 miles) away, beyond the Alsatian plain and the Rhine, were the dark heights of the Black Forest. To the south and east, further away still, loomed the indistinct mass of the Jura. Without the sun, the landscapes seemed sombre. I thought about the battle of the Colmar Pocket in the awful winter of 1944: the desperate fighting that had left so much of this now so peaceful wine country in ruins. Just over a kilometre away, beyond the shoulder of the Mont de Sigolsheim, was the necropolis where the remains of some 1600 French soldiers, casualties of that time, are interred. On the western side of the Vosges, near Epinal, more than 5000 Americans are buried. Below lay Beblenheim and Mittelwihr and Benn-wihr, all more or less devastated in that winter of 1944, all renowned for their wines. Soon it began to rain. It was now mid-afternoon, and as before breakfast I had abandoned Haut Koenigsbourg, so now I gave up Eguisheim.

In wilder country there might be a satisfaction to be derived from braving the elements; in the well-ordered, peaceful, undemanding vineyards of Alsace such heroics seemed out of place. Collected from a rendezvous outside the post office in Kaysersberg, I was taken back to Riquewihr and the Dopff-au-Moulin cellars, where we tasted a Riesling or two, and a Gewürztraminer. There was a lot of talk as the evening drew on and my sense of wellbeing after even so short a walk as I had accomplished that day improved by the minute. Then, just when I thought we had finished tasting and were about to go to dinner, my host went off in order to return with a solemn look and a half-bottle of something that he proceeded to open without comment. It was a lovely golden wine with a 'nose', a fragrance, that instantly signalled something very special. Its taste was a luscious yet wholly uncloying sweetness of the kind one expects from a great sauternes such as a Château d'Yquem or from a German Trockenbeerenauslese. 'Sélection des Grains Nobles, '83,' said Monsieur Dopff. A Sélection des Grains Nobles is made in especially favourable years when the grapes have been left on the vine long enough to be affected by the *Botrytis cinerea* fungus: '*la pourriture noble*' or 'noble rot'. The very high concentration of natural sugar is balanced by an appropriate degree of acidity to give a wine that at its best ought to be drunk almost reverently, and certainly on its own. 1983 was a remarkable year, and what my host had so generously given me was a very remarkable and rare wine. By the time we had finished the half-bottle it was not far from dark outside.

*More than half of Riquewihr, built before the seventeenth century, managed to survive the centuries of savage wars and destruction.*

# SUMMER
# BENEATH THE VOSGES

It was the following July. Rising soon after the sun, I had walked up the hill to the north of Riquewihr and back again before breakfast. At half past seven I was sitting on the terrace of the Hôtel Schoenenbourg with a *café complet*, hoping that the weather forecast in *Le Figaro* – set fair for several days – was to be relied upon. Soon after nine o'clock, when my taxi dropped me on the outskirts of Kintzheim, some dozen kilometres (seven or eight miles) to the north, I was wondering with some apprehension just how hot it was going to be. That day's walk back to Riquewihr through the vines left me with the conviction that nowhere that I know more closely resembles the popular idea and the romantic ideal of wine country than the wine country of Alsace. Except for one short diversion through the forest, and for the villages themselves, hardly a hundred continuous metres of the path were not borderd by the growing vines. And from time to time, wishing to go higher up or lower down the slope, I would simply walk between the rows, glad of the shade, resting once on a cool, green carpet of vine leaves left lying after the trimming that went on throughout the vineyards at that time of year – sometimes by machine, more often than not by hand, with secateurs or shears. Surely, I twice asked provocatively, the pruning ought to have been done much earlier in the year? Oh no, the workers replied: this pruning was not being done to determine how many fruit-bearing shoots would be left to develop; it was to get rid of excess foliage that would otherwise use up nourishment which ought to be going to the grapes and that would keep the fruit too much in the shade. Sometimes, walking along the cool, leafy aisles of vines that typically were a metre and a half (over five feet) high, I seemed to be bathed in a blue-green light, reflected by the copper sulphate solution with which the vines are periodically sprayed against mildew and oidium. In the vineyards there is generally something going on.

It was easy walking: never so steep as seriously to test limbs or lungs; never, except for that one excursion through the forest, demanding careful attention to either map or compass. To my right was always the guiding line of the Vosges; to my left, the wide plain and valley of the Rhine. Village succeeded village, always within sight of one another, never more than a kilometre or two apart. Unadventurous it may have been, but never dull – not unless sunshine and birdsong and a woodpecker and a brace of hares and the wild flowers and the scent of summer are dull. Not unless it was dull to look up at the ruins of castle and watch-tower on the forest-covered heights and think of the centuries of war and turbulent peace that they had seen. Not unless it was tedious to see village squares and streets, innocent of litter and almost all other ugliness, bright with geraniums (everywhere geraniums), tempting with invitations to *dégustations*, direct from the wine-maker's own premises in timbered and cobbled courtyards.

*Riquewihr is one of the prettiest wine towns in the world. In spite of the savagery of past wars, more than half of the existing buildings date from before the beginning of the seventeenth century.*

*Johnson and Duijker recommend
the wine-maker Koeberlé-Kreyer
in the village of Rodern.*

In St Hippolyte was a geranium-decked fountain with a stone basin painted bright blue on the inside, and a carp and goldfish swimming in it. A notice on the spout from which very cold, brilliantly clear water flowed said '*eau potable*', a rare phenomenon even in those parts. I took a supply, then, tempted by smells of roast chicken and smoked ham, and took my turn in a crowded '*boucherie-charcuterie*' where half the other customers seemed to be speaking in the Alsace dialect. Now for wine. Johnson and Duijker recommended a wine-maker in the village of Rodern: 'Koeberlé-Kreyer; Charles Koehly & Fils: Christian Koehly makes fine, stylish wines . . .' The path I took across the verdant little valley of the Eckenbach stream led down from what must have been all of 28 degrees Celsius into a brief but delicious *fraîcheur*, then up again into the noonday glare. Fearing the approach of lunch and with it closing time, I hurried along, almost trotting down the last short slope before the village before toiling briskly up the other side to arrive breathless and perspiring in the attractive Koeberlé-Kreyer courtyard as the church clock struck twelve.

Nobody was about, but an electronic alarm had sounded as I entered the courtyard, and now a bespectacled, grey-haired head appeared at an upstairs window. '*Monsieur?*'

'*Bonjour madame. Je voudrais acheter du vin, si ça ne vous dérangera pas trop.*'

'*Pas du tout, Monsieur. Pas du tout. Je serai avec vous dans un petit instant.*' In a cool and spacious ground-floor room she took already uncorked bottles of Riesling and Pinot Blanc from a refrigerator and poured generously. Both wines, but the Riesling in particular, seemed to me more than delicious. Here again was the lovely, clean, cool freshness of a summer morning. There was no conscientious or ritualistic 'nosing', swirling, 'chewing' or spitting. Emptying both glasses, I asked to buy a bottle of each wine, wrapped the Pinot Blanc up well inside my rucksack and went out again into a village abandoned to the heat, and to a tabby cat asleep on an upturned cask. A few hundred metres took me up a forest track into the trees. Another kilometre and a half (one mile) led down into the wooded valley of the Bergenbach stream; yet another up and out on to the edge of the wide, sweeping, vine-covered Kirchberg slope overlooking Ribeauvillé. It was past one o'clock and high time for lunch, but what to do for indispensable shade? Scant space is surrendered to anything but vines on the best slopes of viticultural Alsace, but soon, on a little knoll, I found a lone, well-laden walnut tree closely hedged in by vines on three sides but commanding a view of the plain. Luxuriously extended in the long grass, boots off, shirt unbuttoned, rejoicing in a gentle, heaven-sent breeze, I poured myself a glass, and then another, of what seemed at the time, and for all I know may indeed have been, one of the most delicious Pinot Blancs in the world. Then I fell asleep.

It was well after four o'clock when I awoke. Little of the heat had gone out of the afternoon sun as I went on down to Ribeauvillé, and the prospect of a meeting at the headquarters of F.E. Trimbach on the edge of the town seemed especially appealing. Nor was I disappointed. In the deep, cool cellars I was taken through the whole range of the firm's wines, from Sylvaner to a Gewürztraminer Sélection des Grains Nobles. Some of the previous year's wines, still a few days away from bottling, were drawn direct from the vats into our glasses. 'A very wonderful year,' said my Trimbach acquaintance. 'Lovely at three or four years old,' (this of the Riesling Réserve) 'marvellous at ten or even much older.' So much for the widely-held belief that Riesling is a wine to be drunk young.

It was getting on for half past six by the time we had finished tasting, but the sun was still high. Rather to my surprise, Monsieur Trimbach had welcomed my suggestion of his walking on with me as far as Hunawihr, and soon we were in the vines at an altitude of about 300 metres (1000 feet), south of Ribeauvillé and looking back across the town to the hillside I had descended earlier. 'You came down across the Osterberg,' said my companion. 'Clay and chalk. That's where our Riesling *cuvée* Frédérick Emile comes from.' As we walked on, he recited at my request what he considered to be the outstanding characteristics of the best of Alsace wines. Purest wines in the world. Clean. Fresh. Single grape varieties. No second (malolactic) fermentation or ageing in wood. In other words, vinification to bring out the full flavour of the grape. In view of my lunchtime Pinot Blanc, I had no difficulty in believing all he said.

It was a lovely gentle five-kilometre (three-mile) stroll next morning from Riquewihr to Kaysersberg, following vineyard tracks and sometimes walking between the rows of vines. From a *camionette* a man in the usual *bleus de travail* was unloading a cultivator with a spraying attachment and I gave him a hand with it. Lovely weather, I remarked. Yes, he said, but with this heat after the wet of a few days ago there was always a chance of mildew, so he had to spray. Were they his own vines, I asked? Yes: only a hectare and a bit, but he had a couple more further down, closer to Bennwihr. No, he didn't make his own wine; his grapes went to the *cave coopérative* in Bennwihr, a big one, and a good one. It even had its own restaurant. I ought to try it some time.

It was a lovely gentle summer morning, too. Birds sang. There were white daisies, purple vetch and blue harebells in the grass. An isolated tree still had black cherries on it. The sun was warm, but from time to time there was a welcome breeze. Though I was going to lunch with one of the most stylish and respected wine-makers in France I was reluctant to come down out of the vines. Come down I did though, past the monastery at Sigolsheim, then behind the villages of Sigolsheim and Kientzheim, so as to avoid the busy D 28 until the last possible moment.

Owned for centuries by monastic orders, like so many other famous wine-making estates in France, Domaine Weinbach stands back from the D 28, halfway between Kientzheim and Kaysersberg, in a broad expanse of vines to the north of the Weisbach stream. 'Clos des Capucins' is writ large on a wall beside the road, but otherwise the domaine is easily missed, for the old house and its attendant red-brick buildings are wholly unobtrusive. Glancing at them from the road, across the vines, one would hardly suspect

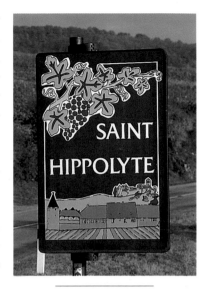

*St Hippolyte was dragged to a martyr's death by wild horses, his bones being eventually laid to rest in the fourteenth-century church of the village named after him. Some of the best Pinot Noir – red grapes of Alsace are grown in the commune.*

that in their cellars are made some of the finest wines in the world.

I had been asked to lunch, but it was only eleven o'clock when I arrived, and we sat down at a table in a panelled room crowded with beautiful old furniture that included a tall ceramic heating stove typical of the region, and started a tasting of virtually the whole range of Domaine Weinbach wines, beginning with a young Sylvaner. 'It's lovely, isn't it?' said my hostess dreamily, eyes half closed, holding her glass by the stem and moving it slowly from side to side under her nose. The Sylvaner does not command much respect among wine critics, and it is not often that it produces a wine to enthuse over. Colette Faller's Sylvaner was a charming exception. '*Belle acidité*', she said, looking at me over her glass, emphasizing the importance of the observation and inviting mine. Acidity *is* of vital importance in any wine. Some kinds of acidity are good, some bad. To most of us, a wine with the right kind and degree of acidity is probably 'smooth' or 'mellow'. With the wrong kind and the wrong degree of acidity it is more likely to be described simply as 'acid'. This Domaine Weinbach Sylvaner was not at all

*Bergheim, freely translated, means 'home on the hill'. With its fourteenth-century fortifications, its nineteenth-century 'medieval' Château de Reichenberg and its wine-makers' houses in both Gothic and Renaissance style, it is one of the most attractive of the wine villages of Alsace. Gewürztraminer is the speciality of the commune and there are marked footpaths through the vineyards.*

acid, nor was it dull and rather flabby, as all too many Sylvaners are. It was clean, refreshing, almost zestful, but not in the least sharp or aggressive.

So I agreed, '*Oui. Belle acidité!*' but awaited more observations. Madame Faller sipped once more, considered again, and said *à propos* of the whole character of the wine, '*Il accroche. Il reste en bouche. Il n'est pas fugitif*'; literally, it hangs on, or clings; it lingers in the mouth; it's not fleeting. Then, '*Belle charpente*': good structure. Thus enlightened, I said in all sincerity that it seemed to me all of those things, and delicious. 'Oh, it's quite a modest wine,' said Colette Faller, 'but then, one needs a modest wine for modest occasions and to go with certain foods, doesn't one?' This would go very well with sausage for instance, wouldn't it?' Just then I thought it would be perfect with almost anything except liquorice allsorts, especially outside in the garden on a summer's day.

So we progressed from Sylvaner to Pinot Blanc, then to a Riesling which had been only a month in bottle and which, Colette Faller said, was 'still not quite settled down', but I thought it sheer delight; then to another

*The famous fortified church of Hunawihr, built in the fourteenth and fifteenth centuries, overlooks the viticulturally famous vineyard of the Clos Ste Hune, owned by Trimbach and producing one of the most renowned Riesling wines of Alsace.*

*Ribeauvillé is an exceptionally
attractive medieval town set
against a backdrop of vine-covered
hills and wooded slopes.*

Riesling that had been harvested later, about 20 November, Madame Faller said: the last harvest before Vendange Tardive. There was a fleeting moment when I thought it sweet, but no sooner had the impression come than it was gone again: this was a most elegantly dry princess of a wine such as the Riesling grape never produced anywhere but in Alsace.

Muscat followed. '*Croquant*', said my teacher, 'Crisp. A very good aperitif, and marvellous with asparagus.' Of the Tokay, or Pinot Gris, that came next I am tempted to enthuse beyond reason. Peaches. Honey. Herbs. Smokey. Smooth. Ample yet beautifully proportioned. Rich yet dry. A gorgeous greeny-gold. 'Late-harvested again, but not *tardive*,' said Colette Faller. (The Faller Vendange Tardive wines, I knew, were famous.)

'It's one of the most delectable wines I've ever tasted,' I said. 'I've fallen head over heels in love with it.' She smiled tolerantly but was pleased.

'Yes,' she said, 'That's easy to do.'

Our tasting had taken the best part of an hour. We ended it with a Gewürztraminer '89, Vendange Tardive. I said that it seemed to me simply one of the loveliest wines I had ever had or was likely to have. 'Yes; it calls forth a lot of emotion,' said Madame Faller as we went into the big kitchen for what she had modestly described as 'just an ordinary midday family meal'. The company consisted of the *caviste*, or cellarman, the foreman responsible for the vineyards and the vines themselves, the oenologist who supervised all processes of vinification, and a matronly young woman who normally looked after despatch, though that day she was standing in for the cook. We ate cold food, all home-grown or home-made, except for the cheese. We drank water or Sylvaner, and – for my benefit – a Gewürztraminer with the cheese. It really wasn't a special lunch, said my hostess. Everybody worked hard at the domaine, and needed proper food. If the weather had been cool, she added, the main dish would have been hot, of course.

The weather was not cool; it was sizzling. Soon after three o'clock I set out on the last six or eight kilometres of the day's purposeful march. At half past six I was standing with a wine-maker of Turckheim on the famous Grand Cru slopes called Brand. Geologically, he said, they were part of a *cône de déjection* underlaid by granite, and like many granitic soils they gave wines of remarkable structure and finesse. He told me much more, and I nodded and exclaimed, hoping that he would believe I was taking it all in. Later, he took me home to meet his wife and we tasted his Riesling and his Gewürztraminer, not in the cellar but in the parlour. No spitting. The wine-maker had an interest in a restaurant in Turckheim, where we dined very well, and although we were drinking a Pinot Gris with our breast of duck I was pressed to try an Alsace Pinot Noir. After the pudding an irresistible Sélection des Grains Nobles was generously produced in my honour, while outside the night-watchman proclaimed that it was ten o'clock and all was well. It certainly was, but when at last my host suggested 'a little nightcap: a *poire Williams* perhaps, or a *mirabelle*, just to taste,' I told him thank you, but no; I had probably done enough tasting for one day.

# THE WINE

The essential feature of the wines of Alsace is the significance of the grape varieties used. Though identification and sale by the name of the grape, once rare in France, has increased in recent years, still for the great majority of wine drinkers the names of any wine region's principal grape varieties tend to be of only secondary importance. In Alsace they ought to be of the very first consideration, for while champagne is largely sold under the name of a particular brand or 'house', the wines of Burgundy are known first and foremost by the appropriate village names and in the Rhône valley the vineyards themselves provide the chief element of identification, in Alsace it is the grape variety that counts above all else. Whereas the best, and best-known wines of other regions may be blends of wine from more than one variety of grape, those of Alsace are in each case made from one variety, and one only. Here, then, are brief descriptions of the more important wine grapes of Alsace, in roughly descending order of merit, and with personal predilections playing their part.

**Riesling:** the 'aristocrat' of Alsace. The same grape as is grown in Germany, but vinified quite differently to make wines that are vastly more attractive than is usual across the Rhine: 'steely' dry, with no marked tendency to sweetness; fruity, yet with an elegant acidity.

**Pinot Gris, or Tokay d'Alsace:** not the same Tokay as the one that produces the famous, lusciously sweet wine of Hungary, this variety gives wines that are 'round' and rich yet elegantly dry; in many a wine-maker's view (and in mine) it is no less aristocratic than the Riesling.

**Gewürztraminer:** aromatic, spicy, richly fruity, yet dry, this is probably by far the most easily recognizable of all white wine grape varieties.

**Pinot Blanc:** gives a wine which can be very good indeed and easily mistaken for a chablis or a Chardonnay by a less-than-expert palate.

**Muscat:** the grapes are very 'raisiny', with the aroma of ripe dessert grapes, but vinify dry. Muscat is often recommended both as an aperitif and as an accompaniment to *foie gras*; but then, which white wine in Alsace is not?

**Sylvaner:** the lowliest of the best-known grapes of Alsace is nevertheless capable, in the hands of a wine-maker as good as Colette Faller, for example, of giving a very pleasing, quaffable, light-hearted wine.

**Pinot Noir:** the same grape that gives red Burgundy is now being used increasingly in Alsace for both red and rosé wines.

# CHAMPAGNE

## INTRODUCTION

The vineyards of *la* Champagne, the province, (as opposed to *le* champagne, the wine) are the most northerly of all the wine-making regions of France. Lying astride the *autoroute* between Calais and Dijon, they are also by far the most accessible vineyards to travellers going south from the northern Channel ports.

Three areas of viticultural Champagne are of outstanding significance: the Montagne de Reims, between Reims and the River Marne; the valley of the Marne itself, bisecting the whole vineyard area; and the Côte des Blancs. Some 100 kilometres (60 miles) south of the southern end of the Côte des Blancs and about 40 kilometres (25 miles) east of Troyes, yet curiously still within the viticultural appellation, there also lies the comparatively obscure but increasingly important champagne district of the Aube.

For most of us, champagne the wine is a matter of big names: Moët et Chandon, Bollinger, Krug, Lanson and half a dozen others. To visit their cellars one must look to Reims and Epernay, or thereabouts, though since the big 'houses' may buy grapes from whichever vineyards they choose in Champagne, it would be virtually impossible to walk for more than a few kilometres in vineyards devoted exclusively to Moët, or Bollinger, or any of the other big names. Outside Reims and Epernay, champagne producers whose names few of us may ever have heard of are to be found in the villages of the several distinct vineyard areas. Walkers are therefore not obliged to go to town in order to sample the *vin du pays*.

---

*The Marne was the scene of one of the most significant of all the battles of the First World War. In some of the best of its vineyards, overlooking the river, the* vendange *was accompanied by the roaring of German batteries.*

---

# BRIEFING

## THE LIE OF THE LAND

All of the wine country of Champagne, and in particular the best-known, most northerly area in the triangle formed by Reims, Châlons-sur-Marne and Epernay, offers more or less easy walking – that is to say without the excessively steep gradients that virtually prohibit pleasurable walking in the vineyards of the Côte Rôtie and Condrieu in the northern Rhône; without the forests and harsh hillsides and ravines that are the cause of so much inconvenient, albeit picturesque fragmentation of much of the wine country of Provence; and without the all-too-frequent hard-top roads of the Loire valley. In the 'golden triangle' of Champagne the vines sweep round shallow amphitheatres formed by the chalk hills, overflowing from one to the next and coming close to engulfing the deceptively unpretentious wine villages and the undulating roads that run between them. Overlooked by woods but seldom interrupted by them, as open as the ocean, they make only the most modest of demands upon the walker's navigational skills.

For good walking in close association with the wine of Champagne it is hardly possible to improve on the three most significant vineyard areas of the region: the Montagne de Reims, the Vallée de la Marne, and the Côte des Blancs. They present no unavoidable difficulties of terrain or other impediments to more or less free and easy progress, while offering fine prospects of the very heart of the wine country. Without exception, all the famous wine villages and best-quality vineyards, as well as the overwhelming majority of the champagne houses, lie within their embrace.

## WALKS

**Winter on the Côte des Blancs** Vertus to Cuis, by way of le Mesnil-sur-Oger, Avize and Cramant. About 16 kilometres/10 miles; allow 3–4 hours.

This route provides very satisfactory walking in the region where the white – Chardonnay – grapes of the champagne blend are mostly grown; for, as Patrick Forbes notes, 'Every presentable champagne contains a percentage of wine made from grapes grown on the Côte des Blancs.' The walk follows long, uninterrupted vineyard paths, offering fine views and, with the exception of Cramant, avoiding villages if so desired. Four kilometres (2½ miles) more from Cuis on straight paths across unexciting arable fields bring one to the outskirts of Epernay.

**September Harvest** Rilly-la-Montagne to Ay, by way of Ludes, Verzenay, Verzy, Villers-Marmery, Trépail,

Ambonnay, Bouzy and Avenay-Val-d'Or. About 32 kilometres/20 miles; allow 9–12 hours.

Because the wine villages lie hard up against the forest edge of the 'mountain', keeping to vineyard paths alone is complicated to the point of being close to impracticable, especially in the first half of the walk, roughly to Villers-Marmery. Nevertheless, for the determined walker there are many uninterrupted stretches through the vines. If more woodland than vines is acceptable, the GR 142 and GR 141, which run more up in the forest than out of it, offer a good compromise.

**Vallée de la Marne** Reuil to Champillon, by way of Tincourt, Venteuil, Arty, Damery and Hautvillers. About 20 kilometres/12 miles; allow 5–6 hours.

This is some of the best walking in *la Champagne viticole*, presenting classic views of the Marne valley and the Canal Latéral, passing through some of the most renowned of all the wine villages, and ending at one of the very best – and most expensive – hotel-restaurants of the region.

The GR 14, coming from Port-à-Binson and following the river, passes through Reuil, providing a path that is not only way-marked but also very rewarding. Climbing the slope north-east of Reuil, it runs for some 4 or 5 kilometres (2½–3 miles) through the Bois du Roi, passing the Ferme Harnotay before coming down again to Damery to cross the valley of the Brunet stream, then climb again to the high ground and the edge of the trees, which it follows all the way to Dom Pérignon's Hautvillers, after which a kilometre or two through the wood brings the walker to Champillon.

| Maps | | | |
|---|---|---|---|
| 1:25,000 | 2713 est | Epernay | Côte des Blancs, |
| | | | Montagne de Reims |
| | | | and Vallée de la |
| | | | Marne |
| | 2713 ouest | Epernay | Montagne de Reims |
| | 2812 ouest | Reims | Montagne de Reims |
| | 2812 est | Verzy | Montagne de Reims |
| | 2813 ouest | Mareuil-sur-Ay | Montagne de Reims |
| | 2814 ouest | Vertus | Côte des Blancs |
| 1:50,000 | 2713 | Epernay | Vallée de la Marne |
| | 2812 | Reims | Montagne de Reims |
| | 2813 | Avize | Côte des Blancs and |
| | | | Montagne de Reims |
| | 2814 | Vertus | Côte des Blancs |
| 1:100,000 | 10 | Reims – | |
| | | Verdun | |
| *Topo-Guide* | GR 14 | Brie – Champagne – Ardennes de | |
| | | Dormans à Bar-le-Duc par le | |
| | | vignoble champenois; Tour de la | |
| | | Montagne de Reims | |

Alternatively, walkers who prefer to stay with the vines (Pinot Noir and Pinot Meunier: the black grapes of champagne) should simply follow a line from Venteuil through Damery to Cumières, taking vineyard paths shown on the 1:25,000 map, running more or less parallel (and perhaps rather too close) to the D1.

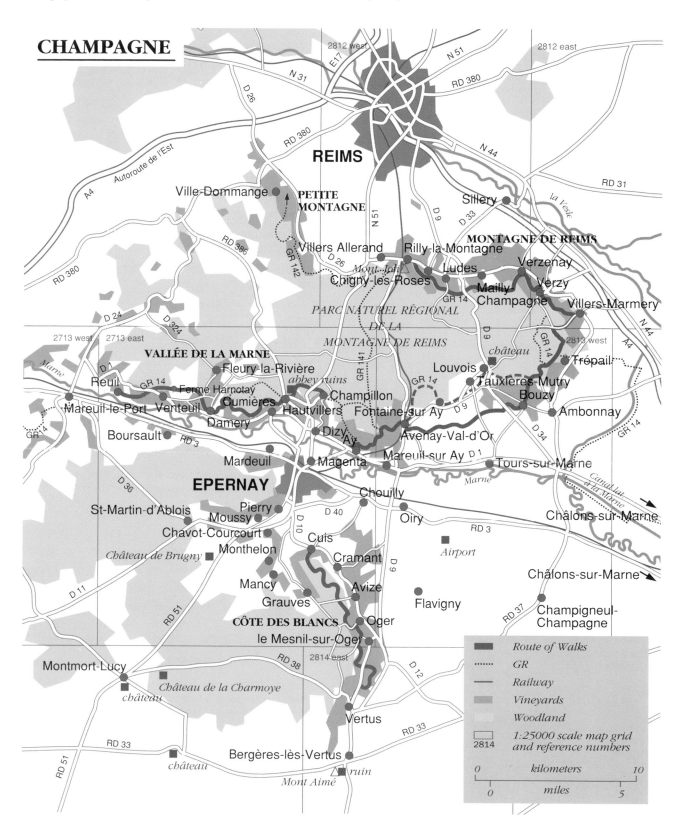

# CHAMPAGNE

Legend:
- **Route of Walks**
- ······ **GR**
- —— **Railway**
- **Vineyards**
- **Woodland**
- 2814 **1:25000 scale map grid and reference numbers**

kilometers 0 — 10
miles 0 — 5

# WINTER ON
# THE CÔTE DES BLANCS

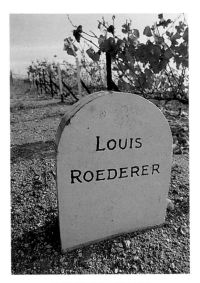

*Not a memorial stone, but a marker on the Côte des Blancs. The meticulous maintenance of vineyards belonging to firms with names such as this is consistent with the quality of their wines.*

It was late March in Champagne. On the Côte des Blancs winter would soon be obliged to yield to spring but was fighting a determined rearguard action. Forsythia was almost in bloom, but little growth could be discerned on the vines and I was none too warm though wearing five layers of clothing. My intention was this: starting from the Hôtel Reine Blanche in Vertus, where I had spent the night after arriving very late by car from Paris, I would follow the Côte des Blancs from one end to the other by way of le Mesnil-sur-Oger, Avize and Cramant, cross into the vineyards of the southern slopes of the Montagne de Reims by the bridge over the Marne down at Mareuil-sur-Aÿ, and so on and up to the Hôtel Royal Champagne at Champillon, north of Epernay. It was an itinerary amounting to perhaps 28 or 30 kilometres (17 or 18 miles).

At eight o'clock that morning the prospects were not encouraging: the sky was threatening, the wind unfriendly, the ground so wet as to be forbidding. Thirty kilometres is not a formidable distance, but in hostile weather and with mud heavy on one's boots it may seem significantly longer. For this reason I made a precautionary contract with myself and attached a penalty clause: promising to complete the course on my own two feet, I accepted that failure to do so would entail my giving up wine or any other form of alcohol whatever for a month. Socks and boots were checked with special care before I put them on.

Every season in the vineyards has its pros and cons. In winter and early spring Champagne seems to me more beautiful than at any other time of the year. The vines – generally trained low and almost parallel to the earth – have been rigorously pruned. In their disciplined rows, plot by plot, running now in one direction, now in another, they present a great undulating patchwork of browns and sepia and dark greys. Later, the essential shape of the land will be half lost in green luxuriance; now, it is revealed in stylish severity. What was needed that morning was a sky that was hard and blue; but it was sullen grey. Here and there in the vineyards, workers wearing gloves, bundled up in padded jackets and sporting woolly hats were tidying between the vines and burning old prunings in oil drums cut in half and mounted on pram chassis. The smell was pleasing and the sight of fire comforting. The Royal Champagne (owned by Moët) has a Michelin star and a good cellar and I determined to keep my eye on those goals if morale should sink. As I slogged along the vineyard paths below le Bois de St Jean, le Bois de la Houppé and le Mont Gaillard, over and down to le Mesnil-sur-Oger, larks were as noisy as on a fine summer's morning, though what they had to sing about I could not think. At about ten o'clock a Scotch mist began and I stopped only to put on my over-jacket. By the time I reached Avize, only eight kilometres (five miles) from Vertus, it was eleven o'clock: at that rate I would be lucky to reach Champillon before dark.

Pausing in the shelter of a doorway to study the map, I stayed to shelter from rain that was now falling in earnest. I was no stranger to Avize in such weather. One November weekend I had walked from Epernay up the valley of the Cubry stream south and west to Vinay, then south and east to Mancy and Grauves and across the Montagne d'Avize to come down into the village by the very street now facing me. Rain had fallen almost all day and dusk had come by the time I climbed the last hill and left the woods and come upon the village immediately below. Feet hurt. Shoulders ached. When I paused I felt the chill of damp clothes. Suddenly the 20 kilometres (12 miles) back to Epernay had appeared impossibly long, and to walk even one more had seemed beyond my strength.

At the Hôtel St Nicolas in Avize the reception desk was also the bar, and I accepted a registration card with one hand and a glass of cognac with the other while my pack lay in a slowly widening pool of water. The large, rubicund *patronne*, wearing a blue woollen dressing gown though it was no more than six o'clock in the evening, had observed that I looked as if I needed a bath. It was an understatement, but I did not hurry the cognac. Later, safe from the rain, shoulders free of the pack, sitting on the edge of my bed savouring a delicious awareness of comfort and wellbeing, I was startled by a perfunctory knock at the door and the entry of the *patronne* bearing towels and (a generous and uncommon gesture in France at that time) a tablet of soap. She led the way down a spiral staircase to a courtyard where rain still danced on the cobbles as I followed the blue dressing gown

*Unknown horseman outside the Musée des Vins in Epernay. Popular though the Musée des Vins is, the many miles of cellars deep in the chalk below the town are far more so. Many of the larger champagne 'houses' have their headquarters here.*

and bedroom slippers through what proved to be the kitchen door.

'Now,' said the *patronne*, 'a little heat so that you do not catch cold.' She lit all the burners of the two gas ranges and turned the flames up as high as they would go. 'And now, *voilà le système*.' Over the sink was a gas heater. A cold water supply had been plumbed into the outlet pipe to the end of which she now fitted a hand shower on a length of rubber tube. '*Nous sommes à la campagne*,' she said, '*mais nous ne sommes pas primitifs*.' 'Don't worry about the water,' she added. 'The floor slopes, and it runs away by itself.' She gave me the key so that I might lock the door against surprise. Standing there by the sink, I let hot water run luxuriously over me until I feared that the kitchen was in danger of flooding and that the bunches of herbs hanging from the ceiling might suffer from the steam. It was, I thought, a kitchen in which good cooking might be done, with well-used and well-ordered pots and pans and knives. I looked forward to dinner that night.

It began with soup, then *charcuterie* and a *pâté* that was served with a certain suggestion of conspiracy. The *patronne* came over when I had eaten and asked if I had enjoyed it. Delicious. And did I know what it was? No idea. 'Cod's liver!' she said triumphantly. 'If I'd told you before, you would never have eaten it; people never do.'

Rabbit came next, cooked in a mushroom sauce with a touch of curry (the *patronne* insisted that I try it: she herself had cooked it), then pigeon served on thin rounds of fried bread. I had drunk half a bottle of Blanc de Blancs with the soup and the second course. With the rabbit and the pigeon I had a Beaujolais-Villages. Then the *patronne's* daughter brought an apple tart whose pastry, she said, had been made with *crème fraîche*. I had already declined the cheese.

Coffee followed, and with it armagnac. At the bar I sat on a high stool and was introduced to Victor and Paul and Jean-Claude. Like most of the men in that bar, like most people in Avize, they lived by the vines. Show interest, and such people will tell you almost all you care to know about champagne. 'Come and look round tomorrow,' they said. 'You walked *that* way? Ah, you would have done better to have walked *this*. Now if *la patronne* has such a thing as a pencil under the counter we'll draw you a map. You're leaving tomorrow? A pity; come back in spring and we'll show you . . .'

Midnight came and we were still talking. One o'clock sounded from the clocks in the village and I was involved in discussions on the Common Market and the Channel Tunnel and the English taste in champagne. '*Patronne*, another glass for Monsieur. Ah, but I insist: you must fortify yourself for tomorrow. It keeps out the rain.'

My going to bed an hour later was defended by Madame: so many kilometres walked yesterday; so many to be walked today. Yes; today! My room was warm. The bed was large and very comfortable. My walking clothes were drying on an old-fashioned radiator; the rain-soaked map hung over the back of a chair. Outside were the dark and the rain and the wind. I listened to them, drew the quilt higher over my shoulders, stretched myself in the warm sheets, heard the murmur of voices and bursts of laughter from the bar, and slept.

But now the Hôtel St Nicolas had been closed for years and in any case my destination was on the far side of the Marne. Putting up the hood of my over-jacket, I went on out of the village. Reluctant to weave a way on sodden dirt paths through the vines below, I kept to the road that hugs the steep slope between Avize and Cramant. Roederer was the name on several stone markers at the edge of a marvellously well-kept plot, and if I had been wearing a hat I would have raised it out of respect for one of the very finest of champagnes. The church clock struck noon behind me as I left Cramant on the way down towards Chouilly. Traffic was negligible, but a heavy lorry managed to spray me liberally with the water that was streaming down beside the raised verge. The view out over several square miles of vines was impressive and I thought how good it would be to sit up there on the hillside on a fine day. As it was, I envied four men in a *camionette* who were taking off muddy rubber boots before settling down to lunch. I wanted shelter in which to delve into my pack for waterproof over-trousers. More, I wanted the flask of Courvoisier VSOP which I knew to be wrapped inside the trousers.

But where to find refuge from the rain? To my right and ahead were only vines, sloping down to the plain. To my left was the *côte* that forms the eastern edge of the Butte de Saran: very steep, but with woods at the top. In the edge of the trees I found a hollow, made long ago by the uprooting of a tree in a gale perhaps, though more likely by a vigneron digging for earth to replace eroded topsoil in the vines. Here, sheltered from a chill breeze, above a thick carpet of dead leaves, I rigged a roof with the groundsheet that is never absent from my winter walking gear, pulled on the waterproof trousers, buttoned up the collar of my down-filled waistcoat, zipped the Gore-tex overjacket up to the neck and unscrewed the flask.

The satisfaction I now derived from that modest cognac in the March woods above the Côte des Blancs was as great as I have ever had from any brandy in the world, or ever could have. First, I had a good dram of it neat. Next, I drank it half-and-half with water. Then, considering that there were still 16 kilometres (10 miles) between me and Champillon and dinner, I thought that perhaps a *casse-croûte* might be sensible. The Courvoisier-à-*l'eau* went very well with that too.

At two o'clock it was time to be off again. Black, heavy clouds were blowing in from the west, but the rain had stopped and the whole panorama in subtle shades of brown criss-crossed by grey-white paths was bathed in an extraordinary golden light from a sun that was itself concealed behind a bank of cloud. For the best part of the next two hours I followed a surfaced road all the way down to the Marne, where the low-lying land to the south was flooded. It was on the other side of the river, with three-quarters of the day's journey done, that resolution faltered. Immediately behind the deceptively modest streets of Mareuil, some of the best vines of all Champagne – Bollinger vines, some of them – rose almost as steeply as those to be found overlooking the Rhône or the Rhine. To the north-west, far wider expanses of vines, though on gentler slopes, promised a testing ascent to Champillon in the conditions then prevailing. Could I make it? *Need* I make it? Not five minutes' walk away was the ever-hospitable house of Bollinger, with friends of long standing. But what of my contract, and that self-denying clause? And what of pride? A little of the VSOP helped again.

Soon after four o'clock, looking back and down to the village I thought that with luck one and three-quarter hours might see me undoing the wire round the cork of a bottle of something or other at the hotel. But five forty-five saw me doing nothing of the sort.

It was all uncomplicated enough for the couple of miles or so along open roads and paths that reached almost to the highest extremity of the vines. There, however, the map showed a track running up through the wood, skirting an almost vertical curving cliff (probably marking an ancient quarry that in past centuries had provided material for the rehabilitation of the vineyards) and emerging at last on to the road above Champillon. If I entered the trees I would lose sight of all landmarks, as well as of the Dizy-Champillon road. If I kept outside them, taking paths through the vines which would certainly have brought me to the road, I would lose height.

It is a sound rule of cross-country travel never to give away height if one can possibly avoid doing so. Uneasy, but obedient to the rule, I found the track, which did indeed begin to skirt a fearsome pit, but which then petered out among fallen trees. Casting about, I found another one which obliged me to glissade perilously down a 45-degree mud slope. Again the path, or what passed for one, mysteriously vanished. Now following only the distant sound of traffic, clambering under and over fallen trunks, crashing through undergrowth, slithering on ledges above dark, sinister pools of water many feet below, and all the while fearing another storm and fading light, I at last reached another great hollow where – blessed reassurance – the gables of a house rose above the tops of pines. Dragging myself up by clumps of hazel rooted in the face of the precipitous cliff, I finally emerged into a well-to-do housing estate, and thence – joyfully – on to the Reims road. 'How far is it to the hotel?' I asked a woman getting out of her car. 'Oh, quite a walk; at least a kilometre and a half' she replied solemnly. No more than a minute later, round a bend, a sign said 'Royal Champagne 300 metres'. I counted every stride to the hotel entrance and they came to 510.

# SEPTEMBER HARVEST

A nd now at last it was harvest time and the 'golden triangle' of *la Champagne viticole* was a scene of almost ant-like activity. From seven or eight o'clock in the morning and from near and far, vehicles of all sorts and sizes, from venerable little Citroën *deux-chevaux* to 40-seater coaches, were delivering their occupants to the Montagne de Reims, the valley of the Marne and the Côte des Blancs. In vineyards belonging to firms whose brands are household names, teams of men and women, mostly young, moved slowly but surely up and down the green corridors, stooping, snipping, chattering at first, but then tending to lapse into purposeful silence. Meanwhile, machines on long spindly legs, like grotesque predatory insects, were carrying stacks of plastic containers filled with grapes from the pickers' baskets and buckets to be emptied into the great steel wagons that would be towed behind tractors to the *pressoirs*. To ing and fro-ing between a family acre or two, the humble *camionettes* of small private growers were speeding their loads to the *coopérative*, or by contract to the premises of this or that individual champagne-maker. Minor roads that vein the hillsides, and that for the rest of the year may be as quiet as the woods in winter, had become hazardous for the unwary and way-marked with squashed grapes. Even the ubiquitous larks seemed noisier than in spring.

All systems were go. In *pressoirs* from Vertus to Verzy and from Boursault to Bouzy men in boiler suits were observing electronic weighing machines and devices for measuring sugar content, while their fellow workers in aprons and rubber boots forked Pinot Noir and Pinot Meunier and Chardonnay (but never together!) into horizontal hydraulic presses, or ensured that the requirements of other juice-extracting contraptions were satisfied. In offices in Reims and Aÿ and Epernay other men in smart suits (a few of them) were scanning charts and computer print-outs and discussing yields and programmes, when not peering anxiously at meteorological predictions on Minitel.

Returning to the Côte des Blancs for the first of three September days, I took particular pleasure from warm sun on my face at half past eight in the morning, and from dry ground underfoot, where before I had trudged in winter clothes and a chill March wind and where roadside drains had been noisy with rain water. At the edge of vines beside a dirt road that traverses slopes below the Bois de la Houppé, to the north of Vertus, two men and two women were drinking coffee and eating croissants while standing at the open back of a large estate car, to which was attached a trailer already holding two or three full containers of white grapes. When they returned my '*bonjour*' with a cheerful '*Vous êtes bien chargé*' ('you're well loaded': my pack looked heavier than it was) I took the opportunity to stop and ask if the picking was going well. Not bad at all, they said: quantity quite good

*Many little-known champagne producers are to be found in the villages of the several distinct vineyard areas, allowing the walker to avoid Reims and Epernay.*

and condition of the grapes excellent. Was I going far? I told them I intended ranging the Côte des Blancs to Avize, crossing over to Grauves through the woods on the Montagne d'Avize, then continuing to Moussy and Pierry in the valley of the Cubry stream before working back to a place not far from Cramant where I was to spend the night.

It was an itinerary amounting to little more than 24 kilometres (15 miles), but they cautioned that it was '*assez loin, vous savez*' (rather a long way you know), then asked if I would like some coffee. I had taken time for no more than a token breakfast before leaving the hotel in Vertus and accepted eagerly. And what about a croissant, they added. No vacuum-flask coffee or croissants (the latter fresh earlier from a *boulangerie* in Epernay, they said) had ever tasted better. My hosts were two brothers and their wives, working a family-owned two-hectare (five-acre) spread of Chardonnay vines. They didn't make any wine themselves; the grapes were sold under contract to one of the best-known champagne houses. I asked them what they thought of the popular notion that it was possible to buy from small, 'unknown' producers champagne that was just as good and half as expensive as the famous brands. Well, they replied, it was certainly possible to find very good champagne from some of the small producers for a lot less than one paid for the *grandes marques*, but what one had to remember was that, unlike the big houses, the small producer couldn't afford to hold reserves of still wine from good years so as to be able to make satisfactory sparkling wine in poor years, so you might find really good buys from a 'little man' today, but not tomorrow. What the well-known brands ought to be able to offer (though they didn't always) was consistent quality, but someone, of course, had to pay for the cost of keeping cellars full of reserve wines instead of turning the grapes into cash within less than eighteen months of the harvest. Another thing was that although the law allowed champagne to be sold after only a year in bottle, the best of the big houses might give their wines at least three years in bottle before putting it on the market; another advantage which had to be paid for. But would I care for a little armagnac to give me courage for the long walk ahead?

I have yet to meet inhospitable vignerons, but at harvest time, particularly when the harvest promises to be a good one, the tendency to congeniality seems especially marked. An hour or so after my second breakfast, I fell into conversation with a man who was overseeing about twenty pickers busy among the vines. He was a vineyard foreman from one of the big houses that my earlier acquaintances had been talking about and was intrigued by my love of walking in France in general and the wine country above all. If I cared to be at the *mairie* in Avize at about noon, he offered, he would be happy to pick me up and take me to lunch with the pickers, as long as I didn't mind a very simple sort of meal. Two hours later he and the deputy foreman and I finished a bottle of the 'house' non-vintage champagne before joining the pickers for a hearty soup, followed by delicious sausages, potatoes and lentils, accompanied by a very acceptable if unidentified red wine. I was duly returned to Avize, fighting a desire to find a place

*Famous landmark of the Montagne de Reims, the windmill of Verzenay, owned by the equally famous firm of Charles Heidsieck and used by them for hospitality. The vines are Pinot Noir, one of the two 'black' grapes (the other is Pinot meunier) which together with the 'white' Chardonnay constitute the blend for a conventional champagne. Coincidentally, 'meunier' is French for miller.*

in the sun where I might take a siesta, and instead of being set down again at the *mairie* was mercifully taken up the steep hill and almost to the western edge of the wooded plateau of the Montagne before beginning the rest of my journey. 'You'll never be in time for your dinner otherwise,' observed the foreman. He was altogether a worthy ambassador for a firm whose guests are usually accommodated in a château so grand that when I arrived there at seven o'clock in the evening I thought it proper to remove ruck-sack and boots before so much as ringing the bell.

Next day was rather more action-packed. A few kilometres further north, in the valley of the Marne, I paid a fleeting visit to the cellars of the family firm of Gaston Chiquet in Dizy, and had a ridiculously early glass of one of their best vintages before walking westwards along the river to Damery with its part-Romanesque, part-Gothic church. Next I crossed to the south bank of the river again to call with an introduction on another family firm in Boursault (which hitherto I thought of only as a very distinctive cheese) where I gladly accepted a spur-of-the-moment suggestion that I should sit down to lunch with the *vendangeurs*, who gave me a warm, not to say boisterous, welcome. Later, heading back towards Epernay, I caught sight of quite a large gipsy encampment up ahead. Fearing an almost certain encounter with a band of hideous, unrestrained dogs, I made a detour through a wood, where I encountered both a swampy dell and a bramble thicket, got bloodily scratched, lost my cool and kept my direction only with the aid of my compass. After a leisurely bath at the Hôtel Berceaux in

*The vineyards of St Martin-d'Ablois in the valley of the Cubry are not among the best situated, but they contribute to the blends of some of the best-known champagnes.*

Epernay, I dined very well at nearby Vinay and La Briqueterie, where a half-bottle of Louis Roederer non-vintage as an aperitif seemed not a drop too much.

On the morning of the third day, in glorious weather, I started at Rilly-la-Montagne on the northern edge of the Montagne-de-Reims, with the idea of walking east and south for some 24 kilometres (15 miles) to within a few kilometres of the Marne. With notable inaccuracy, the forecast in a national newspaper that morning had said that the sky would be '*très nuageux*', but at nine o'clock the sun was already warm. When I enquired about the harvest, people said that although so far the quantity was *moyen* – middling – the quality was *superbe*. Perhaps it would be a vintage year. Everyone seemed in high spirits, pickers included. Often they waved at me and shouted greetings. Most belonged to fairly large parties organized by the big champagne houses: Lanson, Veuve Clicquot or Canard Duchêne. But near Ludes I was hailed by a very elderly man in *bleus de travail* and a black beret who was working alongside two equally elderly women on what proved to be a very small family-owned plot. He tried his limited English on me to recount that he had once been in the French merchant navy and had visited India. I went on my way carrying a large bunch of his black grapes, some of which I ate but most of which I left on top of a cemetery wall, hoping that the birds might enjoy them. The old man might have been hurt if I had refused his gift, but apart from having misgivings about the consequences of a surfeit of Pinot Noir, I also seriously feared being

*Cumières in the valley of the Marne is the scene of a monster bonfire and fair at the end of June.*

mistaken for a pilferer, and so dishonouring myself as a walker. 'Visitors,' warned a notice among the vines at Verzenay, 'Respect the labour of others. Do not pick the fruit.'

My next concern was wine. I had spent a lot of time talking with pickers working for one of the big champagne houses – only eight hours a day but the work was very hard. Their conditions were good and they were fed very well: breakfast, a mid-morning snack on the job, a hot lunch out of insulated containers in the vineyards, and a good evening meal with meat again. It was already past noon by the time I reached Mailly-Champagne, and I feared that such shops as I might find would be closed. One very small shop was open, but they had no half-bottles of anything, let alone champagne, cold or warm, and I left with a dark red wine from Cahors. At Verzenay, half an hour or so later, my desire for a glass or two of the wine of the country was not diminished by a chance visit to the Lanson *pressoir*, close beside the road and wide open to passers by. 'Come in and look around,' called a cheerful foreman wearing blue shorts, a white apron and a white tee-shirt, as I paused in the forecourt. The hospitable traditions of that particular champagne house were well known to me, and my hopes rose suddenly. Were they having a good *vendange*, I asked the foreman? Very good, he said. Perhaps just a touch of rot (*pourriture*), but nothing to worry about. Just a touch!, echoed the head of another famous champagne house ironically when I told him of the incident at lunch next day. Just a touch! I had come across not a few large puddles on the paths through the vines there on the Montagne, souvenirs of the heavy rains of a few days earlier. Rain followed by sun such as the *vendangeurs* were now enjoying is a sure recipe for *la pourriture*, which can ruin an otherwise bumper harvest. But no winemaker likes to advertise his or her difficulties or disasters. I stayed for a few minutes more at the Lanson *pressoir* until the sight of the workmen refreshing themselves with the rewards of other years became too tantalizing, then with a shouted *merci* and *au'voir* I departed in quest not only of a glass of champagne, but also of lunch.

The delicious smell of morning-baked bread led me to a corner shop where an attractive young woman sold me a *baguette*. '*Vous venez d'où?*', she asked. I told her. '*Et vous allez loin?*' *Pas loin*, I told her. Bouzy perhaps, or Ambonnay. '*Oh là là! Quel courage! C'est au bout du monde* (at the end of the world).' Heartened by such flattery, I stuck the bread under the flap of my pack and followed the young woman's directions to the nearest café. On its door was posted a Tarif des Consommations which included a *coupe* of champagne for 12 francs. Leaving pack and stick just inside the door, I asked for what I wanted at the bar. '*Une coupe*', repeated the disagreeable-looking woman who was serving. She took a champagne bottle from a cold cabinet. Evidently it had been open for too long: there was not so much as a bubble to be seen. '*Oh merde! C'est du vin blanc!*', she exclaimed. Indeed it was. Could she not open another bottle, or half-bottle, I asked? '*Pas possible*,' she replied unapologetically, emptying the glass into the sink with one hand and in a single, ill-tempered gesture with the other wiping the counter clean both of the wasted wine and the troublesome customer.

Great was my thirst now as I toiled out of Verzenay, initially on the road and then up what seemed a 45-degree slope between vines, to reach a crest and a view over the Canal de l'Aisne à la Marne and far away across the plain towards the Aisne itself and beyond to the Ardennes. On a grassy bank I slipped off the rucksack. There were lovely touches of autumn in the woods behind and a gentle breeze was blowing. Had I been sprawling on that spot some three-quarters of a century earlier I would have been within reach of German shells. 'How beautiful the view is here, over the sunny vineyards! And what a curious anomaly,' wrote an American poet who served with the French Foreign Legion on the Marne. 'On this slope the grape-pickers are singing merrily at their work, on the other the batteries are roaring. Boom! Boom!'

A steady advance was called for: Verzy, Villers-Marmery, Trépail, Ambonnay (a small diversion), and finally Bouzy; 12 more kilometres (7 miles) of pickers, tractors, lorries and *camionettes*, assailed here and there by the sweet scent of grape juice from a *pressoir*. The work of the *pressoir* is not simply a matter of loading the press and applying the squeeze: there are several separate squeezes for each load of grapes, giving juice of different qualities, not all of which is allowed to be made into champagne. And not all of the juice which may legally be used for champagne is used in practice for the very highest quality of wine. So day and night the men in rubber boots and aprons work their shifts, and are well fed. And night and day the business of removing any unacceptable odds and ends and impurities and of transferring the precious juice to the fermentation vats goes on, until at last, well before the broad-leaved trees in the forest on the Montagne are bare, the presses are clean and dry and the press houses are silent for another year.

To the stranger in the land it is only for the two or three weeks of the harvest and on the occasional *jour de fête* that most of the wine villages of France seem to come fully to life. By the time I reached Ambonnay and Bouzy their café-bars and food shops were busy. Suddenly Tours-sur-Marne, no more than four or five kilometres (two or three miles) down the road into the valley, seemed painfully distant. No vines grew between there and Bouzy, I knew, so it was with a clear conscience that I decided to call a halt. Once before I had been tempted to end a walk in Aÿ, but out of pride had not done so. Now, taking up a generously open invitation, I telephoned the wine-maker I knew there and asked if perhaps he could pick me up. He did so, and we had dinner together, celebrating what he said promised to be a great vintage with Bollinger Vieilles Vignes, which is simply one of the most delicious champagnes that it is possible to find. His wife, who is fiercely proud of the history of the region, told me about the ancient Roman road that runs between the Marne and Reims and suggested that I might walk it one day; tomorrow, for example. I said it was a lovely thought, and perhaps we could talk about it again next year.

# THE WINE

The process by which champagne is made – which is by no means confined to the region from which it takes its name – is so different from the way in which the vast majority of wines are made that it calls for a brief explanation.

Champagne is a blended wine, a fact which may come as a shock to many who accord it an admiration bordering on reverence. The romantic idea of wine has the juice from the appropriate – and single – variety of grapes, grown in a particular vineyard, being fermented in the vat before in due course being transferred to cask or bottle. With the best wines of Alsace and Burgundy this may not be so terribly far from the truth. In many others (even those in which only one grape variety is used, such as a great Meursault or a modest beaujolais), the juice in the vat – which is as likely to be of stainless steel as of wood – may have come from grapes grown in several vineyards. Indeed, more than half the art of many a wine-maker consists precisely in the skill with which that blending is done. Some of the greatest wines are 'blended'. A Margaux may be a blend of Cabernet Sauvignon, Merlot and Cabernet Franc. A Latour may be a blend of the same, plus a little Petit Verdot. A superb Châteauneuf-du-Pape may owe its character to as many as thirteen different varieties of grape.

Three varieties go to the making of a conventional champagne: white Chardonnay, black Pinot Noir and black Pinot Meunier. The first stage of the *méthode champenoise* is the making of an ordinary – which is to say still – wine from each of them. Each of these wines will have its own distinctive character, with its own qualities of firmness, delicacy, bouquet, body and so on, and the proportions in which each is used in relation to the whole volume of the blend will decide the character of the final sparkling wine. In the best champagne firms, or 'houses', an enormous amount of experimental tasting is involved. The ultimate criterion which guides those who do the tasting and make the crucial decisions is the desirability of arriving at a sparkling champagne faithful to the established style (that is, the 'personality' and general quality) associated with the 'house' or brand name. Champagne is not bought by geographical appellations, but by the names of the firms who make it: Bollinger, Moët et Chandon, Gaston Chiquet, Veuve Clicquot and all the rest.

When the blend of still white wines is made, it is unlikely to be distinguishable in appearance from any other still white wine, except to experts. But, as Henry Vizatelly, a great nineteenth-century authority on the subject, noted, 'the special characteristic of Champagne is that its manufacture only just commences when that of other wines ordinarily ends.' So now another process essential to the *méthode champenoise* is carried out: a very small quantity of high-quality sugar is added to the blended wine. The purpose, at this stage, is most definitely not to determine the sweetness or dry-

*Dom Perignon is properly credited not with having invented champagne, but with having been the first caviste to contrive a satisfactory way of keeping the bubbles in the bottle.*

*The traditional shape of the champagne bottle has a lot to do with strength; it must be capable of withstanding enormous pressure.*

*Winter clearance. Tireless care and vigilance are needed to maintain a healthy vineyard. On the lower slopes of the Montagne de Reims, near Epernay, November sees the cutting back and burning of – now – unwanted wood in the vines prior to later pruning.*

ness of the eventual sparkling wine, but rather to enable the still wine to produce the natural gas by which the sparkle itself is achieved. To assist the process a minute quantity of selected natural yeast is usually also added.

When all this has been done bottling takes place, and the as yet non-sparkling champagne, sealed with a temporary cork, is consigned to the cellars. It is now that the vital second fermentation occurs and the sugar in the wine is attacked by enzymes and wholly converted to alcohol and carbonic gas. The gas is retained by the temporary stopper, and – unless it breaks the bottle, which it sometimes does – remains under pressure in the wine. Hence the sparkle.

In the bottles, which are stacked neck downwards in great rows, the ageing of the now sparkling wine begins. The term 'ageing' covers a whole process of change: a process which will never cease until the wine is drunk or destroyed, and which will determine the quality of the champagne when eventually it reaches the drinker's glass. At this stage the wine is far from being ready even to leave the cellar. Sediment produced by the second fermentation must be concentrated, then removed, by the separate processes respectively of *remuage* and *dégorgement* (literally, shaking and disgorging). After *dégorgement* the wine is sparkling, clear, and ready for what are almost the last attentions of the champagne-maker. Firstly any wine lost from the bottle must be replaced. Secondly, since all the sugar that was added before bottling has been consumed by the second fermentation and the wine is now generally too dry for any but the most eccentric of tastes, a *dosage* of

*Near Trépail. Good walking paths are sometimes to be found at the head of the slopes beneath the woods of the Montagne de Reims.*

sugar must be added before the bottle is sealed. The amount varies according to the character required of the wine at its eventual peak condition (after some considerable time in bottle), from *brut*, or very dry, to *doux*, or extremely sweet. The appropriate quantity of sugar is dissolved in wine taken from the same blend of still wine that supplied the bottles before the second fermentation. The second and – until drinking time – permanent cork is now put into the bottle and secured with wire.

According to Patrick Forbes, writing some 25 years ago, nearly 300 pairs of hands assist in the making of a bottle of champagne. Granted, a great many labour-saving devices have been introduced since that time, but – within the wine business – champagne-making must still be uniquely labour-intensive. 'And one of the reasons why it is so expensive,' chorus the champagne-makers defensively. They may have a point.

**Vintage and non-vintage Champagne** Vintage champagne, though a blend of non-sparkling champagne wines to begin with, is made from those of a single, outstandingly good year and is therefore likely to be of higher quality than a non-vintage wine. It cannot lawfully be sold until at least three years after the particular harvest that provided the constituent wines. Most good producers give it longer.

Non-vintage champagne, as we have seen, is made from the wines of several years: good and sometimes not-so-good.

**Blanc de Blancs** Whereas most champagne derives from both white and black grapes, a Blanc de Blancs, as the name suggests, has to be made from the white – Chardonnay – grape only; at its best it ought therefore to be rather lighter (many champagne purists would say slighter), less robust and conceivably (but by no means certainly) more elegant than many conventional champagnes, though greater elegance is what the makers of Blanc de Blancs would like us to perceive as one of its attributes.

**Blanc de Noirs** Made from white wines derived exclusively from black grapes and consequently more robust, fuller, perhaps fruitier than conventional champagnes. Not common. Bollinger's extraordinary, comparatively rare and very expensive Vieilles Vignes, for example, is made exclusively from black grapes – Pinot Noir – grown on old vines that escaped the dread phylloxera.

# BURGUNDY

## INTRODUCTION

The popular image of Burgundy tends to the romantic: a richly pastoral, picturesque region somewhere in the depths of France, where archetypal *paysans* – every one a rubicund, prosperous Jacques Bonhomme – produce hearty red wine.

It is a conception that is not absurdly far from the truth, but geographically Burgundy is a very large territory embracing four major administrative departments: Yonne (with its capital in Auxerre); Nièvre (Nevers); Côte d'Or (Dijon); and Saône-et-Loire, with its capital in Mâcon. That Chablis is a burgundy often comes as a surprise. No less surprising may be the discovery that Pouilly-sur-Loire, which produces the white Pouilly-Fumé, classified as Val-de-Loire, is also just within Burgundy's boundaries. Then again, few of us think of beaujolais as a burgundy. Administratively, the Beaujolais is almost all in the department of the Rhône, but Moulin-à-Vent, often said to be the most distinguished of the ten *crus* of Beaujolais, is in Saône-et-Loire. As for the famous Pouilly-Fuissé, which is in the Mâconnais, or for the comparatively little-known Mercurey, Givry, Montagny and Rully, all in the Chalonnais, given an ordinary motoring map of France and asked to point to their approximate whereabouts, more than a few of us would be as likely to put a finger at random on the Médoc or Châteaunuf-du-Pape as, correctly, on Mâcon or Chagny or Chalon-sur-Saône.

The five chapters that follow trace the wines of Burgundy from north to south; from Chablis through the Côte d'Or, the Côte Chalonnaise and the Mâconnais to the Beaujolais. For our purposes the great city of Lyon, just south of the Beaujolais, marks the end of Burgundy and the beginning of the Rhône.

*Vineyards of a size suggesting small proprietors and domaines of varied character interspersed with woods and pasture make walking in the Yonne particulary pleasing.*

# CHABLIS AND THE YONNE

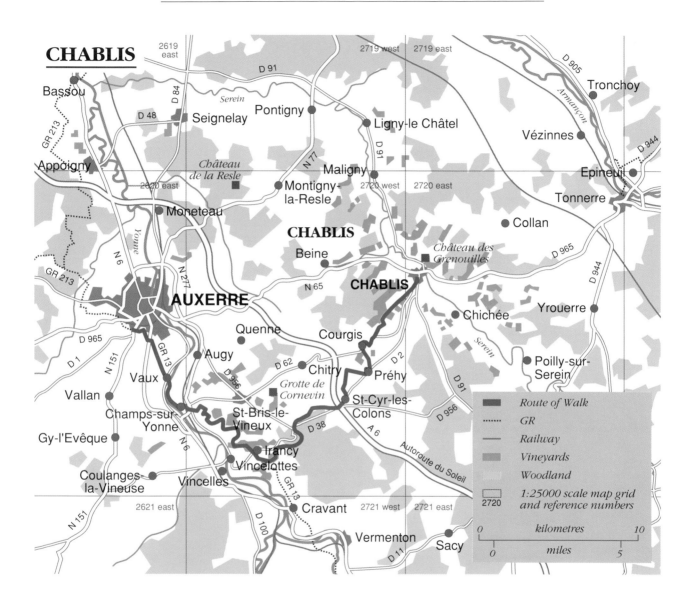

**CHABLIS**

Bassou
Seignelay
Pontigny
Ligny-le Châtel
Tronchoy
Vézinnes
Appoigny
Château de la Resle
Maligny
Epineuil
Montigny-la-Resle
Tonnerre
Moneteau
**CHABLIS**
Collan
Beine
Château des Grenouilles
**AUXERRE**
Chichée
Yrouerre
Quenne
Courgis
Augy
Chitry
Préhy
Poilly-sur-Serein
Vaux
Grotte de Cornevin
St-Cyr-les-Colons
Vallan
St-Bris-le-Vineux
Champs-sur-Yonne
Gy-l'Evêque
Irancy
Vincelottes
Coulanges-la-Vineuse
Vincelles
Cravant
Vermenton
Sacy

2619 east
2719 west
2719 east
2620 east
2720 west
2720 east
2621 east
2721 west
2721 east

Serein
Yonne
Armançon
Serein

| | |
|---|---|
| ▬ | *Route of Walk* |
| ······ | *GR* |
| — | *Railway* |
| ▨ | *Vineyards* |
| | *Woodland* |
| 2720 | *1:25000 scale map grid and reference numbers* |

0                    kilometres                    10
0                    miles                    5

# BRIEFING

## THE LIE OF THE LAND

Chablis and the Yonne are respectively one of the most illustrious and one of the least known of all the viticultural regions of France. Historically, they are no more than the vestigial remains of the Auxerrois, which in the eighteenth century, before the disasters of oidium and phylloxera and before the coming of the railway between Paris and Languedoc, may have comprised up to 40,000 hectares (100,000 acres) of vineyards, supplying the capital with the bulk of its wine. The territory is conveniently distinguished and embraced by three rivers: from west to east, the Yonne, the Serein and the Armançon, the last two being tributaries of the first and mere streams by comparison. Auxerre is on the Yonne; Chablis on the Serein; Tonnerre on the Armançon.

Of the several romantic scenarios first envisaged for this book, one of the most engaging required nothing more complicated than a simple, uninterrupted, north-to-south progress through Champagne, Chablis (the Yonne), the rest of Burgundy and the Rhône valley to Provence. As a plan, however, it had one considerable flaw: for the best part of 80 kilometres (50 miles) between Vertus and Troyes the going would be through a region of vast acreages of cereals, oilseed rape, flax and other crops. The fact that none of France's many long-distance walking paths crossed the territory probably told its own tale.

At Tonnerre and Armançon there appeared to be a very significant change. Studying the maps, I was delighted to see that I was looking at at least 30 kilometres (some 20 miles) of modest hills and valleys and ravines and hidden, sometimes vine-covered plateaux; a land well-husbanded for many centuries, but still wholly rural, agricultural, sparsely populated. And almost everywhere that my chosen route would be likely to take me were vineyards mostly of a size that suggested small proprietors and domaines of varied character, though more often than not widely interspersed with woods and pastures and arable acres not devoted to the vine. Here, I thought, must be wealth of good, firm, clearly identifiable, well-mapped paths demanding little effort but the putting of one foot comfortably in front of the other: in brief, two days of wine country walking that would not be easy to beat. Largely, I was right.

The rivers, the valleys, the hills, the forests, the vineyards, the villages and the market towns – all are part of that quintessentially French rurality loved by so many. Auxerre is a city worthy in every way of such a region. Gallo-Roman in origin (Hugh Johnson thinks its vineyards may date from that period), splendidly situated above a waterfront on one of the country's most delightful rivers, distinguished by its cathedral, its churches and its notably attractive town centre, its appeal may lie as much in its contemporary bustle as in the well-preserved vestiges of its medieval past.

Just east of Chablis is Tonnerre, a port on the Canal de Bourgogne as well as market town on the River Armançon, is about 16 kilometres (10 miles) from Château d'Ancy-le-Franc and about eight kilometres (five miles) from the Château de Tanlay, two of the most impressive châteaux in France. Modest Chablis has comparatively little but its vineyards as a claim to fame, but the church of the ruined Abbaye de Pontigny, a celebrated example of Cistercian architecture, is only some 11 kilometres (seven miles) away on the Serein. Walkers who like to have well-defined, worthwhile objectives for their expeditions will find no shortage in the department of the Yonne.

Chablis town and its environs might usefully, if very roughly, be thought of as the hub of a wheel, the spokes of which are the several valleys running back from the Serein stream; it is easy enough to cross from one valley to another, so that very satisfactory, fairly long walks of 16 kilometres (10 miles) or more – may be made without either doubling back on one's tracks or venturing outside the Chablis appellation.

Auxerre gives easy access to good walking in the wine country on the right bank of the Yonne, especially to the south-east, by way of the GR 13 and bridges over the river at Champs-sur-Yonne and Vincelles.

## WALK

**Chablis to Auxerre** by way of Courgis, St Cyr-les-Colons, Irancy, Champs-sur-Yonne, Vaux (by towpath), Auxerre (by GR 13). About 32 kilometres/20 miles; allow 8–9 hours.

This route provides easy – but by no means all level – walking virtually all of the way, though with steeper ups and downs in the hills bordering the Yonne, depending upon the chosen path.

| Maps | | | |
|---|---|---|---|
| 1:25,000 | 2720 est | Chablis | |
| | 2720 ouest | Champs-sur-Yonne | |
| 1:50,000 | 2720 | Chablis | |
| 1:100,000 | 28 | Auxerre-Saulieu | |
| Topo-Guide | GR 13-132 | Fontainbleu–Auxerre | |
| | GR 13-131 | Auxerre–Vezelay–Autun | |

# FROM THE
# SEREIN TO THE YONNE

*Near Chablis a signpost bears witness to the importance that so many communes all over France now give to the interests of walkers. Details of marked pedestrian routes are more often than not obtainable from the local Syndicat d'Initiative. All the same, the serious walker needs to be equipped with suitable maps.*

Among the assorted umbrellas and walking sticks in the hall at home is a hazel staff, whittled away so that one end is much thicker than the other, giving it the appearance of an elongated club. It was cut one September in a hanging wood overlooking the valley of the Armançon, not far from the Hôtel Abbaye Saint Michel, near Tonnerre. It was whittled on a hillside some 30 kilometres (18 miles) distant overlooking Irancy, just north of the valley of the River Yonne, a few miles south-east of Auxerre. Between the cutting and the whittling I walked through a region that produces one of the most famous – and most infamously imitated and abused – wines in the world.

One late autumn weekend, I had gone to the Hôtel Abbaye Saint Michel near Tonnerre with the intention of walking the 16 kilometres (10 or more miles) south-westwards to Chablis on the Sunday, and the following day covering about the same distance again from Chablis up to Maligny, at the top end of the appellation, and back. But on the Sunday morning, freezing, impenetrable fog cloaked the valley of the Serein and its vine-covered hillsides. Not a chance, the locals had insisted when I asked if it was likely to lift by the afternoon. 'It might clear by tomorrow, but I wouldn't count on it,' said Daniel Cussac, the proprietor of the Abbaye. Apologising for my far-from-elegant walking clothes, I had lunched delectably at a table near a log fire in the charming, vaulted restaurant, lingered over coffee, regretfully declined '*un petit digestif*' in view of the fact that I had more than 160 kilometres (100 miles) to drive afterwards, looked at the weather forecast on Minitel, and three hours later caught a flight back to London.

It was a glorious early autumn when I returned by train from Paris a year later. Between the little villages of Beine and Poinchy on the 19-kilometre (12-mile) drive from Auxerre to Chablis the road runs above a pretty valley, on the northern side of which are the Côte de Savant and the Côte de Troêmes, the latter including vineyards that produce the Premier Cru chablis Beauroy. Now they were bathed in sunshine so warm that an hour later I walked out from the Hôtel Abbaye Saint Michel in shirt-sleeves. 'Magnificent for the *vendanges*,' said Daniel Cussac. 'Marvellous for walking,' I thought.

That evening, dining exactly where I had lunched a year earlier, I was surprised to hear someone at the next table ordering Pouilly-Fuissé. True, the cheapest chablis on the list at the time happened to cost 30 francs more, but could that be the reason why he had chosen a white burgundy from the Mâconnais, 200 kilometres (120 miles) distant, rather than a white burgundy that might reasonably be regarded as the '*vin du pays*'? Or had the diner's experience of chablis so far been unfortunate? If so, it was a very great pity. 'Though chablis is more imitated than any other wine', wrote Morton Shand, 'it remains serenely inimitable and sovereignly apart. Chalk and cheese are not more dissimilar than a true chablis and a "chablis-type" wine, whatever the geographical credentials of the pretender may be.'

Strictly speaking, the Abbaye Saint Michel's local wine is not chablis at all, but the little-known red wine of Epineuil, above the River Armançon just to the north of Tonnerre, and I would have made an earlier start towards my true objective for the day, 16 kilometres (10 miles) distant, had I not accepted Daniel Cussac's suggestion of a 'quick visit' to his friend Monsieur Beau, who – he informed me irresistibly – 'makes a very good Pinot Noir that has won medals in Mâcon'. The quick visit included a tour of Monsieur Beau's three and a half hectares (eight and a half acres) of vines looking south towards the valley of the Armançon and the Canal de Bourgogne, followed by a tasting in his cellars. This included a beautifully light, ruby-coloured, freshly run, unfermented grape juice from the vat: 'Better than grapefruit juice for breakfast,' remarked Cussac, and I agreed.

I was glad to have met Monsieur Beau, who gave me a bottle of his Epineuil rosé when I left, but in consequence it was one o'clock before I reached a hillside commanding a view out over the Serein stream to vines on slopes beyond Chemilly-sur-Serein, and estimated myself to be properly within the appellation of Chablis. Here I chose a place among young pines and wild rose bushes heavy with bright hips and opened Monsieur Beau's parting gift. White and yellow butterflies fluttered about. The sun came out and almost all the sky was blue. The rosé went very well indeed with the *baguette* that I had bought in Tonnerre, and now I never think of chablis

*Almost a part of Chablis town, the village of Milly owes its name to the family of Miles de Noyers, which for centuries exercized feudal authority over the district and its Premier Crus vineyards of Côte de Lachet and les Lys.*

*The church of St Martin in Chablis dates from the end of the twelfth century and is one of the earliest examples of Gothic architecture in France. A chapter of the church of St Martin in Tours, fleeing the Viking invasions, asked Charles the Bold for a safe site further inland. They were granted one at Chablis and there built a resting place for the bones of their patron saint.*

without recalling that hillside and the rosehips and blue sky and warm September sun and – perversely – Epineuil rosé.

After lunch, it was time to test the expectations I had formed from my study of the map and I was pleased to find that the track leading north-west, parallel to the Serein, was as wide and open as I had imagined it would be. Maize and beans seemed to have been harvested from much of the almost flat land, but according to the map there were a few acres of vineyards up on the plateau of the Champs Boisons, out of sight above and beyond the woods to the south-west. Many more lay beyond the open arable land to the right of my path, between 180 and 250 metres (600–800 feet) up on the hillside overlooking Chichée, and on those other hillsides that face north-west but leading north-east up the valley of les Grands Prés (the big meadows) to Fleys.

That afternoon's progress was easy going, nor can I think of anywhere in France that offers such unhindered walking at the very gates of the place from which any particular wine country takes its name. After no more than a few hundred metres of busy road, I walked straight from the beans and maize into the Grands Crus of the magnificent slopes overlooking the town: Blanchots, les Clos, Valmur, Grenouilles, Vaudésir, les Preuses, Bougros. Following the contours of the hillside well above the valley road, climbing up and down (here and there quite steeply), now and then abandoning a track and climbing up and down between the vines, I traversed the hugely expensive acres, wondering if I might have the luck to see a bottle bearing any one of those famous names on the dinner table later on.

What I saw was a 'Fourchaume', which is not a Grand Cru but a Premier Cru, at an informal supper in the kitchen of Michel Laroche, whose family firm is one of the largest and most successful in Chablis. 'We pride ourselves on a happy marriage of the modern and the traditional,' he remarked next morning as we watched a mechanical harvester at work on the Fourchaume slopes. How on earth could any mechanical 'hands' ever remove the bunches of grapes without grabbing and removing half the vines themselves, I wanted to know. 'They don't,' said Laroche. 'It's all done by vibration. Watch.'

The 'hands' of the machine were very large, flat metal plates that were lowered to each side of the row of vines, barely touching the neatly trimmed plants. The vibrating plates simply shook the vines vigorously from side to side. Loose leaves were removed by a blower as the grapes moved on a conveyor belt into the tank on the harvester. 'Other undesirable bits and pieces get picked out at the *pressoir*,' explained Laroche. 'There are good arguments for and against mechanization, but on balance we are for. Being able to get the ripe grapes, and only the ripe grapes, to the *pressoir* when they are exactly at their best is not the least of the advantages.'

Time and place enough elsewhere, I thought, to enquire about the disadvantages. How was the harvest coming along? Down in quantity because of spring freezing and the long, dry summer, replied Laroche. 'Definitely up in quality, so that we'll ferment the Premier Cru and the Grand Cru in new oak and keep it there for at least five months. The bigger the wine, the more wood it can stand. Put a weak wine in new oak and you'll end up with more wood than wine.' To him, oak in the bigger wines was very much like salt and pepper with food: too little and the dish is bland; too much, and you spoil the flavour of the food itself.

The analogy reminded me of an observation by Emile Peynaud, one of France's foremost authorities on wine, in *The Taste of Wine*: 'Wood should be used for wines in the same way that spices are used in cooking, simply to bring out the other flavours.' Most chablis does not see any wood at all.

The Laroche premises in the heart of Chablis town are built of mellowed stone; a massive, very ancient timber wine press still works on special occasions; there are vaulted cellars said to have been part of a ninth-century monastic foundation; the bones of St Martin are believed to have lain here for some years. There we tasted half a dozen wines, three of them over ten years old. 'Chablis', noted Morton Shand, 'has considerable body lurking under a very subtle bouquet, inimitable limpidity, and virginal freshness, with a clean, pebbly flavour.' An earlier writer, he reminded his readers, had claimed that its flintiness was such an incentive to appetite that 'it would tempt a man to eat a carrion crow'. I was not entirely sure about the pebbly flavour in the delectable ten-year-olds, but as an aperitif chablis seems to me to have few rivals outside of Champagne, and when I left the Laroche tasting cellars I went in search of bread. Laroche have interests beyond Chablis and as I was going Michel gave me a bottle of their Côte de

*A spread of Chardonnay near Chablis, with the River Serein in the middle distance. River valleys as far north as this are subject to spring freeze-ups which can be disastrous for the budding vines. No effort is spared to counter the danger, including the use of air heaters of one sort or another and – oddly – the spraying of a mist of water over the burgeoning shoots. The resulting film of ice protects the buds against lower, more damaging temperatures.*

Nuits-Villages ('You'd better tuck this into your pack for lunch').

Sixteen kilometres (10 miles) to the south-west, and more than three hours later – over the hill, across the *autoroute* and down into the valley, through Chitry with its extraordinary church, its cats with slit eyes on sunny windowsills and its cottage gardens riotous with dahlias, up again through the vines where pickers were at work, down through woods where the light was green and birds sang, and up again on a sunken track that looked as if it had been there for ever – I raised a glass to my *chablisien* benefactor while relishing the crust of a particularly good loaf of rye bread.

It was quite wrong, of course. Just as it had been inappropriate to drink a rosé of Epineuil on arriving in the appellation of Chablis, so it was hardly fitting to be enchanted with a Côte de Nuits-Villages from the Côte d'Or, 160 kilometres (100 miles) away, while overlooking Irancy in the vineyards of the Yonne. Down in the sleepy little village were the cellars of Léon Bienvenu, whose wine would have been no less pleasing than the Laroche burgundy, but I had not yet been to Irancy, or tasted Monsieur Bienvenu's Pinot Noir. I had neither the time nor, in the heat of the afternoon, the stamina to descend into the valley: not if I was going to reach Auxerre before dark.

Anyway, I was supremely happy where I was. The scene suggested the sort of medieval painting in which the depth of field is conveyed only by a vertical arrangement of the subject matter. A few hundred metres below me a band of pickers was at work among the vines. The hillside was crossed by a minor road running roughly from lower right to upper left. Beyond, in the middle distance, the ground rose again, and here were more *vendangeurs* in a colourful variety of shirts and vests. Further off still were the roofs of Irancy, which was otherwise hidden, and above it the wide, largely vine-covered hillside rose to a plateau aptly named la Belle Vue. A prettier picture would be hard to find.

Côte de Nuits-Villages, says Serena Sutcliffe, 'can be quite blunt and tannic when young, but a graph of development is more rapid with a better appellation, so that at 3–5 years they are usually at their most appealing.' The appeal of this one, which had been four years in bottle, was very great. So were the view and the sound of a breeze in the little pine trees behind me and the *pain de seigle* and *pâté en croûte*. It was half past three by the time I set off again, but soon I was on the way-marked path of the GR 13 and making good time, keeping to the high ground above the Yonne. Clouds were coming up out of the west, but now and then there was a bright gleam of gold on the river. The view northwards, to St Bris-le-Vineux, was very lovely. 'Rich in vines' is a fair translation of *vineux*, and the beautiful, rolling countryside seemed almost as well endowed with vineyards as it was with the woods and orchards that are so significant a part of its economy.

The GR 13 descends to the river at Champs-sur-Yonne, following the towpath for a couple of kilometres to Vaux before it climbs away over the plateau south of Auxerre. At Vaux, old, solid and very handsome stone buildings with wide double doors distinguish the waterfront, monuments to the heavy commercial traffic that the river used to bear: timber from the forest of the Morvan on great rafts, and wine in casks. Now two couples on the deck of a brightly painted cabin cruiser motoring upstream raised their glasses and wished me '*Bonsoir*'. There are more pleasure boats than barges on most of France's waterways today. At Vaux, too, was another witness to nobler times – a fine, very substantial mansion with the gates to its unkempt courtyard rusty and open and windows shabbily shuttered. The yellowing leaves of tall poplars rustled softly and there was a scent of autumn.

Curiously and deeply saddened, I found the GR 13 markings again and followed them steeply up out of the village by a narrow track. At the top were cherry and apple orchards and vines and a splendid view eastwards to Chitry and all the country I had come through since that morning. Five kilometres (three miles) away, Auxerre's cathedral of Saint Etienne was highlighted by the last few seconds of the setting sun.

*Nestling in a valley close to the river, Irancy produces red and rosé wines, mostly from the Pinot Noir and usually listed in wine books under 'Other wines of the Yonne'. The sleepy village is on the route of the GR 13 between the Morvan, in central Burgundy, and Auxerre.*

# THE WINE

### CHABLIS

There are strong affinites between Chablis and Champagne. Both share the geology of the eastern edge of the Paris basin. Though limestone and clay largely determine the essential character of chablis, and chalk is the foundation of Champagne *viticole classique*, there are significant outcroppings of chalk in the Chablis region. Chardonnay is the white grape indispensable to both, but is the only one used for chablis.

Whereas most Burgundy wines are subject to infinitely intricate subtleties of appellation, there are only four straightforward categories of chablis: Grand Cru, Premier Cru, Chablis AC and Petit Chablis. All the Grand Cru vineyards, occupying only some 100 hectares (250 acres), are on the wide, open slopes just to the north and east of Chablis town. The 30 Premier Cru vineyards, totalling about 600 hectares (1500 acres), are widely distributed on slopes overlooking the little Serein stream or its tributary valleys. Ordinary Chablis AC comes from roughly 1200 hectares (3000 acres) throughout the rest of the appellation. Petit Chablis accounts for about 240 hectares (600 acres) mostly on the outer edges of Chablis AC areas to the north-west and south-west of Chablis town.

All chablis is dry, or meant to be. All is white. None is sparkling in the sense that champagne is a sparkling wine. Generally speaking, the higher the quality, the more important the age of chablis. Because of the extreme climatic difficulties of the region, vintage years are very significant.

### THE YONNE

Because chablis is usually considered in relation not to the Serein, but to the far larger River Yonne to which the Serein is a tributary, the other wines of the area, where they are acknowledged at all, are generally lumped together as 'other wines of the Yonne'. To the west of the Yonne, south of Auxerre, is the commune of Coulanges-la-Vineuse, which produces light red and rosé wines from the Pinot Noir. To the east of the river, that is on the Chablis side, are the only three other communes likely to feature in any wine literature. Chitry and St Bris-le-Vineux each have no fewer than seven varieties of vine: Pinot Noir, Gamay and César for red and rosé wines, and Sauvignon, Aligoté, Chardonnay and Sacy for white. Serena Sutcliffe names the Aligoté (from the grape of that name), and the Bourgogne Blanc (from the Chardonnay) as being particularly promising in Chitry, and the Aligoté as being superior to the Sauvignon in St Bris. She mentions only in passing that commune's Crémant de Bourgogne, a subject on which local tourist literature tends to be expansive since at Bailly, on the river near Champs-sur-Yonne, the great limestone quarries that supplied stone for the Panthéon in Paris now house an impressive quantity of the sparkling wine. Robert Joseph has described the wine as being of 'high quality'. Irancy, lastly, grows mostly Pinot Noir and a little César to make reds and rosés.

*'Chablis, Aligoté Bourgogne', says the neck label of this giant bottle in the village of Collan, between Chablis and Tonnerre. Aligoté is a white grape which has steadily – and literally – been losing ground to the more fashionable Chardonnay, the only grape legally permitted in Chablis AOC wines. The price of a bottle of Aligoté is always appreciably less than that of a Chablis.*

*'And almost everywhere that my chosen route would be likely to take me were vineyards, mostly of a size that suggested small proprietors and domaines of varied character, though more often than not widely interspersed with woods and pastures and arable acres not devoted to the vine.'*

# THE CÔTE D'OR

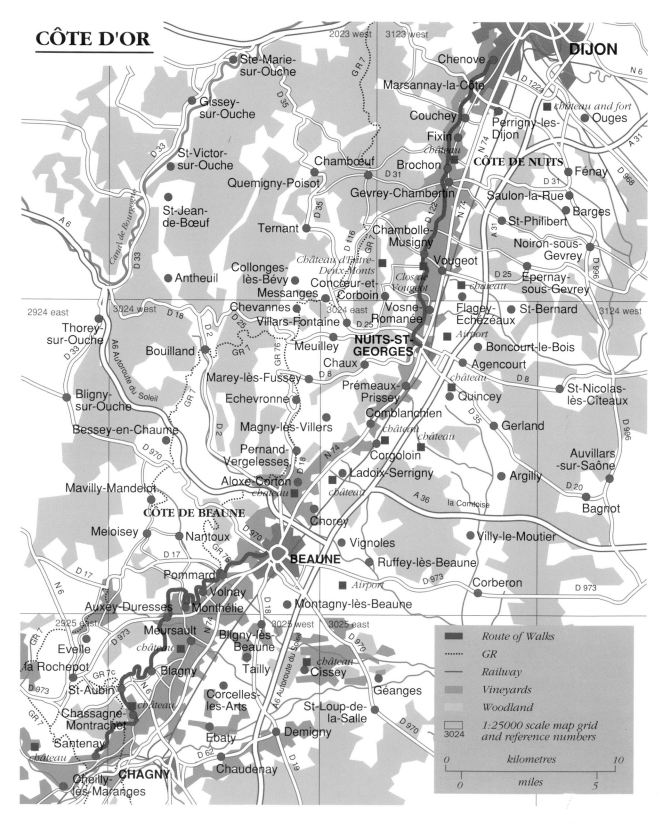

**CÔTE D'OR**

DIJON

2023 west    3123 west

Ste-Marie-sur-Ouche

Chenove

Marsannay-la-Côte

Gissey-sur-Ouche

Couchey

Perrigny-les-Dijon

Ouges

*château and fort*

St-Victor-sur-Ouche

Fixin
*château*

Chambœuf

Brochon

**CÔTE DE NUITS**

Fénay

Quemigny-Poisot

Gevrey-Chambertin

Saulon-la-Rue

St-Jean-de-Bœuf

Barges

St-Philibert

Ternant

Chambolle-Musigny

Noiron-sous-Gevrey

*Château d'Entre-Deux-Monts*

Antheuil

Collonges-lès-Bévy

Messanges

Concœur-et-Corboin

Vougeot

*Clos de Vougeot*

*château*

Epernay-sous-Gevrey

2924 east    3024 west

Chevannes

Villars-Fontaine

3024 east

Vosne-Romanée

Flagey-Echézeaux

St-Bernard

3124 west

*Airport*

Thorey-sur-Ouche

**NUITS-ST-GEORGES**

Boncourt-le-Bois

Bouilland

Meuilley

Chaux

Agencourt
*château*

Marey-lès-Fussey

Prémeaux-Prissey

Quincey

St-Nicolas-lès-Cîteaux

Bligny-sur-Ouche

Echevronne

Comblanchien

Gerland

Bessey-en-Chaume

Magny-les-Villers

*château*  *château*

Corgoloin

Auvillars-sur-Saône

Pernand-Vergelesses

Ladoix-Serrigny

Argilly

Mavilly-Mandelot

Aloxe-Corton
*château*

*château*

*la Comtoise*

Bagnot

**CÔTE DE BEAUNE**

Chorey

Meloisey

Nantoux

Vignoles

Villy-le-Moutier

**BEAUNE**

Ruffey-lès-Beaune

Corberon

Pommard

*Airport*

Volnay

Auxey-Duresses

Monthélie

Montagny-lès-Beaune

2925 east

Meursault
*château*

Bligny-lès-Beaune

3025 west    3025 east

Evelle

Tailly

*château*
Cissey

la Rochepot

Blagny

Géanges

St-Aubin

*château*

Corcelles-les-Arts

St-Loup-de-la-Salle

Chassagne-Montrachet

Ebaty

Demigny

Santenay
*château*

Chaudenay

**CHAGNY**

Cheilly-les-Maranges

| | Route of Walks |
|---|---|
| | GR |
| | Railway |
| | Vineyards |
| | Woodland |
| 3024 | 1:25000 scale map grid and reference numbers |

0    kilometres    10

0    miles    5

# BRIEFING

## THE LIE OF THE LAND

Think of the Côte d'Or as a vine-covered slope running north to south between Dijon and Chagny, roughly 50 kilometres (30 miles) long but seldom as much as a mile wide, and facing eastwards towards the River Saône. Rarely very steep, mostly only gently tilted and sometimes almost imperceptibly so, it is interrupted at intervals by little valleys – *combes* – reaching back into the limestone plateau of which the Côte as a whole constitutes the eastern edge.

Think of it also as the world of wine and wine literature thinks of it, which is to say in two parts: the Côte de Nuits and the Côte de Beaune. The Côte de Nuits starts at Fixin, south of Dijon, and runs down to Prémaux, just south of Nuits-St Georges. The Côte de Beaune begins at Aloxe-Corton, just north of Beaune, and ends at Santenay.

Strictly speaking, the Côte also includes the immediate hinterland to the vine-covered territory between the plain and the plateau. Here, westwards of all the famous villages, on the slopes of the *combes* and of valleys yet further to the west – not in great, impressive sweeps, but interspersed with woods and orchards and pastures – are the modest vineyards of the Hautes Côtes. The wines of this back country of the Côte d'Or may offer burgundies that are bargains by comparison with those of their far better-known neighbours; the walking, however, cannot claim the wide views and long, clear paths of the renowned vineyards between the plateau and the plain of the Saône.

Think of the Côte d'Or mainly, then, as this narrow, irregularly drawn corridor of vines and villages between the often wooded edge of the plateau and the N 74, which runs parallel to the Autoroute du Soleil between Dijon and Beaune and between Beaune and Chagny.

## WALKS

**Côte de Nuits** Dijon (Chenôve) to Nuits-St Georges. 20 kilometres/12.5 miles; allow 5–6 hours.

The wine presses of the Dukes of Burgundy in Chenôve offer an appropriate start. The initial 5 or 6 kilometres (3 or 4 miles) to Fixin (the first important village of the Côte) are likely to be the least captivating stage of the walk. Two kilometres (1.25 miles) further on, just south of Gevrey-Chambertin, the walker may take the comparatively high road at the top of the vine-covered slopes to Chambolle-Musigny and on to south of Clos de Vougeot. Having descended for a kilometre or two, it is then possible to climb up to scrubland beyond the vines, in order to reach a track which again descends

diagonally through Premier Cru vineyards to about a kilometre (just over half a mile) north-west of Nuits-St Georges.

**Côte de Beaune** Beaune to Santenay, by way of Pommard, Monthélie, Auxey-Duresses, Blagny and Chassagne-Montrachet. 20 kilometres/12.5 miles; allow 5–7 hours.

Out of Beaune, keep well north of the N 74 by taking the Pommard road, then vineyard paths to choice. The 10 kilometres (6 miles) or so from just short of Pommard to just before Chassagne-Montrachet represent some of the best walking on the Côte d'Or, with paths that are far from straight and level, lovely views and varied terrain. Careful attention to map-reading is required, however.

**Maps**

| 1:25,000 | 3123 ouest | Dijon | includes city of Dijon to Vosne-Romanée, north of Nuits-St Georges |
|---|---|---|---|
| | 3024 est | Nuits-St Georges | includes Nuits-St Georges to outskirts of Beaune |
| | 3024 ouest | Beaune | includes city of Beaune to outskirts of Meursault |
| | 3025 ouest | Chagny | includes village of Meursault to St Jean-de-Vaux (Chalonnaise), south of Chagny |
| 1:50,000 | 3123 | Dijon | to just south of Tournus |
| | 3024 | Beaune | includes city to outskirts of Chagny |
| 1:100,000 | 37 | Dijon–Tournus | just south of Dijon to just south of Tournus |

# APRIL ON
# THE CÔTE DE NUITS

*Dijon is full of fine architecture
and noble façades in the local pale
limestone, many of them adorned
with decorative carvings such as
this garlanded female.*

Standing on the Boulevard de la Trémouille in Dijon on a fine, clear day, looking south to the hills of the Côte d'Or, it is possible to entertain the happy illusion that by continuing straight ahead one must surely be able to walk unhindered into the vineyards of the Côte de Nuits. An illusion it must remain, however. Where vineyards once almost hugged the walls of the city, now Californian-type suburbs sprawl for some three kilometres (two miles) before more than a few isolated and uninspiring plots of viticulture are reached. Untidily interspersed with patches of maize, assorted vegetables and fruit trees, limited on the one side by the unlovely building developments bordering the Dijon to Beaune road and on the other by the nondescript slopes of the Hautes Côtes, they have nothing of the dignity to be found further south along the Côte d'Or. Later, after Fixin say, the vineyards are recognizably the be-all and end-all of local existence. Here, even around Marsannay and Couchey, where red, a little white and a famous rosé are made, they might be mistaken for an afterthought, incidental to ever-spreading suburbs. At Chenôve, once a country village, are nevertheless the beginnings of tracks that enable the walker to set off southwards without braving hard-top roads and backyard dogs. There also are the much-photographed wine presses of the Dukes of Burgundy, which may help to sustain a romantic idea of wine and wine-making in an increasingly technological age. Many a modest stone-built outhouse of the Côte d'Or shelters an old press, still in use, that functions according to the same mechanical principles.

It was a fine morning in April when I set out. Impatient to get well beyond the petrol stations and housing estates, I set a good pace for three kilometres (two miles) or more, until just short of Couchey. There, where cherry trees were in blossom among the vines, I was wished a friendly '*Bonjour*' by a luxuriantly bearded man who was walking down between the rows of Pinot Noir in what seemed to me a proprietoral sort of way. And, indeed, he was Monsieur Huguenot *père*, of Huguenot Père et Fils of Marsannay, 'just running an eye over things'. What were the two men further off among the vines doing, I asked him. Tying the canes of pruned vines to the supporting wires, replied Monsieur Huguenot. How many hectares of vines did Huguenot Père et Fils own, I asked. A good twenty, he said, but only six of them here, and the rest in other appellations. Did 20 hectares (50 acres) constitute a large holding? No, only a good medium-sized one. Some people had a lot more. Hundreds had far less. He and his son made red, white and a little rosé; but mostly red, and mostly to be drunk fairly young; not for long keeping, like a lot of wines from the more famous vineyards of the Côte, where they had different soils. There (Monsieur Huguenot gestured towards Fixin, Gevrey-Chambertin and Chambolle-Musigny) – there the better slopes had a different balance of chalk or limestone and clay.

More clay, as here, where we stood on level ground close to the village of Couchey made for less finely structured wines. 'The best thing would be for you to come and taste them.'

But having got into my stride I did not want to break it. Already it was eleven o'clock and I wanted to reach Gevrey-Chambertin, more than three kilometres (two miles) away, before everything shut for lunch. Not only had I ideas of visiting the château, I also needed to shop for a picnic. Might I come another day, I asked. Any time, said Monsieur Huguenot. Thus I hurried on through Fixey, with its very prettily placed Romanesque church, and through Fixin (pronounced 'Fissin'), which in retrospect seems to nestle among cherry and plum blossom, reaching Gevrey-Chambertin as the clocks struck twelve.

The château was closed all that day, but I was able to buy what I needed for lunch, including wine. Notwithstanding the locality, I had intended nothing out of the ordinary when I chanced across a serious-looking corner shop with a well-known wine-maker's name over the door. I expected it to be locked, but it was open. The interior was attractively Dickensian and silent. After a little while a grandmotherly person appeared, apologising for keeping me waiting. '*Les jeunes*', who really looked after the shop, were all '*à table*'. It was clearly not the occasion for tasting or deliberation, so with some extravagance I bought a cellar-cool bottle of the proprietor's three-year-old Gevrey-Chambertin AC. As soon as I had left the shop I tucked it down inside my shirt, buttoned and zipped everything else over it, and

*'Think of the Côte d'Or mainly as this narrow, irregularly drawn corridor of vines and villages between the wooded edge of the plateau and the N 74.'*

went on my way hoping that nobody would remark my curious anatomy and that by picnic time my expensive acquisition would be agreeably *chambré*. I was not at all sorry that the château had been closed.

In his autobiographical book *A Traveller's Life*, Eric Newby tells of asking Evelyn Waugh to write an introduction to *A Short Walk in the Hindu Kush*. In the course of the brief correspondence that followed, Newby had occasion to point out that there was no such wine as the 'Clos de Bère' which features in *Brideshead Revisited*. Waugh replied that it was a misprint for Clos de Bèze. Newby got his introduction, and as a gesture of thanks sent Waugh three magnums of Clos de Bèze. Newby and I were friends. We had talked about the incident, and about Waugh, and (as always in Newby's company) had laughed a lot. Such were my slender motives for wanting to sit with a glass of burgundy overlooking the Clos de Bèze, though I had never tasted the product of its precious 15 hectares (37 acres). Taking the tarred minor road that leads up the hill out of Gevrey into the Bois du Forey, I came to a track running between the topmost vines and the wood, just below the 300 metre contour line. Two or three minutes more brought me to a little grassy recess in the bank that formed both the border of the track and the margin of the wood. 'The Grand Crus shelter under the woods of the Montagne de la Combe Grisard, a good barrier against the winds from the north,' notes Serena Sutcliffe of the highest vineyards of Gevrey-Chambertin, in my dog-eared and wine-stained copy of her invaluable *Pocket Guide to the Wines of Burgundy*. With the north wind sighing in the trees, I gratefully shed my pack, settled myself comfortably, and ritually poured a little of the Gevrey-Chambertin AC on to the ground, there above one of the most celebrated of all the Grands Crus. Not ten metres below were the precisely ordered, immaculately tended vines of the Clos de Bèze.

It is not the recommended treatment for any decent wine that it should be translated from cellar to luncheon underneath the consumer's thermal vest in the course of a purposeful 1200-metre walk; nevertheless, the little burgundy seemed to have taken no harm. It was a trifle too young, I thought, and still a touch too cold; all the same, it was better than drinkable right from the start, and much better half an hour later, and by the time I reflected that half a bottle would have been absurdly too little I began to think also that Serena Sutcliffe's remark about the top wines of the appellation combining 'finesse with power' might not be inappropriate for the humbler ones too. What a delight it was to sit in that privileged place, watching cloud shadows passing over the burgeoning vines of Grands and Premiers Crus, looking at the map, and noting that the good, wide track ran southwards all the way along the edge of the wood and out into the vines, promising fine, steady walking with – except for the wine villages and the Château du Clos de Vougeot – not a dwelling (and so probably not a dog) in sight.

So it proved, though in order not to descend to the D 122 and the village of Morey-St Denis I had to follow a narrow track steeply up behind the Clos de Tart and along the brow of the largely scrub-covered hillside before

*The gates of the Clos de Vougeot open on to vineyards with a multiplicity of owners producing wines of widely varying quality.*

*At Gevrey-Chambertin, on the Côte de Nuits, a vigneron takes time off from wine-making to harvest his crop of cherries.*

coming down into the *combe* and the village of Chambolle-Musigny.

Not five kilometres (three miles) had yet been covered since lunch at the Clos de Bèze, but there were good reasons to pause here on the way to Nuits-St Georges. First, there was the village of Chambolle-Musigny. The Romans, says one book, called it Campus Ebulliens because of the stream that flowed out of the *combe* and in times of heavy rain inconveniently overflowed its narrow course. Campus Ebulliens became Champ Bouillant, and then Chambolle. On looking into such matters, one soon learns caution if not scepticism. One of the two Grand Crus of the appellation is Bonnes Mares (Musigny is the other). *Mare* means stagnant pool, says one reference; *mares* comes from the word *marer*, an ancient word meaning the annual husbandry of the vines, says another, so that *bonnes mares* could mean well-tended acres. No, says a third, 'Bonnes Mares' is obviously a corruption of '*Bonnes Mères*', the property having once belonged to Bernadine nuns. Whatever the etymology of its place names, with its solidly handsome houses, its inclined streets and alleys, its geranium-decked courtyards of ochre-coloured stone and its lime trees, Chambolle-Musigny is among the prettiest villages of the Côte d'Or.

It is also an appropriate place in which to touch lightly upon the weighty subject of soil. The Côte d'Or consists of a multiplicity of individual vineyards known as *climats*. The soil of one *climat* may be significantly different from that of another, in which case the wines from them, if skilfully made, will reflect those differences. The vineyards of Chambolle-Musigny and neighbouring Morey-St Denis offer a good example. 'It is here that the wines of the Côte de Nuits change,' remarks Alexis Lichine of Morey-St Denis. 'The Morey vineyards of Clos de la Roche and Clos Saint Denis serve as a bridge between the hard sturdiness of the northern part of the commune and the softer, elegant distinction of the Bonne Mares, Musignys, and other wines from Chambolle, the next commune southward. To

*Nuits-St Georges, end of the Côte de Nuits, en fête. The grapes of its vineyards are usually the first to ripen on the whole of the Côte, according to Morton Shand.*

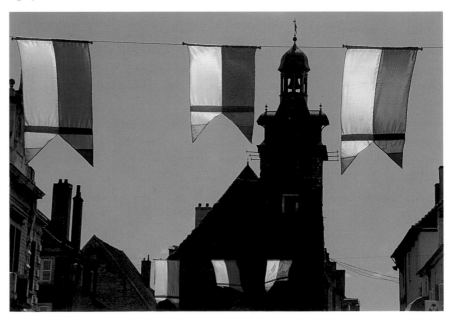

the eye there is no distinction between the vines of the two communes [but] ... having once owned a small parcel in Bonnes Mares ... I always marvelled at these infinite variations of the soil, which year in year out created consistent differences between my wines on the Chambolle side and those of my neighbours in Morey.'

As I continued along the eastern edge of the woods of la Montagne de la Combe Grisard, with the vines of Chambertin and Latricières immediately below me, and then across the slope through the heart of the Clos de la Roche, Clos de Tart and Bonnes Mares, I noted the variations in the soil (here the colour of milk chocolate with many small pebbles, there much darker with fewer pebbles), the density with which the vines were planted, how they were trained and pruned, the pitch of the ground in this place or that, and whether a vineyard faced due east, or east with a southern inclination, and so on. In short, I tried to notice all those things which, we are assured, so influence the character of a wine that the true expert can with ease taste a wine labelled only — say — 'Chambertin', or even not labelled at all, and tell us whether it is from the vines of Chambolle-Musigny-les-Amoureuses, which are on one side of the D 122, or from those of Chambolle-Musigny-les-Charmes, which are just on the other. I noticed them, but I did not dwell on them, for the sky had become so blue and the sun so warm that opposite the Clos de Vougeot, and above the wide, lovely and seemingly endless sweep of vines, I was tempted to climb up into the long grass on the hillside bordering the track, and there to lie in the sun among the box and briar roses.

I was sitting looking at my map on a low stone wall between the vines of Romanée-Conti and Romanée-St Vivant (what names for a booted wanderer to conjure with!) when a middle-aged man who was driving slowly along the track in a modest Renault stopped to enquire if I needed help. I said that I had been given the address of a certain well-reputed wine-maker in the locality and that I was now trying to find him. What was the wine-maker's name, the man asked. 'Trapet,' I told him. 'Well,' he said, 'You'll have no difficulty in tracking him down because he's talking to you. Put your pack on the back seat and jump in.' Thus I made the acquaintance of one of the best-known wine-makers of the Côte de Nuits. His car was modest. His wine-making premises, like those of so many others whose names are music to a wine-lover's ears, would be unlikely to attract so much as a passing glance, nor were they tricked out with any of the refinements so frequently to be found in a business that is only too aware of the value of appearances. There was no rustically elegant, candle-lit tasting cellar gleaming with polished oak and sparkling glass; no poker-worked wooden boxes of wine for 'VIP' guests. There was oak in plenty, the deliciously fragrant new oak of neatly marshalled rows of casks stained purple around the bungs by young wines, but we tasted by electric light, spitting into a plastic bucket. 'Violets, perhaps', Monsieur Trapet replied thoughtfully when I asked him to give his own impressions of the 'nose' of this wine or that, 'and red berry fruit. *Epices*, of course. Spice.' Admiring the very

*All wine, said Hilaire Belloc, is conditioned by circumstances. Among the vineyards, with the appetite and thirst stimulated by a good walk, even a very modest bottle may give pleasure for which there can be no price.*

beautiful colour (*robe*) and limpidity of the sample in the glass, I asked how much he filtered. 'Very little,' he said. Too much filtration could take the heart out of a wine.

It was the easiest and most agreeable of marches into Nuits-St Georges thereafter, so that I was already reviewing with satisfaction my 16-kilometre (10-mile) day on the Côte de Nuits and looking forward to the Côte de Beaune. Nuits-St Georges only sustained and improved the mood. On a previous visit a year or two before I had stayed grandly as a paying guest in the house of the Comtesse de Loisy, where dinner had started with truffled eggs and the lamb that followed had been accompanied by a superb Nuits-St Georges from the very distinguished house of Faiveley. Now I lodged less nobly and chose to have dinner at a hugely busy, ordinary restaurant in the centre of town. The three-course menu cost what one might expect to pay for the soup in London's West End, and was wholly acceptable. There were house wines at charitable prices, and when the bustling, good-humoured *patronne* told me, *sotto voce*, that there was a bottle or two of 'réserve spéciale' left if I would like to try it, I gladly accepted and found myself drinking a wine which, although no Richebourg or Romanée-Conti, was far superior to the sort of burgundies that I might normally afford. What exactly was it, I asked. Ah, said the *patronne*, she couldn't tell me that, though her husband might know; but at any rate it was from '*d'ici quelque part*': somewhere around here. It went wonderfully well with the chicken and chips.

*Collonges-lès-Bévy in the Hautes Côtes-de-Nuits: 'the wines of this back country of the Côte d'Or may offer burgundies that are bargains by comparison with those of their far better-known neighbours. The walking is good too, but different.*

# LUNCHING ON
# THE CÔTE DE BEAUNE

*The famous polychrome tiles of
the Hospices de Beaune, where the*
cour d'honneur *has been
described as 'a lodging fit
for a prince rather than a
hospital for the poor'.*

The Côte de Beaune began rather less modestly than the Côte de Nuits had ended, for I stayed at the Hôtel le Cep in Beaune's Rue Marfoux and dined in the Restaurant Bernard Morillon at the same address. Morillon has a well-deserved Michelin star. Late after dinner on the Saturday night, chatting with him over an especially good marc de Bourgogne, I asked if he might suggest one or two wine-makers I might visit. I had to stop him in full spate after I had listed six, knowing that if I managed to meet two I would be lucky. The difficulty for the walker in wine country is not so much the introductions as the time.

Next day I was up very early in order to take photographs in the vineyards while the sun was still low, and when I looked about for some where to buy a few things for a picnic lunch I found nothing open in the centre of the city except a *boulangerie*. Was there anywhere that I might buy other food and drink, I asked? Well, they said, just round the corner was a *traiteur* whom they knew to be getting things ready for a party he was doing that day: there was just a chance that he might help. The *traiteur* was civility itself. He sold me some food, and when I asked where I might get wine he shrugged his shoulders and said that everything was shut, but added that, provided I kept quiet about it, he might forget about the law and let me have a bottle of something. Which did I prefer: red or white? Taking a bottle of red at ten francs a litre, I enquired what it was, meaning mostly where did it come from. He smiled. '*C'est un bon vin de traiteur. Pas plus.*' It was a kindly answer to a silly question. Gratefully, I went on my way.

After almost two hours of the sort of frustrations that professional photographers are paid to endure and that walkers and writers are best ad- vised to avoid I was among the vines of the Premiers Crus of the Pommard appellation. Then I was past Pommard (Pomona, the Roman goddess of fruits and gardens, had a temple there) and climbing up to Volnay, whose wine I have been especially fond of ever since I first acquired any prefer- ences in burgundy. I dare say it has something to do with the name and its associations of flight, lightness and airiness, just as the name Fleurie un- doubtedly has a lot to do with the popularity of that delightful *cru* of the Beaujolais. And Volnay is indeed exceptionally light and elegant: Hugh Johnson has described it as the Château Lafite of the Côte de Beaune.

Now it was lunchtime. The place where I slipped off my pack was a very small, flat piece of turf cut into the pine-and-shrub-covered summit of the slope at the extremity of the vines to the south of Volnay village, sheltered from a keen little north-west breeze and commanding a very lovely view. If I had chosen the place on the grounds of viticultural distinction alone, however, I could not conceivably have done better. A few metres down the slope to the left were the vines of Taille Pied; below and to the right were those of the Clos des Chênes. Below Taille Pied was the vineyard or *climat*

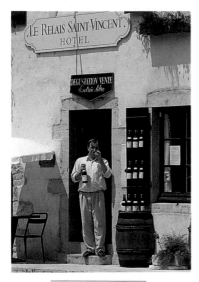

*The name St Vincent, patron saint of wine-makers, is attached to a multiplicity of things in the wine regions of France, including many an establishment not distinguished in the guidebooks. The suggestion of free entry and* dégustation *is commonplace in Meursault. The entry may be free, but the* dégustation *more often than not assumes the purchase of a bottle or two of wine.*

of en Champans. Below the Clos des Chênes was Cailleret Dessus. It would have been fitting, as I sat there enjoying this prospect of the wide valley of the Saône and the Doubs and the distant Jura, had I been able to draw the cork from a bottle of one of these same Volnay Premiers Crus. In fact I had only the *bon vin de traiteur*, with '*12% vol. Vin de table de France*' printed on its cork, but it would have been extravagant to ask for anything better to go with the cold chicken and cheese, and in the end I poured away no more than a quarter-bottle before going on up to Monthélie in search of one of Bernard Morillon's friends.

With its old stone houses, its hidden courtyards and its steep streets, Monthélie is as close as one is likely to get to the romantic idea of what a Burgundian wine village ought to be, and is as convincing a proof as might be needed that contemporary wine-making is far from being all stainless steel and eagle-eyed accountants. The domaine was not easy to find. Though lunchtime was still some way off, Monthélie seemed deserted. 'Round the corner and on the right,' directed a woman whom I caught sight of through a half-open window. But there was no sign to identify the premises, and I walked past them twice before finding the entrance. In a courtyard hidden from the street, on a floor of cobbles, hard-beaten earth and gravel, lay a score of oak casks, no more than a few years old, in one stage or another of being cleaned. A sliding door of unpainted, weathered timber gave access to a *cuverie* of large oak vats, where two youngish men were scrubbing down the cement floor with long brooms. One of them, by his own description 'a sort of foreman', paused in his task and came forward to meet me. I introduced myself and we shook hands. Of course, said the man, Monsieur Morillon was a good friend and client of the *patronne*, who unfortunately was away in Lyon; could he be of help? Thus, beside the open fermentation vats at courtyard level, then down in a cellar where the white Monthélie-'villages', Meursault-'villages' and Volnay Premier Cru les Santenots were in cask, and where the red Monthélie Premier Cru les Duresses and Premier Cru le Meix Bataille were also ageing in wood, there began an hour of talk and tasting. The property was now in the hands of the fifth generation of the same family, I was told. There were 6.3 hectares (15.5 acres) of vines in 17 different *parcelles*, '*très morcelés*' (very fragmented), in a number of different appellations: Monthélie, Volnay, Auxey-Duresses, Pommard, Meursault and so on. All their wines were made in the wood, always had been. Yes, they exported quite a bit, and sold a lot to tourists. Would I like to try anything special?

Already, by the very nature of the property, I had been given a useful reminder of the essential character of the Burgundy wine scene: the astounding fragmentation by ownership of the vineyards, and in consequence, the enormous variations to be encountered in wines bearing the same vineyard name. Three different domaines, for example, may own *parcelles* of vines in the appellation of Pommard, in the vineyard called, say, les Gavottes. Each may make its own estate-bottled 'Pommard Premier Cru les Gavottes, Appellation Pommard Premier Cru Contrôlée'. The wine of one might be excellent, that of the second could be mediocre, while that of the third might well be a downright disgrace. Or, to take a famous true example, at the time of writing the tiny Clos de Vougeot, covering only some 50 hectares (125 acres), is divided between no fewer than 78 owners, many of whom make their own wine and sell it under the Clos de Vougeot name. Some owners who have too few vines for a wine of their own contribute their grapes to a cooperative vinification. Others who make too small a quantity of wine to justify an individual label sell it to a *négociant-éleveur* who will make it part of his own blend. Then again, some plots of vines are on the least favourable soil of the Clos, down on the flat ground, while others lie on the better soil higher up. Morton Shand states that in the Middle Ages, when Cistercian monks owned the Clos, three different qualities of wine were made from the upper, middle and lower levels. And yet again, some of the vines are more mature than others. Inevitably, the quality of wine that is sold quite legitimately as 'Clos de Vougeot' varies from the superb to the very ordinary. 'I pity the consumer', says Alexis Lichine, 'who tries to distinguish from the label the quality of the wine inside.'

So there in Monthélie, in those ancient cellars redolent of oak and many vintages, in the company of the foreman, of the other man who had been working with him when I arrived and of another who said that he did 'a little of everything' on the property, I tasted half a dozen of the domaines's wines, and thought I saw why the chef admired them. There was an '89 Meursault which, the foreman said, needed five or six years before drink-

*On the path to Blagny between Meursault and Puligny-Montrachet. Blagny produces both red and white wines, but only the red are entitled to the appellation of the commune. The best whites are classified as either Meursault or Puligny-Montrachet.*

*Well-drained, with underlying limestone, like the vines themselves, the vineyard paths of the Côte d'Or offer many miles of easy walking with no direction-finding problems whatever.*

ing. ('Burgundy whites need ageing, and the big ones just as much ageing as the reds.') There was an '88 ('a great year') les Duresses, which in the opinion of my three tasting companions needed 'at least ten years' before it would be ready for drinking. How was it then, I asked, that '88 red burgundies like that were everywhere to be found on restaurant wine lists? 'Because it's too expensive to pay for them and then keep them lying in the cellar, earning nothing,' was the answer. So they were drunk much too young, which was what had earned such a lot of good wine a bad name.

Though people in the trade are often obliged to do it at that time, half past three in the afternoon is not the best time for tasting, and to tell the truth I was considerably less interested in my own impressions than in observing my companions. Here, 'nosing' each sample briefly; holding it up to the light by the stem or the base of the glass; swirling it expertly; nosing it again; taking half a mouthful; 'chewing' it; sucking air through it; in short, going through all the performances by which a wine of stature is encouraged to reveal its character, were not pin-stripe-suited directors of smart wine-shipping houses, or public relations account executives who had been to evening classes, but men in *bleus de travail* whose job was not even to sell the wine, but to grow the grapes and make it. Here were individuals who could tell you whether the soil of the *climat* of le Meix Bataille had more pebbles in it than the soil of Sur la Velle, or less, or none at all, or whether the vines of the Clos des Chênes got more sun than those of en Chevret, or whether Jean-Paul X. was inclined to use chemicals rather than harrowing to control weeds in the vineyard, or if it had rained excessively in April of the year before last. Here, I thought, was the Burgundy one liked to imagine behind the labels. And it was no rarity. I departed with warm encouragement to return and with the names of other vignerons to be visited in neighbouring Meursault and Auxey-Duresses. Truly there is a *confrérie* of respect and admiration among the makers of good wine.

But an appointment for seven o'clock that evening in Chagny was still at least ten kilometres (six miles) away, and after leaving Monthélie I was obliged to bypass both Auxey-Duresses and Meursault, which saddened me. Each November, unless the year has been especially bad for Burgundy wines, and usually on the third Sunday in the month, the great auction of the new vintage takes place at the famous Hospices de Beaune. On the Saturday evening before the sale there is a dinner under the auspices of the Chevaliers du Tastevin at the Clos de Vougeot. On the Sunday evening, after the sale, there is the 'Dîner aux Chandelles' in the Bastion de Beaune. And on the Monday, at the Château de Meursault, there is the much-sought-after Paulée de Meursault, the last of the three great social events collectively known as les Trois Glorieuses. The first strikes me as being eminently missable. The second would not see me if it clashed with an invitation to dine with friends. But for the Paulée de Meursault almost no sacrifice would be too great.

In the Burgundian *patois* a *paulée* is a midday break, which in the past (I am told) used to be enjoyed by the workers in the fields. It is above all the unpretentious, down-to-earth nature of the Paulée that constitutes so much of its worth. It begins very formally, all *Monsieur* and *Madame* and polite enquiries as to what one thought about the price at yesterday's auction, and whether it is one's first time in Burgundy. An hour later, people who had been total strangers before sitting down are emphasizing a point or securing a neighbour's attention with a hand resting fleetingly on a forearm, or a head brought ever so slightly closer than is really justified even by the rapidly rising tide of noisy conversation. Soon, glasses are clinking one against another in that universal expression of bonhomie.

It begins with champagne at about noon. It ends with cognac and other *petits digestifs* long after night has fallen. The food is very good, and as for the wine, I have never tasted such a variety of burgundies before, and I shall be fortunate ever to do so again. At the Paulée, growers and merchants delight in producing examples of their best, Meursault, naturally, being in overwhelming predominance. Bottles pass up and down the long tables, and names far beyond one's pocket and any but academic acquaintance appear on labels half-hidden now and then by slim, bejewelled fingers.

So I walked on from Meursault to Montrachet (the 't' is silent), through plot after expensive and virtually flat plot of names that are unlikely to be found on any supermarket shelves: les Gouttes d'Or, les Bouchères, les Genevrières Dessus and Dessous (literally, the upper and lower junipers). At the top of the vineyards was a patch of uncultivated land and – curiously shocking – a hideous rubbish tip. Feeling immensely tired, though I could hardly have walked more than a dozen kilometres (seven miles) in the day, I lay on the grass beside a drystone wall and closed my eyes for twenty minutes between les Charmes Dessus and Dessous, the first to the north of the track, the second to the south. Checking the map, I noted that the church spire of Puligny-Montrachet was ahead of me, and that a kilometre (just over half a mile) up the slopes was Blagny, which Serena Sutcliffe says is often a very good alternative to the more expensive Meursault. Then came les Combettes and les Perrières, where massive limestone slabs in deep and disused quarry were a lesson in the geology of the fabled vineyards. Then on through les Pucelles (the virgins) and the quaintly named Bienvenues Bâtard Montrachet, below le Montrachet itself, over which poets have drooled, to the outskirts of Chassagne-Montrachet.

Ideally, the day ought to have ended with my striding on to Santenay and Sampigny-les-Maranges and the end of the Côte de Beaune and the Côte d'Or. Instead, I was sitting on a high stool in the handsome little communal *caveau* at Chassagne-Montrachet in the chance company of a Belgian and two Swedes, sampling some of the lesser local wines. As for the end of the Côte de Beaune, there was no denying that I had stiffened up during my half hour at the bar, and that even the three kilometres (just under two miles) to Chagny, let alone twice as many to Sampigny, now seemed formidable. When the Belgian said that he was going on south to Lyon and would be glad to drop me off in Chagny I accepted with great pleasure, swallowing my pride along with a sample of a Chassagne-Montrachet red.

*The* côte *occupied by the great vineyards of the Côte d'Or is mostly crowned with woodlands crossed by paths leading to vineyards of the Hautes Côtes, where the wines may sometimes rival those which have far better-known names and are sold at far higher prices.*

# THE WINE

The Côte de Nuits is overwhelmingly red wine country: red wine made from a single grape, the 'noble' Pinot Noir. No other red wine grape – the Gamay which is the staple of Beaujolais, for instance – has any significance here, and white wines are rare. The Côte de Beaune is planted with both Pinot Noir for red wine and Chardonnay for white. There is also some Aligoté. All the famous whites of the Côte d'Or, most notably Meursault and Montrachet, come from the Côte de Beaune.

The system of appellation – or categorization – of Côte d'Or wines is not simple, and the whole subject is further complicated by the custom of the wine villages of joining their names to those of the most renowned vineyards in their area (thus Gevrey was the village, Chambertin the vineyard). At the bottom, which carries no derogatory implications whatever, are generic or regional names, for example Bourgogne, Bourgogne Passe-Tout-Grains (Passe-Tout-Grains being a blend of Pinot Noir and Gamay), or Bourgogne Hautes Côtes de Beaune. Next come communal or village names: Gevrey-Chambertin or Chambolle-Musigny, for instance. In this case the label might indicate simply 'Gevrey-Chambertin, Appellation Contrôlée', with no other identification except the name of the producer. It might also name the specific vineyard attached, as for example 'CHAMBOLLE-MUSIGNY les Herbues', but the vineyard name (les Herbues) must always be printed in a smaller typeface than the name of the commune. Next are the Premier Cru wines, which also go by the name of the commune, but with 'Premier Cru' displayed prominently on the label. Finally, at the top of this noble hierarchy, are the Grands Crus. These wines, in sharp and significant contrast to all the others, are identified first and foremost by the names of their individual vineyards, of which there are some thirty: thus 'CHAMBERTIN – CLOSE DE BEZE. Appellation Contrôlée', plus the producer's name. To summarize, then, these are the categories of Côte d'Or wines, this time from the top:

Grand Cru: for example, CHAMBERTIN – CLOSE DE BEZE
Premier Cru: for example, GEVREY-CHAMBERTIN – Les Gémeaux Premier Cru
Commune: for example, GEVREY-CHAMBERTIN
Generic: for example, BOURGOGNE

# THE CÔTE CHALONNAISE

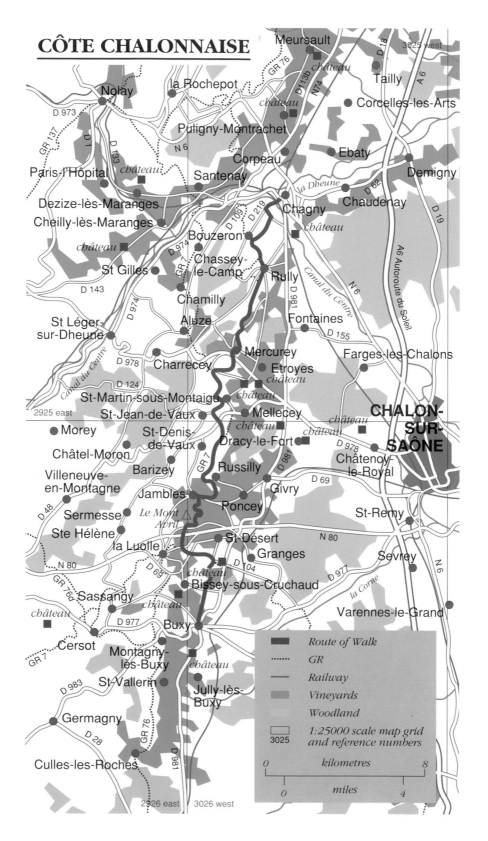

**CÔTE CHALONNAISE**

Meursault

3025 west

Tailly

Nolay

la Rochepot

Corcelles-les-Arts

D 973

château

château

D 113b

N 74

A 6

D 18

GR 76

Puligny-Montrachet

Ebaty

Demigny

GR 137

D 1

D 133

N 6

château

Corpeau

Santenay

Chaudenay

D 62

D 19

Paris-l'Hôpital

Dezize-lès-Maranges

Cheilly-lès-Maranges

la Dheune

Chagny

château

D 109

D 219

château

A6 Autoroute du Soleil

N 6

Bouzeron

château

D 974

GR 7

Chassey-le-Camp

Rully

Canal du Centre

D 981

St Gilles

D 143

Chamilly

Fontaines

D 155

St Léger-sur-Dheune

Aluze

Mercurey

Farges-les-Chalons

D 978

Charrecey

Etroyes

château

Canal du Centre

D 124

St-Martin-sous-Montaigu

château

CHALON-SUR-SAÔNE

2925 east

St-Jean-de-Vaux

Mellecey

château

château

château

Morey

St-Denis-de-Vaux

Dracy-le-Fort

D 978

Châtel-Moron

GR 7

Russilly

D 981

Châtenoy-le-Royal

Barizey

D 69

Villeneuve-en-Montagne

Jambles

Givry

St-Remy

D 48

Sermesse

Poncey

Le Mont Avril

Ste Hélène

la Luolle

St-Désert

N 80

N 80

Granges

D 977

Sevrey

N 6

GR 76d

D 68

château

D 104

la Corne

Sassangy

château

Bissey-sous-Cruchaud

château

D 977

Buxy

Varennes-le-Grand

Cersot

GR 7

Montagny-lès-Buxy

château

D 983

St-Vallerin

Jully-lès-Buxy

Germagny

GR 76

D 28

D 981

Culles-les-Roches

2926 east    3026 west

| | Route of Walk |
| | GR |
| | Railway |
| | Vineyards |
| | Woodland |
| 3025 | 1:25000 scale map grid and reference numbers |

0    kilometres    8

0    miles    4

# BRIEFING

## THE LIE OF THE LAND

At Santenay in the valley of the River Dheune, the 56-kilometre (35-mile) long, one and a half-kilometre (one-mile) wide, almost unbroken stretch of vineyards of the Côte d'Or ends, and the Côte Chalonnaise begins. Between the wines of the two *côtes* there may be certain strong similarities, but the characters of their countrysides are as dissimilar as, say, Pommard is from Pouilly-Fuissé. No longer may one go for kilometre after kilometre without a gap between one wine appellation and the next. Between Dijon and Santenay there can be no doubt whatever that the vine rules, but south of Chagny is a region altogether more bucolic than the Côte d'Or, more rustic and less sophisticated. Some 30 kilometres (20 miles) further south, between the valleys of the Dheune and the Grosne around St Gengoux-le-National, the vine may even at times seem incidental to a landscape that reflects a rich, general agriculture, with forests, orchards, arable lands and grazing cattle. The villages here, unlike those of the Côte d'Or, are not devoted almost exclusively to wine and what has come to be called 'wine tourism', and are less obviously affluent.

From the walker's point of view, these differences are chiefly reflected in a deeper rurality and a considerably more varied and interesting topography, which requires in consequence more careful use of the 1:25,000 map than may generally be the case on the other side of the Dheune.

## WALK

**Chagny to Buxy or Montagny** by way of Rully and Mercurey. About 24 kilometres/15 miles; allow 6–8 hours.

Close to the railway station in Chagny a bridge over the Canal du Centre to the Rue Croisée marks the start of the minor D 219 road to Bouzeron (2.5 kilometres or 1.5 miles). At the first crossroads after the canal turn south-eastwards off the D 219 and continue for 500 metres to another crossroads, where a wide track climbs through scrub to la Folie, a substantial wine domaine on the Montagne de la Folie.

From the southern edge of the domaine a path (not always clear) runs across the plateau, descending past vines (because of high scrub not always visible) to fine views of Rully on its hillside and to a wide, unpaved track between Rully and Chagny, which becomes a paved lane through low-lying vines on the northern edge of Rully village.

The prominent church at the top of Rully village provides a marker for the start of the lane that passes the east-facing château and looks down over its vines before forking down towards Aluze and ahead towards Mercurey. Soon after the fork the tarred surface gives way to a wide dirt track along the top of a vineyard named on the map as les Fiolles. Mont Morin is a kilometre (just over half a mile) further on, and the unmistakable track provides almost ideal walking through a wide expanse of vines and over a low saddle between woods at the top of les Champs Martin. From here there is a delightful view of Mercurey in the valley of the little Giroux stream.

Well-defined tracks and traffic-free lanes run from Bourgneuf-Val-d'Or up to Touches, over and down to St Martin-sous-Montaigu and St Jean-de-Vaux, then on south to Jambles and le Mont Avril. From St Jean-de-Vaux to Buxy (Givry representing a marked diversion to the east) the land becomes progressively more hilly and uneven, so that although there are paths, tracks and minor roads in plenty there are also many ups and downs, and less uncomplicated, open walking than to the north of St Jean. In this southern half of the walk particularly, time spent on careful route-planning and map-reading is likely to be well repaid.

### Maps

**Maps are specified in order north to south to cover main wine areas, with lateral additions (Montagny and Cluny) where appropriate.**

| 1:25,000 | 3025 | ouest | Chagny | Meursault to Chalon-sur-Saone, includes Mercurey |
|---|---|---|---|---|
| | 3026 | ouest | Chalon-sur-Saone | includes Givry and Buxy, but not Montagny |
| | 2926 | est | Ecuisses | includes Montagny |
| | 3027 | ouest | Lugny | joins Côte Chalonnaise to Mâconnais |
| | | | | |
| 1:50,000 | 3025 | | Chagny | joins Côte de Beaune to Côte Chalonnaise |
| | 3026 | | Chalon-sur-Saone | rest of Côte Chaionnaise |

# MEADOWS, WOODS AND HIDDEN VINEYARDS

Above a great sweep of vines belonging to the imposing Château de Rully, I stood looking across the valley to the Canal du Centre, vainly wondering where it could have been that I had made my first acquaintance with the wines of the district some ten years before. Driving north from Lyon on the N 6, I had turned left beyond Chalon-sur-Saône to find a good place for lunch. Minor roads led me on through what was not immediately recognizable as wine country, but where, on the outskirts of a village, a *vente directe* sign, a bottle on top of an upturned barrel outside an open door and prices chalked on a black-painted board caught my eye. The door gave into a barn of sorts, in which, by such daylight as managed to penetrate its depths, I could make out a circular wine-press and two or three large wooden vats and horizontal casks. On another upturned barrel just inside the door were several more bottles. No one seemed to be about. After half a minute or so I called out, '*Il y a quelqu'un?*' Silence. I called again, and then once more. This time a woman well past middle age appeared from round the corner of an interior wall. She was sorry, she said, her husband was in the fields at the moment and she had been busy in the kitchen. Did I want to taste the wine? I tasted a red and a white and much preferred the white, which seemed to me robust and fruity yet floral and

*The countryside of the Côte Chalonnaise reflects a rich general agriculture: forests, orchards, arable acres, grazing cattle. Here in Jambles the best wines, mostly red, share the appellation of nearby Givry.*

dignified; in short full of character. The name on the label was one I had never heard of, and the price was remarkably low. I took two bottles back to England, where a knowledgeable friend said ah, so I had discovered the poor man's Montrachet! Had I come across Montagny yet? Like the Rully we were drinking, he said, it wasn't really to be confused with Meursault or Montrachet, of course, but at its best it was an outstandingly good Char- donnay, and one that ordinary mortals could afford.

Now, on a September day ten years later, very soon after the *vendanges*, I had become a devoted admirer of the wines of the Côte Chalonnaise, and had increased my knowledge of the appellation by a five- or six-kilometre (three- or four-mile) walk from Chagny after a night at the legendary Hôtel Lameloise. 'Jean-François Delorme, in Rully. Tell him I sent you,' Jacques Lameloise had replied when I asked him for an introduction to the makers of the remarkably good *méthode champenoise* Crémant de Bourgogne Blanc de Blancs that I had drunk before dinner. After a distinctly unfriendly send- off from the outskirts of Chagny by a Dobermann pinscher, I had set off across the high ground known unpropitiously as the Montagne de la Folie, from which I had descended to a terrifyingly vociferous welcome to Rully from a very large and menacing St Bernard. I calmed myself with a drink of wondrously cold water from a public pump in the Grande Rue before mak- ing my way to the Delorme offices, where a brief tasting had included a Pre- mier Cru Rully-Varot. 'Elegant white wine with a scent of newly mown grass,' says Serena Sutcliffe: I have drunk it since in London and pined for

*The village of Mellecy lies in the vallée des Vaux, part of the valley of the Orbise, which is a tributary of the Saône. The wines of the Côte Chalonnaise, according to Serena Sutcliffe, 'have real regional character and a great deal to say for themselves'.*

those meadows and woods and hidden vineyards of the Côte Chalonnaise.

But now it was delightful, peaceful walking the rest of the way from Rully to Mercurey, with vines inconspicuous until the low plateau of Mont Morin, where they stretched for several hundred metres on each side of a wide dirt road, then rose gently and narrowed to a pass between woods before opening out and descending again into the slopes of les Champs Martin – and what seemed to me one of the loveliest of wine-country views that I had ever seen.

I thought so then, in early autumn. I have thought so since when the colours in the tall trees on the southern edge of the village were rivalled by those among the Pinot Noir vines that mostly enfold it. I have thought so in spring, when the scents of blackthorn seemed to fill the air along the way from Rully and a cherry tree in riotous blossom stood isolated in les Champs Martin, and I felt that the remaining 16 kilometres (10 miles) to Montagny-les-Buxy and the southern end of the Côte Chalonnaise might be covered in a few bold strides. In fact, they required all of the rest of that September day. The centre of present-day Mercurey is not around the church, at the bottom of les Champs Martin, but straddles the D 978 a few hundred metres further south. Here are to be found the hôtel-restaurant Hostellerie du Val d'Or, the *boulangerie*, the pharmacy, the *tabac* and all the other appurtenances of a busy, prosperous village. Arriving from Rully, I turned right along the D 978, promising myself to return and explore Mercurey at some future date, but intending meanwhile to take a track shown

*The four kilometres (two and a half miles) between Rully and Mercurey are part of some of the best walking offered by the Côte Chalonnaise, and where the path comes down into Mercurey village the Hostellerie du Val d'Or has a good list of local wines.*

running southwards on the map, through a wood bordering the vines named as la Pilotte. It was an intention soon to be corrected, but had the consequence of acquainting me with Monsieur Liéjon, whom I would otherwise never have met.

His premises were advertised by an upturned barrel with two glasses on it, perilously close, I thought, to the sharp bend that takes the D 978 out of Bourgneuf towards Touches. Noting my pack and my walker's garb as I paused at his open doors, Monsieur Liéjon, as he later acknowledged, did not at first recognize a likely customer; nevertheless, he readily returned my '*bonjour*', and when I asked him if there was a possibility of tasting his wine was ungrudging with his '*Mais bien sûr!*' Although he was still in his sixties, he was retired really, he said, and made only 'a few thousand' bottles of red a year, all of which he sold to private customers, most of them regular ones. He himself did not work in the vines, but had a *métayage* arrangement by which another man held the land in return for supplying Monsieur Liéjon with the grapes he needed. His wine was just 'Mercurey AC', but some of the slopes in the appellation were now rated Premier Cru. He fermented his grapes with the stalks on, which of course increased the tannin content in the finished wines and made them more *vins de garde* (wines for keeping) than ones designed to be drunk young, like a lot of red wines nowadays.

I tasted his two-year-old wine, and his three-year-old. Even the second, he said, needed two or three more years in bottle. 'More like double that,' I thought, and asked if he had anything a bit older still.

'All sold,' he said. Then, thoughtfully, 'Well, there's just a chance that I might find the odd bottle of '85 somewhere since you're obviously so keen on wine (*Un si grand amateur de vin*).'

He found it, and now, my pack heavier by one bottle and my route improved on the vigneron's advice, I went on south out of the village on the minor road that traverses les Pendanches, a wide sweep of vines leading up the hill to Touches. The view back across to Mercurey and beyond to les Champs Martin was very lovely: the tall trees bordering Bourgneuf were beginning to turn colour; the vines were still green, the roofs a weathered orange, the sky blue. In Touches the church clock startled me with its clamorous striking of twelve noon. Nothing else stirred. Red and white parallel bars painted on a wall were a reminder that the GR 7 passes that way. A lane descending southwards out of the village was signed 'Clos du Roi', and I remembered that Givry, some five or six kilometres (three or four miles) distant in a more or less straight line, was reported to have been a favourite wine of Henry IV, whose mistress Diane de Poitiers is supposed to have had a vineyard there. Passing close by an isolated and very pretty farm on the next hill, I caught a scent of fermenting grapes. West of the house the ground fell steeply to a secret little valley, perhaps 500 metres long and half as wide, totally enclosed by woods and planted with what seemed to be beautifully kept vines. The track skirted a wooded hill and the mysterious ruins of the Château de Montaigu, then was bordered by vines all the way to St Jean-de-Vaux. I was still in the appellation of

*The largely medieval Château de Rully is one of the landmarks of the Côte Chalonnaise. Lived in by the same family for some five hundred years, it has its own Chardonnay vineyards that produce a very good white wine.*

Mercurey, I supposed, though the soil seemed to contain more clay and less limestone than it had closer to Mercurey itself. At a quarter past one, St Jean-de-Vaux showed very little sign of life. Alone in the sun at a bright red table on the edge of the deserted village square, I temporarily quenched my considerable thirst on two glasses of beautifully cold *pression*, before asking the *patronne* if she could sell me a bottle of red wine (I was keeping the Liéjon vintage for some future London occasion). She could, she said, but at the restaurant price, which would be seventy francs. I would do better to buy something '*chez un vigneron*': there was one just up the road, and yet another a little further on.

Not far from the locked church a woman was hanging tea towels on a line in front of a modest house in a huddle of venerable stone buildings, bordering on the decrepit. Could she tell me where I might find a vigneron who would sell me a bottle of wine? As if on cue, a man of perhaps sixty, healthy-faced, slightly corpulent, dressed in old, baggy blue trousers, an open-neck, roughly matching shirt with rolled-up sleeves, and old, unpolished brown shoes, now emerged from an open door. One of seven growers in St Jean-de-Vaux, he was descended from two centuries of vignerons, he said. Not big, but not as small as some. Only just over one and a half hectares of Pinot Noir, from which he made a Bourgogne AOC, bottling about 5000 bottles a year; selling the rest to *négociants* in bulk.

In one of the stone buildings that looked as if it had been there for ever, under massive beams that were once whole tree trunks, purple must was bubbling and burbling in great open oak vats. 'The song of the wine,' said the vigneron. After fermentation it would spend a year and a half in barrel before bottling. His accent was deeply rural and I would have found it hard to follow but for the fact that in wine talk a lot can be fairly well guessed at. Might I buy a bottle of his wine, I asked? To take home, or just for my *casse-croûte*, asked the vigneron? Oh, just for a picnic, I replied. An empty bottle was found, rinsed with wine drawn from a barrel, filled and – after a search for a suitable cork in a kitchen drawer – stoppered. What did I owe? Nothing. Please, I said. Very well then, if I insisted, seven francs. '*Et merci pour votre visite.*' With handshakes all round and the bottle in my pack, I left St Jean-de-Vaux, crossed a hillside planted partly with vines and partly with maize, descended to the valley of the Orbise stream, toiled up through St Denis-de-Vaux, and carried on southwards, up and down past vines and woods and pasture in search, as usual, of a picnic place with a view.

I found it on the southern slope of le Mont Avril, south of Jambles, looking down across the vines that almost completely encircle the 'mountain', into the valley and to St Désert, across to the Forêt de Givry, and beyond to the Saône. The simple St Jean-de-Vaux Bourgogne AOC admirably suited the *friand* (a sort of superior sausage roll), wholemeal bread and cheese that I had bought in Chagny, and although I had come no more than 16 kilometres (10 miles) I fell into a doze from which I awoke to the realization that if I wanted to reach Buxy before dark, let alone dinner time, I had no time whatever to lose.

# THE WINE

To earn the respect of good wine-makers in the Côte Chalonnaise, let them see that you do not suppose their Bouzerons and Rullys and Mercureys and Givrys and Montagnys to be much the same as the lesser wines of the Côte d'Or, only cheaper. Some may indignantly deny that it was ever so. Others, acknowledging that limestone and limestone-clay are the basic constituents of the soils of the Chalonnaise, as of those of the Côte d'Or, may concede that there used to be plausible reasons for the misunderstanding, but will cite the many successful efforts that have been made in the past decade or so greatly to improve the quality of the region's wines. The best Pinot Noirs, Chardonnays, Aligotés and Passe-Tout-Grains of the Côte Chalonnaise, they gratefully agree, have their own distinctively native characteristics and deserve to be judged accordingly.

From north to south, the five appellations and top villages are:

**Bouzeron** makes mainly white wine from the Aligoté grape, here distinguished by its own appellation of Aligoté de Bouzeron.

**Rully** produces significantly more white wine than red; the white mostly from the Chardonnay, the red from the Pinot Noir. It also produces a lot of good Crémant de Bourgogne, the white, sparkling wine made by the *méthode champenoise*.

Both **Mercurey** and **Givry** make mostly red wines from the Pinot Noir, but also some white from Chardonnay.

**Montagny** makes exclusively white wines from the Chardonnay.

Apart from the wines entitled to the village names of origin, there are also Bourgogne Rouge, from the Pinot Noir, and Bourgogne Passe-Tout-Grain, which is a blend of Pinot Noir and Gamay.

*Buxy gives the lie to those who still suppose that cooperatives are synonymous with mediocrity, or worse. The cave coopérative on the outskirts of the ancient village is a shining example of what can be achieved through strict attention to quality. Both its wines and its premises are admirable.*

# THE MÂCONNAIS

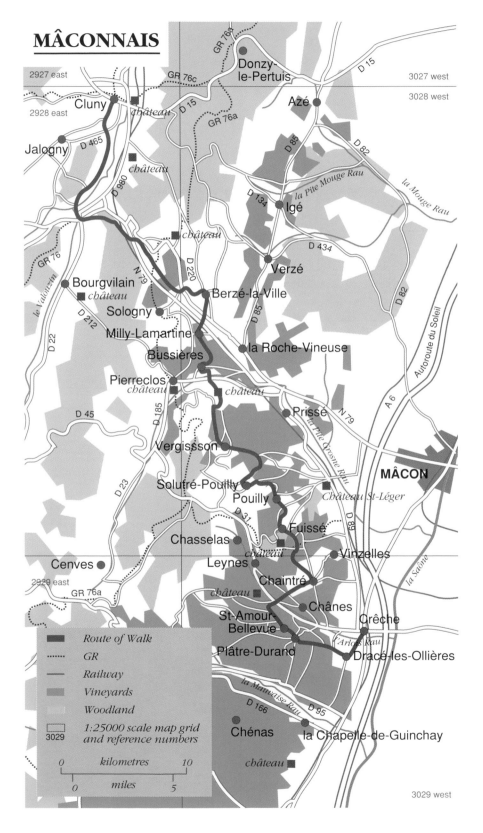

**MÂCONNAIS**

2927 east

GR 76c

GR 76a

Donzy-le-Pertuis

D 15

3027 west

3028 west

Cluny

château

D 15

Azé

2928 east

Jalogny

D 465

GR 76a

D 85

D 82

château

D 980

D 134

la Pite Mouge Rau

la Mouge Rau

Igé

GR 76

château

D 434

le Valouzin

N 79

D 220

Verzé

Bourgvilain

château

Berzé-la-Ville

D 82

Sologny

D 212

D 85

Milly-Lamartine

D 22

Bussières

la Roche-Vineuse

Autoroute du Soleil

Pierreclos

château

château

D 45

D 185

Prissé

N 79

A 6

Vergisson

la Pite Grosne Rau

D 23

MÂCON

Solutré-Pouilly

Pouilly

Château St-Léger

D 31

Fuissé

D 89

Chasselas

château

Vinzelles

Cenves

Leynes

Chaintré

la Saône

2929 east

GR 76a

château

St-Amour-Bellevue

Chânes

Crêche

Plâtre-Durand

l'Arlois Rau

Dracé-les-Ollières

**Route of Walk**

**GR**

**Railway**

**Vineyards**

**Woodland**

3029

*1:25000 scale map grid and reference numbers*

la Mauvaise Rau

D 166

D 95

Chénas

la Chapelle-de-Guinchay

0   kilometres   10

château

0   miles   5

3029 west

# BRIEFING

## THE LIE OF THE LAND

Travellers making a continuous progress through the vineyards of Burgundy have a walk of hardly two or three hours from the end of the Côte Chalonnaise to the beginning of the Mâconnais, nor will they be likely to find any impressively obvious contrasts between the two.

The Mâconnais begins at Tournus and merges with the Beaujolais a little south of Mâcon. The River Saône is its eastern limit, while the River Grosne marks both its northern and western boundaries. At its broadest it measures some 15 kilometres (9 miles) across, but most of the vineyards lie within a span half as wide.

Hugh Johnson has described the Mâconnais aptly as 'all bumps and dips', and here again, comparison with the Côte d'Or is instructive. Instead of some 50 broadly speaking continuous kilometres (30 miles) of viticulture on a more or less continuous and clearly defined slope (it is significant that there is no singular Côte Mâconnaise), the vineyards of the Mâconnais consist of many individual though often very large areas of vines, separated by wooded uplands (on average between 250 and 500 metres, or 825 and 1650 feet, in height), by slopes unsuited by soil or exposure to the grape, and by valleys and hillsides devoted to other kinds of farming. Vineyards seldom dominate the landscape to the extent that they dominate the Côte de Nuits and the Côte de Beaune, or the neighbouring Beaujolais. The exception, perhaps, is in the area between Prissé and Fuissé (with Pouilly in between), where even the landmarks of la Roche de Vergisson and la Roche de Solutré take second place to the region's premier vines.

Consistent with its other characteristics as wine country, the Mâconnais has no Dijon, no Beaune, no Nuits-St Georges. Nor has it any wine villages of a certain sophistication, such as Gevrey-Chambertin, though modest Chaintré, Leynes, Chardonnay, Davaye, Igé, Lugny, Pouilly, Prissé, Solgny, Solutré, Verzé, Viré and others have their charms. And it has the Roche de Solutré, at the foot of which lies a prehistoric 'graveyard' of horses and which is a fine and famous landmark for the walker. Vines grow almost to the door of the unobtrusive archeological museum beside it, and on a clear day the view is superb. The Mâconnais also has Cluny, which although no wine town, has an enduring and poignantly romantic place in the history of wine.

## WALK

**Cluny to Crêches-sur-Saône** by way of Vergisson, Solutré, Pouilly and Fuissé. About 40 kilometres/25 miles; allow 12–14 hours.

Though the suggested walk falls in the heroic, summer dawn-to-dusk category if attempted without an overnight pause, it otherwise offers the possibility of two comfortably full, rich days through the heart of the Mâconnais wine country and into the northern Beaujolais. While I have not followed the itinerary precisely as set out here, I have nevertheless covered the greater part of it. The outlined route is the result of experience allied to a careful study of the 1:25,000 map, the assumption being, as almost always, that other walkers will make their own judgements and adjustments 'in the field'.

Head south from Cluny on the west bank of the Grosne (parallel to the D 980, Cluny to Mâcon road on the east side of the stream), crossing a bridge just south of the end of the Bois de Vaux to join first the D 22, then the N 79 between la Valouze and les Vachets. Turn on to a lane south of les Vachets, which becomes a track through woods bordering the line of the TGV. At the Viaduc de la Roche take an underpass to the D 263, and so to la Croix Blanche and the beginning of the vineyards. Berzé-la-Ville, Milly-Lamartine, Bussières, Vergisson, Solutré is then the recommended line of march, though not necessarily the shortest.

Solutré to Fuissé and the 'higher ground' south of the lovely Fuissé valley is covered in the following pages. Chaintré is the village to aim for, then down to la Roche and across the Arbois stream just south-east of St Vérand. St Amour Bellevue (Beaujolais) is now a kilometre (just over half a mile) to the south, while Crêches is about four kilometres (2.5 miles) to the east. About eight kilometres (5 miles) further south from the Arbois valley brings the walker to the considerable rewards of Fleurie.

**Maps**

| 1:25,000 | 3027 | ouest | Lugny | joins Côte Chalonnaise to Mâconnais |
|---|---|---|---|---|
| | 3028 | ouest | Mâcon | includes virtually whole of wine country to Beaujolais |
| | 2928 | est | Cluny | not needed for wine country |
| 1:50,000 | 3027 | | Tournus | joins Côte Chalonnaise to Mâconnais |
| | 3028 | | Mâcon | rest of Mâconnais to Beaujolais |
| 1:100,000 | 43 | | Lyon, Vichy | |

# FROM CLUNY TO ST AMOUR

My reasons for starting in Cluny were very largely romantic. The place has no significance that I know of in modern wine-making, and strictly speaking is not even in wine country, since the nearest vines appear to be some five kilometres (three miles) distant. But from the end of the Roman Empire the story of wine in Europe was largely the story of the Church. Popular historians are fond of the imagery of the flame of civilization kept burning in monastic cells throughout the so-called Dark Ages. According to the historian H.A.L. Fisher: 'In many cases the monastery was a missionary establishment ... a hostelry for the refreshment of wayfarers, an improving landlord, a centre of education and scholarship.' In a land devastated and depopulated by barbarism, wars, pestilence and famine, agricultural knowledge was no less important than religious philosophy and observances, and viticulture was a prime part of agriculture – necessary, not least, for the supply of sacramental and medicinal wines.

No religious institution was greater or had greater influence than the Benedictine abbey of Cluny. Founded in 909 and granted autonomy by pontifical decree, it became quite independent of all temporal authority and by the middle of the twelfth century had almost 1500 dependencies. It was Pope Urban II who famously described it as 'the light of the world'. But by then, too, Bernard of Cîteaux was bitterly denouncing the ostentation and luxury of an institution whose elders were 'unable to journey four leagues from home unless accompanied by a train of at least sixty horses'. Did the 'light' really have to be in candelabras of gold or silver in order to shine, the ascetic Bernard asked. Cistercian monks were fanatically hard workers, and not least in the vineyards which they acquired in Burgundy. One of their monuments is the Clos de Vougeot.

Already gravely damaged during the wars of religion, Cluny failed to survive the infamous vandalism of the French Revolution, so that what before the building of St Peter's in Rome was the largest church in Christendom, described by architect Viollet-le-Duc as 'the Mother of western civilization', became in the words of historian Jacques-Louis Delpal 'no more than a ghost in stone'.

I had arrived too late the evening before to see the ruins, and so, determined to see them in the morning, found myself attached to a party of Swedish tourists with a French-speaking guide, peering up at the tragic remains of the south transept and the apse when I ought to have been two or three hours on my way. With admirable restraint, the *Blue Guide* to France describes the ruins as 'somewhat disappointing'. Cluny as a whole, as Michelin advises, is 'worth the detour', but that cold, grey morning, listening to a long and lugubrious recitation of past glories and infamies, while the rain fell, was depressing. Soon I slipped away.

*Though it remains worth the journey, Cluny today contains only a few poignant remains of what once was 'the light of the world'.*

*The village of Solutré and vineyards of the heart of the Mâconnais seen from the Roche de Solutré itself: the climb to the lower slopes of the rock is worthwhile for this view alone.*

With some 460 monks in residence at one time, Cluny's consumption of wine must have been very large, I thought. And I wondered if the train of sixty horses had ever travelled where now I set myself a brisk pace on the wide, stone-based, seemingly very ancient track from Cluny towards Mâcon, along the valley of the Grosne. Rain fell unrelentingly and I was glad of the shelter of the woods that border the TGV track between Paris and the south. At two o'clock in the afternoon, 12 kilometres (seven and a half miles) from the abbey by the route I had chosen, I came to the Relais du Mâconnais at la Croix-Blanche on the N 79. In that weather, Thoissey, my ultimate goal, was much too far away to reach by dinner time. Also, an appetizing aroma from the open kitchen window of the hotel was accompanied by a glimpse of cooks in white toques. Better, I thought, to take refuge here for the rest of the day, then begin again tomorrow. A quarter of an hour later, as I was changing clothes, the rain stopped. Fifteen minutes

*The Château de Pierreclos, south of Milly-Lamartine, was home in the seventeenth century to Mademoiselle Jacqueline de Milly, the 'Laurence' of Lamartine's epic poem* Jocelyn.

more saw the sun breaking through.

In my rucksack I had the makings of a picnic, bought in Cluny. Up at Berzé-la-Ville, I thought, there might be a shaded terrace and a glass of Mâcon blanc to linger over, and higher still perhaps a place where I might lunch and enjoy the view. Berzé-la-Ville! Had I not read about a certain Chapelle des Moines at Berzé? The village had been a dependency of Cluny in the twelfth century, and the chapel a favourite retreat of the abbot, St Hugues. Once, a thunderbolt had reduced it to ruins, from which the abbot had nevertheless emerged unharmed. In the chapel, which had recently been presented to the nation by its former owner, Joan Evans, were some remarkable frescoes.

There was more blue sky than grey by the time I left the hotel. Less than a mile on a leafy path beside vines took me up to the chapel standing alone with its outbuildings just below the village. By now the afternoon was very warm and I was glad to sit on a wooden bench in the cool silence, gazing at what one of the books I had read describes as 'the primavera of the twelfth-century renaissance . . . a masterpiece which, of its kind, has no equal in Burgundy and no superior anywhere in France.'

Certainly the colours were charming, but I presumed much muted by time, and I wondered about the emotions they might have engendered in the medieval mind when the flames of the grill beneath St Vincent (or perhaps St Laurence) and the blood gushing from the neck of the decapitated St Blaise were fresh and bright.

A woman in workaday black appeared and told me that the cellar below had once been used for wine. People said it aged especially well there. Thus further encouraged in the thought of a bottle and a terrace, I went on up into the village, but found a peace as deep as in the abbot's retreat.

Following first of all a narrow path between tall hedges of box and thorn behind the village, then a broad track leading straight up the steep hillside beside a spread of Chardonnay vines, I gained the 396-metre (1300-foot) high southern end of the 506-metre (1700-foot) Mont Chevreuil. The 'broussaille' which according to the map covers the dry, stony ground consists mostly of low box and thorn bushes and coarse grass, and here I found a satisfactory place to shed pack and boots and damp shirt and to fetch out the picnic that I had bought before leaving Cluny, including a Mâcon-Villages la Roche-Vineuse – a wine beyond price, as it seemed to me on that glorious afternoon, though it had cost me only about three pounds.

From where I sat I could see la Roche-Vineuse on its hillside, about two and a half kilometres (a mile and a half) away south-east across the valley. To the south-west, on the other side of the main Mâcon–Cluny road and the TGV line, vineyards and uncultivated slopes rose to Milly-Lamartine.

*Souvent sur la montagne, a l'ombre du vieux chêne,*
*Au coucher du soleil, tristement je m'assieds;*
*Je promène au hasard mes regards sur la plaine,*
*Dont le tableau changeant se déroule a mes pieds.*

Lamartine learned by heart at school! There were a few white galleons of clouds now, and idly I followed their shadows across the landscape. In my mind's eye I saw these hills and valleys and woods and vines and villages stretching back northwards to the Côte Chalonnaise and southwards to Beaujolais and the Lyonnais before ending in the heights of the Massif Central. There was a breeze, very soft on my face. There was the wine.

It was almost half past five when I awoke. An hour later, in sleepy little Milly with its locked twelfth-century church, I stood at the massive iron gates of the house where Lamartine is said to have spent much of his childhood, while on the other side of them a large dog let me know that I was not welcome. At the southern end of the village, beyond a commemorative bust of the poet, a track led across the hillside and down through vines to a tunnel under the TGV line and a few hundred metres of N 79 back to the Relais du Mâconnais, a long bath, a *coupe* of Crémant de Bourgogne, and a good dinner. The first course was *coquilles St Jacques* in a white wine sauce and I considered ordering a half-bottle of Pouilly-Fuissé to accompany it. Why not a St Véran, asked *la patronne*? Why not, I agreed, knowing nothing about it, but feeling safe in her hands and noting that the St Véran was appreciably the cheaper of the two. Thus my slender knowledge of the wines of the Mâconnais was happily improved, for the St Véran was so delicious that I promised myself a visit to the St Véran appellation – on the border with Beaujolais, around the village that is spelt St Vérand – the next day. What was the weather forecast, I asked, before going to bed. '*Beau*,' said *la*

*The river-front at Mâcon at night, birthplace of the romantic poet Lamartine in 1790, now hosts the annual Foire Nationale des Vins de France in June.*

*patronne.* 'A little cloudy to begin with, then fine for the rest of the day.'

In Solutré the next morning I stood in a bus shelter and contemplated the rain. The ten or so kilometres (six or seven miles) from la Croix Blanche and the Relais du Mâconnais had left me damp and dispirited. Scribbled in my notebook was the name of a wine-maker I had thought to visit after lunch, if I could find him. Had the lady in the *cave* of the Union des Producteurs de Grands Vin Blancs, just across the road from the bus shelter, who now sold me a glass of excellent Pouilly-Fuissé for nine francs, by any chance heard of him? But yes of course! Monsieur Besson was a good and very well-known wine-maker, and '*super-sympa*' (extremely nice). His place was in Pouilly, not two kilometres (just over a mile) away. It was getting on for noon as I walked down the hill from Solutré. On the outskirts of the village thoughts of lunch, already stimulated by the glass of Pouilly-Fuissé, were sharpened by a glimpse through a half-open door of a long wooden table set with cutlery, glasses and large loaves of bread, obviously awaiting pickers who would soon be returning from the fields. As I looked, thinking of peasant scenes by Breughel and of countless other paintings of flagons of wine and loaves and cheeses, a trailer carrying a bedraggled assortment of men and women went by, bound for just such a *vendangeurs*' lunch, I was sure. I envied them their hot soup, but not the hours of hard, wet work still ahead of them: grape-picking is not unadulterated fun.

Soon I envied nobody. Halfway through the village of Pouilly, which is little more than its own main street, I asked a man in *bleus de travail* and rubber boots if he knew where the Besson property was. 'Here,' he said 'you're standing at the gateway.' In the unpretentious courtyard of a solidly prosperous-looking group of buildings people were coming and going. One of them, an attractive woman with an air of competence and authority about her, came up to me and most politely asked if she could help. I was looking for Monsieur Besson, I told her. 'Unfortunately he's not here,' she said, 'but I'm his wife. What may I do for you?' I knew they were preoccupied with the *vendange*, I said, but I had hoped in passing simply to have a few minutes' conversation with Monsieur Besson and to taste his wine. 'Well,' she replied, 'I'm not an adequate substitute for my husband, but at least I can offer you a glass of wine.'

Thus I found myself in the cellar drinking what seemed to me a most admirable greeny-gold, fruity, fragrant, refreshing Pouilly-Fuissé in company with jovial friends of the family from Holland, and the *caviste*, and others who gripped my hand as if I had been a long-lost brother and shook their heads in mock wonder and said that of course the English were well known for their eccentricities (walking to Thoissey! And in such weather!) and that anyway I could not have come across a better cellar than this one, and now that I had tasted the '91, I must try the '89, and the '86, and ... And would I care to stay to lunch, asked Madame Besson. It was just a simple *déjeuner des vendangeurs*, but she would be pleased if I would sit down with them. I sat very happily. Outside, the rain went on falling. Inside, there reigned that particular quality of contentment which seems only to be

*Communal enterprise at Berzé-la-Ville. The Romanesque Chapelle des Moines, once used as a wine cellar, contains remarkable twelfth-century frescoes painted by Cluniac monks, one of which depicts St Laurence being martyred on a grill.*

born of physical exertion in the open air rewarded by unsophisticated creature comforts, and all in agreeable company.

The pickers were a mixed party of young people from a hotel school in Amsterdam, ravenously hungry after five hours among the vines on about as bad a morning as might be feared for the vintage. The food was simple, good, and extravagantly plentiful, there were pitchers of both red and white wine on the tables, and there was much chatter and laughter. Though my own exertions deserved no such hospitality, still I savoured every minute and morsel of that *déjeuner des vendangeurs*. 'Something for the grown-ups,' said someone at my shoulder, putting a brandy glass down in front of me and pouring an amber liquid. It was a *'très vieux' marc* of the property: smooth, perfumed and worth lingering over in a way that commercial *marc* rarely, if ever, is. But now the very young were on their feet and there was much fun while they cut armholes in large green plastic dustbin bags and put them on over their anoraks. They need not have bothered: outside, the sky had lightened wonderfully and the rain had stopped.

There were cheers and shouts of *'Bonne chance'* and *'Bonne promenade'* as I set off again out of Pouilly and towards Fuissé. Very soon I was on a wide, firm dirt road leading down through a great spread of Chardonnay vines that embraces both villages in their lovely shallow valley. Minute by minute the weather improved, so that by the time I had reached the higher ground south of Fuissé the sky was three-quarters blue. My vantage point, at about 335 metres (1100 feet), was at the northern extremity of a wide, roughly concave sweep of vines stretching two kilometres (a mile and a quarter) down to the valley of the Arlois stream, which if mere neatness and territorial convenience governed such things would form the unequivocal boundary between the Mâconnais and the Beaujolais. In fact it is here that the two are confused, for while Chasselas, Leynes and St Vérand, closely bordering the Arlois, are three of the eight communes that comprise the appellation of St Véran, which is Mâcon, the sweeps of vines immediately below and ahead represent the northerly extent of Beaujolais-Villages; and St Véran may be sold as either a Beaujolais Blanc, or a Bourgogne Blanc, or a Mâcon-Villages.

The view was both glorious and encouraging, for from the southern bank of the Arlois the ground rose steeply to St Amour, that most popular of the ten *crus* of the Beaujolais; perhaps five kilometres (two or three miles) to the south-west, beyond Juliénas, lay the dark green mass of the Bois de Retour; and behind, at 509 metres (1670 feet), the still higher Pic de Remont. A heavenly breeze blew, redolent of woods and vines fresh from the rain and now warm in the sun, and – quite unaccountably, and unmistakably – of the sea.

The autumn day had been wet and dismal: now it might almost have been mistaken for summer. I had been tired and dispirited; now I felt at one with the *vendangeurs* in their loose-knit little groups in the still largely green landscape. After St Amour, I knew, the way was all easy and – before the flatlands bordering the Saône and embracing Thoissey – all downhill.

# THE WINE

Before the Second World War the Mâconnais made far more red wine than white, but the whole consumer market, together with the techniques for making high-quality white wine, has changed hugely since then, so that almost three-quarters of the entire production of the Mâconnais is now white wine, made from the fashionable Chardonnay grape, ideally planted on basically limestone soil. There is also some Aligoté (white). Red wines are made from Gamay and Pinot Noir.

Compared with those of the Côte d'Or, the appellations of the Mâconnais are easy to remember and comprehend. For white, and in ascending order of quality, they are seven: Mâcon Blanc, Mâcon Supérieur, Mâcon-Villages (or just Mâcon) with the name of a village attached, St Véran followed by a village name, and lastly Pouilly-Fuissé and Pouilly-Vinzelles. For red wines there are basically two appellations: Mâcon Rouge (and a little Mâcon Rosé) and Mâcon Supérieur, which is only red.

Pouilly-Fuissé is the most famous and (not always justly) the most expensive of the whites, with Pouilly-Vinzelles tending to run it a close second. St Véran (not to be confused with the village of St Vérand, which is within the appellation) can be very good indeed, and is significantly cheaper than the Pouillys.

*Beneath the cliffs of the Roche de Solutré lie the bones of more than 100,000 wild horses and deer, the detritus (archeologists conjecture) of thousands of prehistoric meals.*

# BEAUJOLAIS

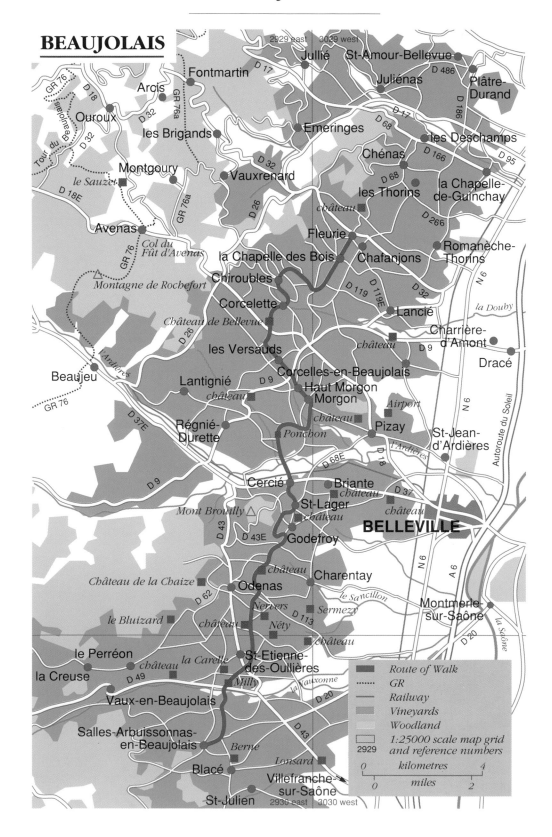

**BEAUJOLAIS**

2929 east | 3039 west
Jullié   St-Amour-Bellevue
D 17
Fontmartin                    Juliénas                    D 486   Plâtre-
Arcis                                                               Durand
GR 76                                                       D 186
D 18                    GR 76a        Emeringes           les Deschamps
Ouroux        D 32                            D 68              D 166
les Brigands                         Chénas           D 95
Tour du Beaujolais  D 32  GR 76a    D 17
le Sauzet                     Vauxrenard   D 32   les Thorins   la Chapelle-
Montgoury                                                de-Guinchay
D 18E                              D 26          château    D 266
Avenas         GR 76                          Fleurie         Romanèche-
Col du                      la Chapelle des Bois   Chafanjons    Thorins
Fût d'Avenas                   Chiroubles                  la Douby
Montagne de Rochefort          Corcelette     D 119  D 119E  Lancié
Château de Bellevue      D 26                  château   Charrière-
les Versauds                                              d'Amont
                                     Corcelles-en-Beaujolais         Dracé
Beaujeu       Lantignié    D 9    Haut Morgon           D 9
GR 76                château    Morgon    Airport
L'Ardières                          château         St-Jean-
D 37E     Régnié-              Ponchon   Pizay   d'Ardières
D 9       Durette                                Autoroute du Soleil
                                            D 68E    D 18   l'Ardières
                        Cercié    Briante
                              château          D 37
Mont Brouilly    D 43      St-Lager  château   château
D 43E          château
                        Godefroy        BELLEVILLE
                      château           N 6   A 6
Château de la Chaize       Charentay
              D 62    Odenas    le Sancillon      Montmerle-
le Bluizard        Nervers   Sermezy           sur-Saône
château      D 113                       D 20   la Saône
Nèty
le Perréon       château   la Carelle  château
la Creuse    D 49    St-Etienne-   la Vauxonne
Vaux-en-Beaujolais   des-Oullières        D 20
              Milly
Salles-Arbuissonnas-
en-Beaujolais    Berne
Blacé       Lonsard      Villefranche-
St-Julien   2930 east | 3030 west  sur-Saône

| | Route of Walk |
|---|---|
| ······· | GR |
| | Railway |
| | Vineyards |
| | Woodland |
| 2929 | 1:25000 scale map grid and reference numbers |

0   kilometres   4
0   miles   2

# BRIEFING

## THE LIE OF THE LAND

The vineyards of the Beaujolais begin just south of Mâcon and continue almost to Lyon, occupying the foothills of the Monts du Beaujolais and their eastern approaches. The Monts du Beaujolais some of which are over 1000 metres (3300 feet) high, are themselves the eastern limit of the Massif Central: from here the land descends eastwards, through the low foothills and across the plain of the Saône to the River Saône itself. The highest of the vineyard hills is the isolated Mont Brouilly, at 484 metres (1588 feet). The average height of the Beaujolais vineyards is 300 metres (984 feet).

The southern part of the whole viticultural region (very roughly south of a line drawn due west from just above Villefranche-sur-Saône) has a more sedimentary soil than the northern part, and is largely not granitic. It is also less open, more wooded, and more divided by valleys (*vallonné*). Consequently, all the best and best-known wines of the Beaujolais come from north of Villefranche, and it is almost exclusively this part which concerns us. In general, the most pleasing walking among the *crus* of the Beaujolais is round and about the famous villages of this more northerly part of the region, closest to the high hills: Chiroubles, Fleurie, Chénas and Juliénas.

No other part of viticultural France that I have walked in has been so densely populated with individual wine farmers, their dwellings and working buildings; nor has any other been so minutely fragmented into so many individually mapped domaines. On the 1:25,000 sheets of the IGN survey covering the Beaujolais the light green of the vines is in places almost obscured by a black-printed chaos of intercommunicating paths and tracks and minor, hard-top roads: for this walker at least, the inevitable consequence is almost incessant reference to the map.

In keeping with its products, the Beaujolais has no pretensions to grandeur, though the seventeenth-century Château de la Chaize, near Odenas, is a noble historical monument with cellars to match and well-reputed Brouilly to be tasted in them. The little town of Belleville on the Saône, humbly wedged between the N 6 and the autoroute, is the 'capital' of the northern Beaujolais, where all the *crus* are to be found. Villefranche, some 16 kilometres (10 miles) to the south, is larger, but is still no Reims or Dijon. Indisputably, the villages that give their names to the *crus* – Fleurie, Morgon, Juliénas, St Amour and the rest – are the places to look for the life and wines of Beaujolais. One of the proudest boasts of the regional tourism authorities is that the village of Vaux-en-Beaujolais was the model for Clochemerle.

## WALK

**Salles-Arbuissonnas-en-Beaujolais to Fleurie** by way of Mont Brouilly, St Lager, Cercié, Morgon and Chiroubles. About 20 kilometres/12.5 miles; allow 5–6 hours.

Just to the east of Salles, the D 19 and D 20 cross almost at right-angles. The path heads north-east from the crossroads through the vines, across the Sallerin stream and towards St Etienne-des-Oullières, by way of Milly or le Darroux. Cross the D 43 and keep St Etienne and Odenas to the west on the way to Pierreux Château. Godefroy and St Lager are on the way to Cercié and a crossing of the Ardières stream. From here, tracks skirt or go through the vines to Ponchon, and thence to Morgon and Haute Morgon.

Les Versauds and les Montillets are now reference points for the line of march over and down to Corcelette, with the Château de Bellevue in between. From Corcelette a track crosses the little Douby stream, leading to by-ways up to Chiroubles. Numerous paths and lanes now traverse the 2 or 3 hilly kilometres (1–2 miles) to Fleurie, with the best views to be had from the high road through la Chapelle des Bois.

| Maps | | | |
|---|---|---|---|
| **1:25,000** | **2929 est** | **Beaujeu** | |
| | **2930 est** | **le Bois d'Oingt** | |
| | **3029 ouest** | **Belleville** | |
| | **3030 ouest** | **Villefranche-sur-Saône** | |
| **1:50,000** | **2929** | **Beaujeu** | |
| | **2930** | **Villefranche-sur-Saône** | |
| | **3029** | **Belleville** | |
| **1:100,000** | **43** | **Vichy** | |
| | **51** | **Lyon** | |

# MORGON BY MOONLIGHT

For a first glimpse of the Beaujolais, picture this fortunate walker at ease on the east-facing slopes of Mont Brouilly, about seven kilometres (four and a half miles) west of Belleville, on a perfect September day. Sitting in the shade of a very small oak at the margin of the trees and brush which descend from the summit of the hill until they yield to the sea of Gamay vines surging up from the plain, I had beside me a substantial outcrop of what I supposed to be Odenas granite, of which this ancient, extinct volcano largely consists. Propped against the rock was my rucksack. Inside it, still wrapped up, but vertical and with the cork drawn, was a bottle of Beaujolais-Villages.

Before me lay an apparently unbounded panorama of most of eastern France: the valley of the Saône; the Bresse plain; the Jura to the north-west; the mountains of Savoy to the south-east; and 160 kilometres (100 miles) or more, away to the east, the high Alps and the massif of Mont Blanc. Immediately below, to right and left and straight ahead, lay half the vines of AOC Côte de Brouilly. Below them were perhaps a third of those of Brouilly. Below again stretched perhaps four or five thousand hectares (10–12,000 acres) of ordinary Beaujolais and a thousand or two (2500–5000 acres) of Beaujolais-Villages. All over this vast patchwork of vineyards parties of grape harvesters were at work, the chemical reds, blues and whites of their clothing vivid against the uniformly green expanse of vines. The sky was unclouded, the light was of Grecian clarity, a wonderfully welcome breeze was blowing and I was about to have lunch.

It was idyllic there on Mont Brouilly. The whole morning had been a good one. Having flown from London to Lyon the evening before and driven to the Hôtel St Vincent at Salles-Arbuissonnas-en-Beaujolais, some nine kilometres (five and a half miles) north-west of Villefranche, I had been pleased to find myself in a chintzy room in the garden annexe, with a view northwards across the Sallerin stream and many square miles of vines. Next morning I had explored the quiet, pretty little village in a leisurely fashion, walking in the twelfth-century cloisters, sitting in the square where the lime trees were in new leaf, and buying the essentials for a picnic, including a cold bottle of Beaujolais-Villages, which according to the woman in the shop came from *un vigneron sérieux* just down the road. Soon I was striding down a track through the view that I had seen from my hotel window, quite transported by the sun and the air and the loveliness of the whole landscape, thinking that if I were to climb to the top of the furthest slope beyond the valley and find a blue sea and islands stretching out below me I would not be surprised.

Two hours on the road had done nothing to impair my mood. Perhaps half the way was literally on the road, since resolutely to have shunned metalled surfaces would have entailed frequent deviations from the general

*St Amour is the most northerly cru of the Beaujolais, and thanks to its name one of the most popular. The white wine of the commune may be called St Véran, which confusingly is an appellation of the neighbouring Mâconnais.*

*The most pleasing walking among the* crus *of the Beaujolais is round and about the famous villages of the more northerly part of the region, closest to the high hills: Chiroubles, Fleurie, Chénas (shown here) and Juliénas. Chénas takes its name from the forests of oak (*chêne*) that used to cover the land.*

line of march for which there was really no need, since with the exception of a few metres here and there the roads were all very minor ones, and the only traffic was the occasional load of grapes travelling from vineyard to *pressoir*. For the first four of the seven or eight kilometres (four or five miles) between Salles and the lower slopes of Mont Brouilly I had been walking in the appellation of Beaujolais-Villages, then for about 500 metres had traversed the *cru* of AOC Brouilly, before reaching the jealously defended *cru* of AOC Côte de Brouilly. Once what is now the AOC Brouilly was merely part of the far larger Villages appellation, the AOC Brouilly being restricted to wines from the slopes of the 'mountain', where the proprietors argued passionately that the lower ground included alluvial soils that made for less well-structured wines than those derived from the granitic and shale soils on the *côtes* above. In an attempt to arrive at a compromise between the two opposing camps, a decree of 1938 created the new *crus* of Brouilly and Côte de Brouilly. The 'mountain' will erupt again before any further encroachment is made upon what the few remaining members of the old guard still regard as the superior *cru*.

No such distinctions bothered me as I lunched there on the hillside overlooking the domaine of Godefroy and the neighbouring village and the château of St Lager. The Beaujolais-Villages I had brought from Salles seemed to me superior enough as I sat on the edge of the highest vineyard in all Beaujolais. All of the other top nine appellations were to be found further north, and with the exception of Regnié, a fairly recent creation, at one time or another over the previous three years I had walked in all of them.

In May the year before, persuaded by the Michelin guide's Bibendum in a rocking chair, printed in red, plus the note that the hotel was *au milieu du vignoble*, I had spent a night at the Château de Pizay near Belleville, and after a tour of the property's own wine-making cellars had set off to walk to Fleurie by way of Morgon and Chiroubles, an itinerary of perhaps 16 kilometres (10 miles) by the route that I had planned only very vaguely. For not much more than 500 metres at first I had been more or less obliged to keep to a hard-top road before striking up into the great expanse of vines that stretches north of the Ardières valley, and westwards from the N 6 towards the wooded hills. There had been showers and sunshine, apple blossom in farmhouse gardens, and easy going on vineyard paths and very minor roads. At mid-morning, consulting my map near Haute Morgon, I had been asked by a man who happened to see me from his garden on the edge of the vines if I needed help. When he learned of my interest in wine and wine country he revealed that he himself was a vigneron in a very small way and that he would be happy to show me his 'cellar' (which he said was really no cellar at all) if I had the time.

It emerged that Monsieur Rideau had been a bank manager until his wife had inherited *quelques vignes*, at which time he had happily changed his occupation. His cellar looked from the outside like a garage going down and back into the artifical mound on which Monsieur Rideau's fairly modern bungalow had been built. One half of the floor space was occupied by a wooden vat, two large wooden *fûts* and several smaller casks. In the other half was a small horizontal press, a number of smaller casks and the usual assortment of plastic hoses and ancillary equipment. Fermentation, Monsieur Rideau said, was by *macération carbonique*. His wine was AOC Morgon; would I care to taste the last vintage, soon to be bottled here on the premises by a specialist firm that came round? He really hadn't the room to do it himself. I tasted the last year's wine, which I thought drinkable but much too young, followed by the vintage before that, and then a five-year-old which seemed to me very good. Yes, said Monsieur Rideau; his grapes were grown on the lower slopes of the Mont du Py, not a kilometre (half a mile) away; one of the best places in the whole appellation. Morgon was generally thought to have as good a 'body' as a fine wine from the Côte d'Or together with the characteristic fruitiness of a good Gamay of Beaujolais. At its best it certainly ought not to be drunk very young. Monsieur Rideau insisted on my taking a bottle of his three-year-old wine with me: I tucked it into my pack, promising myself to let it rest at home for a year or two more. Less than an hour after leaving the bungalow cellars of my kindly, modest ex-bank manager, heading north-west towards Chiroubles and with lunch in mind, I was buying a bottle of two-year-old Morgon at the Château de Bellevue, the domaine of Prince Alexandre Lieven.

Eager now to reach higher ground, I went on up through the hamlet of Vermont, took a path into the vines, climbed a slope and, at the edge of a wood overlooking Chiroubles on its hill beyond the little valley of the

*The chapel of the Madonna of Fleurie overlooks the vineyards upon which her blessing is asked in an annual ceremony.*

Douby stream and with a view of Fleurie further to the north-east, seated myself comfortably against a fallen tree and raised a glass both to Monsieur Rideau's ten thousand and the Prince's two hundred thousand bottles of Morgon a year. Beaujolais had never tasted better than there, with a breeze in the pines and the air scented with hawthorn and blackthorn blossom and yellow broom, and a menu consisting exclusively of wholemeal bread with cheese.

The rest of the walk was all up and down and this way and that by paths and lanes as pretty as the name Fleurie itself, and the views out over the vine-covered plain from the high road leading into Chiroubles were very fine. I had another happy prospect in view, too, for although I intended sleeping in my one-man tent in the verdant and well-ordered municipal site, I had a rendezvous for dinner in the village, at the Auberge du Cep; a not-so-modest little restaurant with a Michelin star.

The following morning I set out north-eastwards towards the Château du Moulin-à-Vent. There is no commune of Moulin-à-Vent, only the mill on the outcropping granite below the village of les Thorins. At the Château they showed me the temperature-controlled stainless-steel fermentation vats and the ranks of oak casks where, unusually, the wine is aged for six months following vinification. 'Textbook Moulin-à-Vent, ideal for laying down. Depth and richness,' notes Serena Sutcliffe of the estate's wines. Tasting under the eye of proprietor Jean-Pierre Bloud, I remembered her words and repeated them sagely, as if they were my own. Monsieur Bloud

*The Monts du Beaujolais are the north-eastern outriders of the Massif Central. The GR 760, Tour du Beaujolais, traverses them parallel to the Saône valley, offering fine views; but to taste the wine of the country the walker must descend to the lower slopes.*

was pleased and impressed. His vines grow on a pinkish soil of granitic sand which contains (it is said) a significant element of manganese: hence the 'nerves and sinews' of the wine, which should never be drunk until it is at least two or three years old, and can profit from much longer in bottle. I sampled a ten-year-old wine there in Monsieur Bloud's cellars and thought that if I had been given it in a blind tasting anywhere else in the world I would almost certainly have mistaken the Gamay for a Pinot Noir. 'Easily done,' agreed Monsieur Bloud.

There was a bottle of his five-year-old wine in my pack as I went on up the road, making for the high ground west and south of Chénas. At the bottom of a slope which the map called le Mont was a lone wild peach tree in glorious blossom, and half an acre or so of abandoned vineyard where the pink earth, deeply fissured by water erosion, made me think of Colorado. At the top of the slope, on a granite spur reaching down from the wooded hill, were dwarf oaks and coarse grass and heather. Here I arranged myself. 'Real breed allied to structure and length,' says Serena Sutcliffe of 'fine' Moulin-à-Vent. There on that May day it seemed to me that the wine I had brought from the château enjoyed all of those attributes. Monsieur Bloud had apologised for not being able to ask me to lunch (he had a business appointment in Villefranche) and had waved aside my reluctance to accept a 'serious' bottle for a picnic: 'The best moment is when you want it most.'

After a long lunch, instead of going down to Chénas I passed only briefly through a corner of the appellation before climbing up into the Bois de Retour and over and down to Juliénas, beyond the valley of the slender River Mauvaise, then gently on up to St Amour, the most northerly of all the *crus*, where I had a five o'clock appointment at the Auberge du Paradis in neighbouring Plâtre-Durand. *Paradis* is the name given to half-fermented wine said to be a local tipple in some parts of the Beaujolais, but I have never been offered it, and to end that May walk I was quite content with draught beer.

Now, a year and a half later, I was obliged to abandon my reminiscences on Mont Brouilly in favour of a rendezvous at the Château de Pizay with a representative from the regional tourist organization who would take me back to Salles for dinner. Lucien was in his middle thirties, anxious to please but all his own man. We could have dinner back at the hotel in Salles, as arranged, he said. Or I might like to try something a little different. A good friend of his was the daughter of a vigneron in Morgon. She and her sister were coming up from Lyon for the weekend and he had promised to meet them off the train at Belleville at five o'clock and take them to their parents' place just a few kilometres along the road. The harvest was in full swing on the family property and we could have supper with the *vendangeurs*. There was absolutely no obligation, but it might be fun. As I often do, I had carried a change of lightweight clothes in my pack and one of the garden guest rooms at the Château de Pizay was now placed at my disposal. Lucien said that while I cleaned up he would meet the train.

*In Beaujolais many a façade such as this conceals venerable cellars where methods of wine-making have not changed fundamentally for centuries. Whole-grape maceration is one such technique.*

The family property was typical of the Beaujolais: a farmhouse of terra-cotta-coloured stone and indeterminate age; a farmyard no tidier nor more elegant than working farmyards normally are, with assorted outbuildings and a litter of farm equipment, including two tractors with metal trailers hooked up. Madame Durance was a good-looking, cheerful woman in her fifties who apologised to me for not shaking hands, since they were covered in flour. Monsieur Durance was not yet back from calling on the wine-maker in Villié-Morgon to whom he sold his grapes. Gabrielle and Véronique, who had explained to us on the way from the station that they had not come for a lazy weekend, but to help their mother feed the grape-pickers, put on aprons and started laying a long trestle table at one side of the very large kitchen. Lucien and I helped. When Monsieur Durance did appear he looked as though he had just had a good scrub. He had slightly greying hair and was wearing a bottle-green corduroy shirt with blue denim trousers. ('*Très gai!*' remarked Gabrielle). Though *accueillant* enough, he was sparing with words. It had been a very good harvest so far, he said: quantity good; quality excellent. '*Pas mal du tout.*'

Grape-harvest suppers are generally jolly, joyful occasions: the work is hard; the hours necessarily long; the pleasure of stopping work particularly great, and the camaraderie usually self-sustaining. Grape-growers and wine-makers have a tradition of feeding their workers well, if only out of self-interest, and wine flows freely at table, even if it is not always literally *du pays*. It is an opportunity for everyone to let their hair down and have a happy time. At first Gabrielle and Véronique were kept busy putting food on the table for the dozen or so hungry and thirsty young men and women pickers, all of whom were French, from Clermont-Ferrand. When everyone had finished the *charcuterie* and was busy with the main course – a hearty beef *ragoût* – the sisters joined their father, Lucien and me at one end of the table and started on their own supper. Glasses were filled with a wine which Monsieur Durance described as '*un bot petit Gamay de la commune*' and then filled again. I encouraged my host to talk about wine, and he was scathing not only about Beaujolais Nouveau, but also about what he called fashions in *crus*: one year Fleurie was all the rage; the next year Brouilly; the year after that, something else. The *négociants* did it just so as to manipulate prices. He was glad he was only a grower, not a wine-maker. His father and grandfather had been growers too. A cobbler ought to stick to his last. 'Not a wine-maker!' exclaimed Véronique. 'What a story!' ('*Quelle histoire!*'). With mock solemnity Monsieur Durance informed her that his '*quelques bouteilles*' were just his little hobby: he was no Georges Dubœuf!

At the end of dinner, Monsieur Durance announced that since the picking was going so well he would like to propose a little celebration: we would go and drink a bottle of 'the '83'. Now the significance of Véronique's ironic remark became fully apparent. In an open barn at one side of the farmyard was a neat, high stack of old, dry vine roots. Behind the stack, a door in the stone wall and some steps led down into a cellar lit by a single bare electric bulb. A wooden vat, an old-fashioned vertical, slatted press, several far-from-new casks and a row of large stainless-steel jugs constituted the image of a traditional wine-making *cave*. Through a low arch another short flight of stone steps gave access to a storage cellar.

While Monsieur Durance left us briefly for the lower level, his daughters lit the six half-burned candles in a pyramid-shaped wrought-iron holder ('*Il est très ritualiste*,' explained Véronique) before switching off the electric bulb. We first tasted a two-year-old wine, which was tannic and without any Beaujolais charm. 'You see: not drinkable! But if I lived by selling wine I would have sold it and someone would be paying to drink it,' scoffed Monsieur Durance. Then we sampled a five-year-old, which I thought very drinkable indeed. ('Promising!'). The '83 was the one of oldest Beaujolais I had ever tasted, a revelation in flavours and appearance. Held up to the candle-flames it was still a lovely garnet colour. Though it was as cool as the lower cellar, its 'nose' was seductive, and the taste so complex as to challenge the imagination and descriptive powers of the taster. 'No chaptalization, no filtering: only racking,' said Monsieur Durance.

It was not very sensible at that hour, but there was no spitting: we drank the wine. It was even less prudent to start on a fifteen-year-old *marc*, which Monsieur Durance said came from a friend of his. When the subject of going to bed was raised at last, it was unanimously agreed that no responsible person could possibly take the wheel of a car, so I would have to stay more or less where I was. My host went off to his own bed. The rest of us took our *marc* and went outside to decide whether the moon was full.

*It is the most open land north of Villefranche-sur-Saône that produces all the best and best-known wines of the Beaujolais.*

# THE WINE

Once in a London restaurant I heard a man ask the waiter for 'a good bottle of beaujolais, nice and cold'. When a bottle labelled 'Fleurie' arrived the customer glanced at it and said that there was a mistake: he had ordered beaujolais. The waiter pointed out the 'Beaujolais' printed in much smaller type on the label, whereupon, to his credit, the man grinned and said oh well, one lived and learned.

Is beaujolais one of the best-known wines in the English-speaking world, or – more likely – one of the most misunderstood? Though most beaujolais is red, there are also both white and rosé beaujolais. And 'Beaujolais' is rarely the name to be found printed most prominently on the labels of the best wines of the region of Beaujolais, in which there are twelve distinct appellations (Fleurie being one).

By far the larger – southern – part of the Beaujolais region produces wines which are entitled to no name other than 'Beaujolais'. It is the north which makes all the finer wines of the area. 'Beaujolais' short and simple also represents the largest of all the twelve appellations. Next going north, and in size, is 'Beaujolais-Villages', which also has vineyards elsewhere in the region, territorial neighbours of all the *crus*. Then there are the ten Grands Crus themselves from south to north: Brouilly, Côte de Brouilly, Regnié, Morgon, Chiroubles, Fleurie, Moulin-à-Vent, Chénas, Juliénas and St Amour. Further north still we are out of Beaujolais and into the Mâconnais.

Grape, soil and method of vinification are always factors of prime importance, but in the case of Beaujolais have special significance. Taking vinification first, in Beaujolais the method of making the wine is different from the method used in the rest of Burgundy, or indeed the method used for most red wines anywhere. It is whole-grape vinification. In the ordinary way the grapes are destalked and crushed wholly or in part before being put into the fermentation vat, or (when they are trodden in the age-old way, for instance) are systematically crushed in the fermentation vats to release the juice as a preliminary to fermentation. In the Beaujolais the vats are loaded, but not completely filled with the grapes still in bunches, whole, as they have come from the vineyard (though free of leaves and other unwanted bits and pieces, of course), complete with stalks and uncrushed. Grapes at the bottom of the vat get crushed by the weight of those above, and fermentation begins, releasing carbonic acid gas. The gas rises to envelop the whole grapes, which then cannot ferment in the normal way. However, fermentation does occur within each separate berry, so that when the grapes burst and the partly fermented juice is released it embodies more of the essential aromas and flavours of the flesh of the fruit and less, if any, of the tannins that are to be found in juice derived from the ordinary vinification process. By this method, too, the colour of the skins is extracted more quickly. A modern variation of the whole-grape process as traditionally practised in the Beaujolais involves filling the vat completely with carbonic acid gas at the outset and is called *macération carbonique*.

Then the grape. The only permissible variety for AC Beaujolais is the Gamay, which does best on sandy or stony soils that are underlaid by granite or schist and that have little clay or lime in them. Large parts of the Beaujolais (not all of it) are granitic or schistous, and many parts are ideally sandy or stony (or sandy and stony) as well. Even at its best the Gamay does not give wines of much character when vinified in the ordinary way, but at its best and vinified by the traditional Beaujolais whole-grape or *macération carbonique* methods it can produce wines low in tannin, but high in fruit, flavour and colour and (because of the low tannin) especially well suited to being drunk when young. Hence Beaujolais Nouveau, or Beaujolais Primeur, officially released on the third Thursday in November.

The best Beaujolais Nouveau has the zest and charm of extreme but well-bred youth. Not-so-good 'Nouveau' may have the zest but little else to recommend it. The best is not ordinary AC Beaujolais from the southern part of the region, but the AC Beaujolais-Villages from the northern part. The ten individual *crus* are not offered as Nouveau or Primeur. When not over-filtered, over-chaptalized or flash-pasteurized to give 'stability', AC Beaujolais-Villages can develop much 'character' with two or three years of age, and many wine-makers in the Beaujolais feel that harm has been done to the image of Beaujolais in general by the relatively recent cult surrounding the immature wines.

*Fleurie possesses the most evocative of all the names of the ten crus of Beaujolais, and produces a delightful wine to match. All the major wine villages have their caves coopératives.*

# THE LOIRE

## INTRODUCTION

At a length of 1005 kilometres (625 miles) from the southeast of the Massif Central to the Atlantic, the Loire is the longest river in France, some 185 kilometres (115 miles) longer than the Rhône. We are overwhelmingly concerned with what is very roughly the lower half of the river, after it has left the Bourbonnais and the Massif Central behind it and has reached the Nivernais and the edge of the Paris basin.

Conveniently and conventionally, going from inland towards the ocean, we look at three distinctly different viticultural areas. First, there is the Sancerrois and its immediate neighbour of Pouilly-sur-Loire, which are respectively the homes of the world-famous wines of Sancerre and Pouilly-Fumé. Contiguous with Sancerre country, to the west, there is the lesser-known appellation of Menetou-Salon. Here in the Sancerrois, where the cathedral city of Bourges is the focal point, it is the Sauvignon grape which rules.

Next, after the Loire has made its great westward bend past Orléans, there are Touraine and Anjou, with famous places such as Blois, Amboise, Tours and Saumur; with famous châteaux such as Chambord, Chenonceaux and Azay-le-Rideau; and with famous wines ranging from red to white and from sweet to dry and from still to sparkling. In this central, 'Valley-of-the Loire' region between Orléans and Angers, the most familiar names on the wine labels are Anjou, Saumur, Vouvray, Chinon and Bourgueil. Here, Chenin is the best-known grape for the white wines, and Cabernet Franc is the leading variety for the reds, but with half a dozen other varieties present in varying degrees of significance.

Lastly, there is the Pays Nantais, more familiarly Muscadet country, which begins roughly 32 kilometres (20 miles) west of Angers and ends roughly 48 kilometres (30 miles) west of the port city of Nantes, almost on the beaches of the Atlantic. Muscadet is also the name of the leading grape here, with Gros Plant the runner up.

*For wide views, firm paths and an absence of hindrances the appellation of Sancerre has no serious competition in its two neighbours.*

# SANCERRE–POUILLY–MENETOU

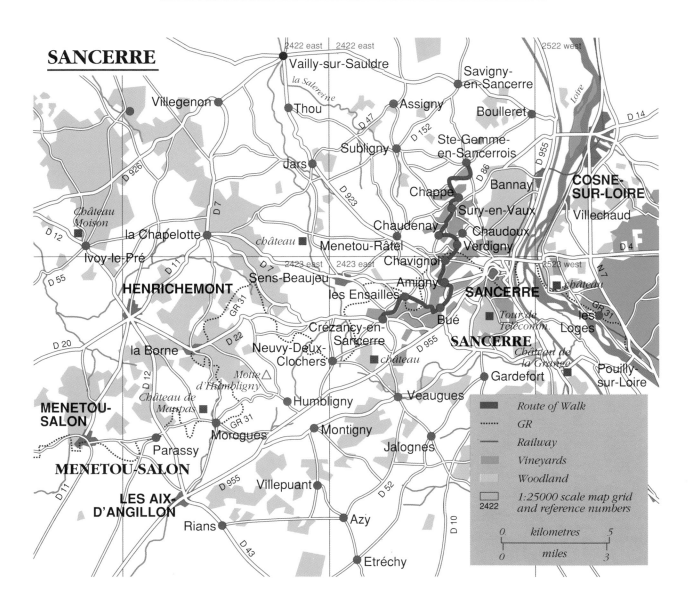

**SANCERRE**

Vailly-sur-Sauldre

2422 east | 2422 east

2522 west

Savigny-en-Sancerre

Villegenon

Thou

Assigny

Boulleret

D 14

*la Salereine*

D 47

D 152

Ste-Gemme-en-Sancerrois

D 955

Subligny

D 86

Bannay

COSNE-SUR-LOIRE

D 926

Jars

Chappe

Sury-en-Vaux

Villechaud

D 923

*Château Moison*

Chaudenay

Chaudoux

*château*

Menetou-Râtel

Verdigny

D 4

D 12

la Chapelotte

D 11

Chavignol

2523 west

*château*

Ivoy-le-Pré

D 7

2423 east | 2423 east

Amigny

GR 31

D 55

Sens-Beaujeu

les Ensailles

SANCERRE

les Loges

**HENRICHEMONT**

GR 31

Bué

SANCERRE

Crezancy-en-Sancerre

*Tour de Télécomm.*

la Borne

D 22

Neuvy-Deux-Clochers

D 955

Pouilly-sur-Loire

D 20

*château*

*Château de la Grange*

*Motte d'Humbligny*

Gardefort

D 12

*Château de Maupas*

GR 31

Humbligny

Veaugues

**MENETOU-SALON**

Morogues

Montigny

D 11

Parassy

Jalognes

**MENETOU-SALON**

**LES AIX-D'ANGILLON**

Villepuant

D 955

D 52

Azy

D 10

Rians

D 43

Etréchy

| | Route of Walk |
| --- | --- |
| | GR |
| | Railway |
| | Vineyards |
| | Woodland |
| 2422 | 1:25000 scale map grid and reference numbers |

0        kilometres        5

0        miles        3

# BRIEFING

## THE LIE OF THE LAND

Sancerre and Pouilly-sur-Loire almost face one another across the River Loire between Orléans and Nevers, some 100 kilometres (60 miles) east and south of Orléans. It was by way of their vineyards, Hugh Johnson has suggested, that the now internationally fashionable Sauvignon Blanc 'varietal' was discovered.

The Sancerrois is the high country (over 300 metres or nearly 1000 feet) at the south-eastern edge of the plain of Sologne, which lies south of the great curve of the Loire between Nevers and Saumur, and north of the Massif Central. Pouilly, on the opposite – right – bank of the river, lies on the lower north-western fringe of the 'high' country of Nièvre.

The underlying structure of the area is chalk. Laid on top of this are deposits of clay with flints: this is what the textbooks mean when they say that the soil is in parts 'siliceous'. In some of the vineyards of Pouilly, which generally are lower than those of Sancerre, there is a good deal of alluvial sand. Conceivably it is the predominance of the chalk in the structure of the land, and the effect that this has on the luminosity of the region, that makes Sancerre somewhat reminiscent of Champagne – even if one does not know that a Comte de Champagne was a progenitor of the Comtes de Sancerre, and that in modern times, before the strict laws of *appellation d'origine*, Pinot Noir grapes from the Sancerrois often augmented Champagne's own supply.

If nearly everyone has heard of Sancerre and Pouilly-Fumé, comparatively few have heard of Menetou-Salon. But Menetou-Salon is the westward geological extension of the ground that underlies the vineyards of Sancerre, which is why the Sauvignon grape is able to do as well there as in the neighbouring, better-known appellation.

For wide views, firm paths and an absence of hindrances the appellation of Sancerre has no serious competition in its two neighbouring appellations of Pouilly-sur-Loire and Menetou-Salon. The wine country on the right bank of the river is less appealingly sculpted and lacks the elevation of Sancerre, though from the Pouilly side there are splendid views to the west. Continuing westwards from Sancerre, one is by contrast in a more enclosed country, more wooded and more variously farmed. As a consequence, path-finding requires rather more attention to the map.

## WALKS

**Ste Gemme-en-Sancerrois to Crézancy-en-Sancerre** by way of Sury-en-Vaux, Chaudenay, Verdigny, Chavignol, Amigny, Bué, les Epsailles. 16–18 kilometres/10–12 miles; allow 4–6 hours.

If there is to be as much visiting and tasting as walking, it will prove impossible to conform to the old military maxim of never willingly giving away the advantage of high ground, since the wine villages here are mostly in the valleys. It is also difficult to avoid hard-top roads, but although the little roads are many, except at harvest time the traffic is wondrously light, so that there is no serious impairment of the rural peace.

Do not expect long, gently undulating paths among the vines, as in Alsace, Champagne or the Côte d'Or. So great has been the demand for Sancerre in the past two or three decades that land with satisfactory soil and good exposure, but which used to be considered too steep for economical viticulture, has now been planted, with the result that not a few of the vineyard slopes might rival those of the northern Rhône for steepness.

**GR 31: Pouilly-sur-Loire to Morogues** About 95 kilometres/60 miles; allow 25–28 hours.

The GR 31, which runs between the Nièvre and the GR 3 near Blois, passes through the edge of the Pouilly vineyards at Pouilly itself and carries on through les Loges (a typical wine village) to cross the Loire below Sancerre; it then continues either through or close to the Sancerre villages of Amigny, Chavignol, Verdigny, les Epsailles and Crézancy, before crossing into the appellation of Menetou-Salon to reach – via a long detour – Morogues, Parassy and the village of Menetou-Salon itself.

| Maps | | |
|---|---|---|
| **1:25,000** | **2323 est** | **St Martin-d'Auxigny** |
| | **2423 ouest** | **les Aix-d'Angillon** |
| | **2423 est** | **Sancerre** |
| | **2523 ouest** | **la Charité-sur-Loire** |
| **1:50,000** | **2323** | **St Martin-d'Auxigny** |
| | **2422** | **Lère** |
| | **2423** | **Sancerre** |
| | **2523** | **Pouilly-sur-Loire** |
| **1:100,000** | **27** | **Orléans – la Charité-sur-Loire** |
| ***Topo-Guide*** | **GR 31:** | ***Sentier Sologne-Sancerrois*** |

# WINTER DESCENDS ON THE SANCERROIS

From where I was sitting by an isolated clump of tall pines at the edge of a ploughed and harrowed field just north-east of Pouilly-sur-Loire, I looked down at the spires and turrets of Baron de Ladoucette's Château du Nozet, wondering how long it might be before the October sun would disperse the mists that shrouded the rest of the château and its noble park. Already quite warm on my back, it was illuminating Sancerre on its hilltop and some of the vine-covered slopes on the far side of the river.

Years before, it had been with the Château du Nozet and its Ladoucette label that my slender knowledge of Sancerre had begun. The occasion was a lunch at London's Connaught Hotel, then hardly known by comparison with its big sister the Savoy, and remarkable for its reasonable prices. Even Chablis and Pouilly-Fuissé did not cost a fortune, and Sancerre and Pouilly-Fumé, recent discoveries when set beside old familiars from a list of white burgundies, were bargains. I had never heard of Sancerre before, and Ladoucette proved a deliciously persuasive encouragement to exploration.

Now there were wide, inspiring views from the vineyards of Pouilly to those of Sancerre from the path that I took down the hill, skirting Pouilly and continuing, quite high above the river, to the villages of les Loges and Bois Gibault. At the Relais Fleurie, Pouilly, where I had spent the night, I had chanced to meet Monsieur Roger Pabiot, 'propriétaire-viticulteur', who had invited me to visit his premises in Bois Gibault, so in passing I now did so. Provoked by my asking with false ingenuousness whether there was really much difference between a good wine from this side of the river and a good one from the other side, Monsieur Pabiot attempted to persuade me of the 'unmistakable' characteristics of Pouilly-Fumé, as opposed to Sancerre: 'More finesse, more complexity, more "gun-flint" in the bouquet...' I inhaled slowly and deeply and tasted very thoughtfully and nodded seriously in acknowledgement of all that he said, but knew that in a blind tasting I would still be as likely as not to identify a Sancerre as a Pouilly-Fumé and a Pouilly-Fumé as a Sancerre.

It would have been an eight-kilometre (five-mile) walk, a lot of it not particulary rewarding, from Bois Gibault to the wine village across the river where I had been invited to visit a vigneron who – I had been told – was an ardent traditionalist. Monsieur Pabiot said he was going into Sancerre in any case and would be glad to put me on my road. At St Satur, between Sancerre and the river, he mischievously proposed my visiting the church, only partly restored after being destroyed by the English in the fourteenth century. Then he dropped me near a path leading to Chavignol, which has given its name to the goat cheeses so unattractively called 'crottins de Chavignol', but which also produces some of the best-reputed wines of the Sancerrois. As in all the wine villages at that season, the air was strongly

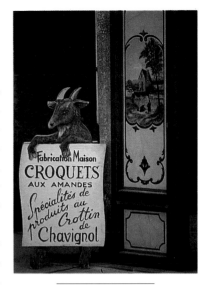

*Though the tradition of making them dates from at least the sixteenth century, the small, cylinder-shaped, individual cheeses of Chavignol were not called* crottins *(in the vernacular, animal droppings) until the nineteenth century. When old they are hard, almost black and far from beautiful.* Croquets *are traditional local biscuits.*

*Great forests occupy much of the Berry country and are no small part of its beauty. When traversing them a compass may be very useful.*

scented with *marc*, the residue of the grapes after the final pressing, from which the spirit of the same name is distilled. A man working in a vegetable patch still flourishing with fat leeks, huge cabbages and late tomatoes confirmed the map's suggestion that a certain path would take me up through woods out of the valley. It did, but so unconvincing was it and so closely crowded with blackthorn that only my faith in the Institut Géographique National prevented me from turning back.

The effort was justified. Emerging at last from the thicket, I climbed on up to the brow of the slope, sat comfortably on a low bank, and – in spite of noting that according to the map I was on les Monts Damnés – was very glad to be alive in such a place on such a day. The sun was warm, the sky blue and almost cloudless. Reaching to right and left and below me were the downland and valleys, woods and villages of the heart of the Sancerrois; and beyond Sancerre itself on its isolated peak, beyond the channels and backwaters and islands and wanderings of the river, were the vineyards of Pouilly, where I had stood earlier that morning. The mists had gone. Further away still were the forested uplands of the Nivernais, and far in the distance the blue-veiled heights of the Monts du Morvan. And now I drew the cork from a half-bottle of Monsieur Pabiot's Pouilly-Fumé. If one cannot have champagne as an aperitif there is no hardship in substituting a good white wine from the upper Loire.

After a while, my appointment took me by road and track across the hill and steeply down again into the village where I was to meet the tradition-

*Owned by the Cordier firm of Bordeaux, Clos de la Poussié, near Bué, is one of the best of all the vineyards of Sancerre. Clos du Chêne Marchand and Clos du Roy are other celebrated names from the commune.*

alist. I found him in the *cuverie* attached to a modest-looking farmhouse on the edge of the small and deeply rural settlement. Rubicund, and after a few minutes of exploratory formality quietly jovial, he showed me the vats in which his grapes fermented for 'about three weeks'. No ageing in wood for Sancerre: the important thing was to keep the freshness and authentic flavours of the Sauvignon. After racking the wine several times, he usually bottled in March. Sitting in his parlour with three or four wines to illustrate the conversation, he talked to me about the *terroir* of Sancerre. True, the soil was basically chalk, but topsoils varied significantly. In some places it was mostly mixed, chalk and clay formed from millions of tiny shells from the time when the whole region was the bed of the sea. In other places there was a preponderance of flints. Then again, there was the ground that had a lot of silex in it and was very pebbly: very hard on the machinery. The land was '*très parcellé*'. He, for instance, owned four different lots of vines in four different locations, two of them on especially good slopes, so he made two distinctly different Sancerres in order to keep the essential characters of the two different *terroirs*. It wasn't too difficult to tell where any particular Sancerre came from, provided it was an honestly made wine. What was I doing about lunch? His wife was in Bourges, visiting her old father in hospital, so he couldn't propose eating at home; but there was a not-half-bad little place in the next village.

It was not bad at all: cosy and without pretension, its corner bar well attended by locals. While the traditionalist and I lunched modestly but well I heard about the problems of maintaining quality in a seller's market, and how the popularity of Sancerre and the resulting prosperity in the region had gone to some heads: too much technology, too much emphasis on volume, too many fast cars. But now, what about *un petit digestif* to see me on my way?

Reinforced, I climbed out of the valley again and took the high roads and tracks westwards to les Epsailles, then down to Reigny and eastwards again to Bué. Few vistas of wine country are more impressive than the one commanded by the path that follows the contours of the 372 metre-high (1221-foot) Côte de Champtin. Much later, and most of it would have been in shadow. As it was, the whole magnificent panorama was floodlit by the setting sun. Below me, below Champtin and Bué, were two of the most famous slopes of the entire region. Sancerres labelled Clos du Roi and Clos du Chêne Marchand had always seemed to me very good before that day: they have tasted even better since.

The path down into Bué crossed a slope of lesser quality and was planted with Pinot Noir, not Sauvignon. Once, at a Michelin-starred restaurant in the Loire, I had left the choice of red wine to the *sommelier*, specifying only that it should be one of the expensive establishment's less expensive bottles. To my astonishment he had produced a red Sancerre, which I had liked very much. Now, in Bué, having tried in vain to order a taxi from a telephone kiosk, I went across to a man whom I had caught sight of as he rolled a barrel out from a dark interior and asked him if he happened to know of any local person who might offer a service. We talked. He asked if I would care for a glass of wine; it sounded to him, he said, as if I had earned one. When I had had a glass of his delicious, cellar-cool Sauvignon, he asked if I was familiar with the red wine of the district. I told him of my only experience of it. Ah, that was an odd coincidence, he exclaimed: it was he who supplied that restaurant with all their Sancerre! Perhaps I would like to try something with a few more years of bottle age than the one I had had before? People were fond of saying that red Sancerre was hardly worth taking seriously, but I could judge for myself. I did, and thought that if I had a dozen or two of that red wine of Sancerre at home it would be offered only to a discerning few. Well, said the vigneron, if I came back one day with my car he would probably be able to let me have a case, but in principle his production was sold in advance of bottling. When I afterwards looked up his name in one of my reference books I found it among the very top wine-makers of Sancerre.

Winter came that October night when autumn was looking the other way. It was no more than four kilometres (two and a half miles) from Bué to Sancerre, and out of pride I chose after all to walk. The beauty of the sunset was awesome. Never in the world had I seen so enormous a sphere; so crimson, molten and incandescent that as it sank into the horizon – and at the end so quickly – I imagined the dark forests erupting into flame. The sky changed from blue to shades of green, then through yellow and orange to the brown of an old red wine. Flawless and unsuspecting, it proclaimed a

*The Château du Nozet, viewed here from its surrounding vineyards, produces La Doucette, one of the best, probably the most famous and certainly one of the most expensive wines of the Pouilly-Fumé appellation. Sauvignon is the grape of Pouilly-Fumé AOC, as of Sancerre AOC. The white wine made from the Chasselas grapes of the region is classified as Pouilly-sur-Loire.*

clear dawn to another brilliant day and I went confidently to bed.

Confident too, I was up early next morning to see the sunrise over the slopes beyond Pouilly. But there was no sun: the sky was unpolished pewter. Gloomily I returned to bed for an hour, suddenly and unreasonably devoid of enthusiasm for persisting with the walk as I had envisaged it, which for the sake of topographical continuity was to begin again at Bué, then follow the GR 31 (but in reverse direction to that given in the *Topo-Guide*) to Menetou-Salon. Instead, reluctant to go back over ground already covered, I took a taxi to Crézancy-en-Sancerre, almost four kilometres (two and a half miles) further west of Bué. There, exchanging small talk at the bar of a café while trying to revive morale with a coffee and cognac, I began to become concerned that I had allowed myself insufficient time to keep a four o'clock appointment with a certain vigneron in Morogues, some 30 or more kilometres (nearly 20 miles) distant by the GR 31, with a fairly heavy pack. I gratefully accepted an offer from a mechanic whose speciality was looking after agricultural machinery of a lift in his *camionette* as far as Neuvy-Deux-Clochers, by which I lost face but gained the better part of two hours. When I told the mechanic whom it was that I was going to see in Morogues, he said that he had worked for Monsieur Pellé often and that he made very good wine.

The kilometres that followed could hardly have been in greater contrast to those of the day before, which had led me mostly through, beside or close to the vineyards. That day, however, as far as I was aware, I went

*'Reaching to right and left and below me were the downland and valleys and woods and villages of the heart of the Sancerrois, and beyond Sancerre itself, beyond the channels and backwaters and islands and wanderings of the river, were the vineyards of Pouilly.'*

nowhere near a vine until I was approaching Morogues. Grapes or no grapes, west of a line drawn from Crézancy south to Veaugues (barring Montigny, which contains the last two names of the Sancerre appellation) the topography of the hills beside the Loire is not repeated. Here instead were fields to skirt, streams to cross, farmyard dogs to be apprehensive of, hamlets to pass through. It was not bad walking, but under a leaden sky, with feet shuffling through the leaves on woodland paths and the sound of a gunshot welcome as the sole sign of other human life, it was walking for little purpose other than getting from A to B. I was glad when, at about the time for tea and buttered toast, I reached Henry Pellé's curious wine cellar at Morogues.

Henry Pellé's name is to be found in numerous books about wine, always under headings such as 'outstanding producers'. His wine-making premises are of a singular appearance, being tunnelled into a hillside from what might at first glance be the entrance to an air-raid shelter. Monsieur Pellé himself is what popular fancy might like all wine-makers to be: a trifle rustic, unaffected, shrewd, jovial and very good-humoured. Two local friends of his, one a vigneron, happened to arrive soon after I did and stayed to taste his Sancerre white and red, followed by his Menetou-Salon Morogues white, red and rosé. There was quite a lot of serious discussion and a good deal of banter. When we had tasted new and very young vintages, we moved on to older ones, talking about all of them in much detail. The wines were indeed outstanding, I thought, one or two of the Menetou-

*On the Route Jacques Coeur in the Berry, Château de la Verrerie was built by sixteenth-century Stuarts of Scotland. It is a member of La Vie de Château, an association of private homes providing bed and breakfast on a noble scale.*

Salon Sauvignons being as pleasing as any I had ever tasted in Sancerre.

By now my plans had changed. Having already visited the largely nineteenth-century restoration of the originally fifteenth-century château at Menetou-Salon on a previous occasion, I decided instead to head north-west to Henrichemont, planned by Sully and named after Henri IV in 1608, where according to the *Topo-Guide* there were hotels. More significantly, some five kilometres (three miles) beyond Henrichemont, near Ivoy-le-Pré, was the domaine of Vignoble de la Loge, which had associations with Henri Alain-Fournier and *Le Grand Meaulnes*, and where Marc Lebrun was reputedly making excellent white and red Menetou-Salon. And some nine or ten kilometres (five or six miles) further north still was the Château de la Verrerie, at which noble estate with close Scottish connections I had an open invitation to stay. With luck, I might reach Henrichemont before dark. Next day I would walk to Ivoy-le-Pré before lunch, then on to the Château de la Verrerie (a member of La Vie de Château), where the Comte de Vogüé was an authority on the wines of the upper Loire.

I failed stage one. Shunning the obvious but hard-top road, I took tracks to the east of it. An hour after leaving Morogues the sky was still leaden, the pace tiring, and I knew that before I could set foot on the D 22 on the other side of the forest that I had too boldly decided to cross (let alone reach Henrichemont) night would fall. Now, while I could still see what I was doing, I would have to make camp for the night.

Looking back, I suspect that I may unconsciously have been seeking an excuse to try out a device that I often carried as emergency equipment but had never used: a Gore-tex 'bivvy' (bivouac) bag, large enough to contain the user as he or she lies inside it in a sleeping bag. Needing neither poles nor pegs, it is considerably lighter than a one-man tent. In a thicket of saplings that gave an illusion of security I found a level space large enough for my needs. For extra shelter, and to enhance the illusion, I rigged my very lightweight groundsheet as a sort of porch. Bits and pieces remained from a lunchtime picnic. I had water. Not least, I had a small flask of whisky. By eight o'clock I was snugly cocooned against the dark.

Few people can claim unbroken sleep in a bivouac, and those who do ought not to be surprised if they are not believed. I slept and woke, slept and woke, drank whisky mixed with water from a bottle which – placed within arm's reach outside the bivvy bag – was almost ice cold, and slept again. Winter tightened its grip while I hid there. It was not a matter simply of temperature, but of impalpable, primordial mood. The silence of the woods seemed to me not the silence of the forest at rest, but of all nature cowering from the dread tyrant, not daring to stir, hoping to be overlooked. But in the morning there was a heavy frost in the clearings and a million leaves had fallen. When I unpacked my rucksack at the Château de la Verrerie that evening the bottle of Marc Lebrun's Menetou-Salon that I had brought from the Vignoble de la Loge was cold enough to drink without further ado. But I knew better than to confess to the Comte and Comtesse de Vogüé that I had brought my own wine.

*St Satur, close to Sancerre, has a church of the fourteenth century and some houses of a still earlier period. It was already described as 'old' in records of the eleventh century. Monks planted vines here in the twelfth century.*

# THE WINE

No wine region of France is less complicated in terms of wine itself than Pouilly-sur-Loire, Sancerre and Menetou-Salon. The best, the best-known and overwhelmingly the most commercially important wines are white, and they are made from a single variety of grape, the famous Sauvignon. Some of the lesser Chasselas is grown in the vineyards of Pouilly-Fumé, but the wine that is made from it may only be sold as Pouilly-sur-Loire.

Hugh Johnson has suggested that the present universal popularity of Sauvignon stems from the success of Pouilly-Fumé and Sancerre, but it is difficult to think of anywhere else in the world, or even in France itself, that produces Sauvignon as distinctive and distinguished as those from this comparatively small viticultural region of the upper Loire. Certainly anyone familiar with the best and most typical Sauvignons of Pouilly-Fumé, Sancerre and Menetou-Salon would be disappointed if expecting to find substitutes in the Sauvignons of the New World, or even in those of Bordeaux.

'Crisp', 'dry' and 'fruity' are the words that come most immediately to mind in the quest for a succinct description of these singularly delicious, uncomplicated white wines. Some of its many champions would argue that Pouilly-Fumé was 'finer', more elegant, and more interestingly complex than its neighbour across the river. Others would say that Sancerre was 'bigger', and that because of its higher acidity it may gain from several years of bottle age (here on the upper Loire Sauvignon is never aged in wood), whereas Pouilly-Fumé does not. Most of us have more than a little difficulty in knowing when we are enjoying one rather than the other without the help of a sight of the label.

The fact that the vineyards of the upper Loire are in a decisively northern climate, so that the Sauvignon takes longer to ripen and acquires a higher acidity here than in, say, Australia, California or Bordeaux, is said to be an important factor in the distinctive character of the wine from these parts. The soil certainly seems to be another. As usual in wine districts of quality, simple and practical rationalizations tend to be elusive, but the presence of underlying, and in some places surface, chalk, and on the Sancerre slopes of flint, is clearly of vital significance. (Gun-flint is another word rarely absent from descriptions of both Pouilly-Fumé and Sancerre.) Certainly to the sensitive palate there are marked differences between the wines derived from vineyards of differing soils, although differences in the angle of exposure to the sun can also play their part.

Although white wine dominates the region, there are also both red and rosé wines. These are made from the Pinot Noir as in Burgundy, but because of the more northerly climate are never the equal of the best of Burgundy wines, and not for long keeping.

# SAUMUR–TOURAINE

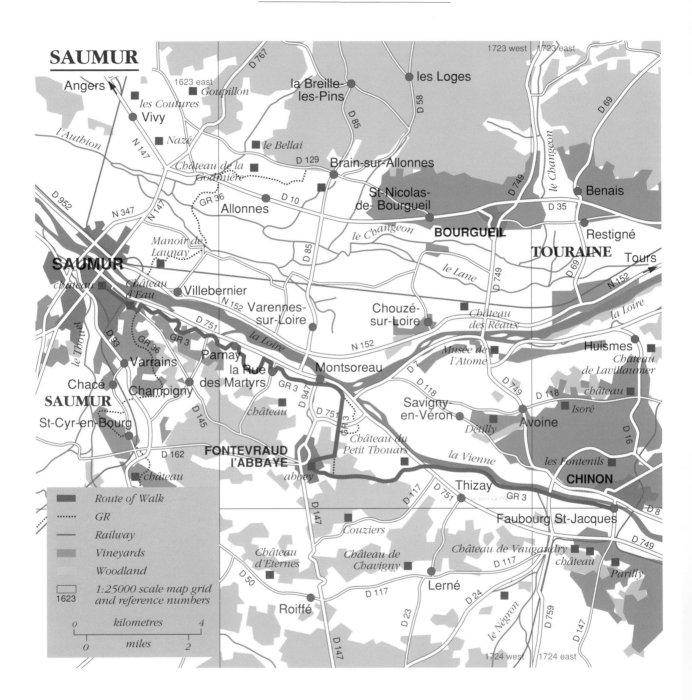

**SAUMUR**

Angers

les Coutures
Vivy
*Goupillon*
*1623 east*

*Nazé*
*le Bellai*

*Château de la*
*Godinière*

la Breille-
les-Pins

les Loges

Brain-sur-Allonnes

l'Authion

N 147

D 767

D 85

D 58

D 69

D 129

GR 36

Allonnes

D 10

St-Nicolas-
de- Bourgueil

le Changeon

Benais

D 952

N 347

N 147

*Manoir de*
*Launay*

D 85

*le Changeon*

**BOURGUEIL**

D 749

le Changeon

D 35

Restigné

**TOURAINE**

Tours

**SAUMUR**

*château*

Château
d'Eau

Villebernier

N 152

Varennes-
sur-Loire

*le Lane*

le Thouet

D 751

GR 36

GR 3

la Loire

Chouzé-
sur-Loire

*Château*
*des Réaux*

D 749

N 152

D 69

N 152

la Loire

D 93

Varrains

Parnay

la Rue
des Martyrs

Montsoreau

*Musée de*
*l'Atome*

Huismes

*Château*
*de Lavillaumer*

Chacé

Champigny

**SAUMUR**

St-Cyr-en-Bourg

D 145

GR 3

*château*

D 947

D 751

GR 3

D 7

D 118

Savigny-
en-Véron

*Détilly*

D 749

D 118

Avoine

*château*

*Isoré*

D 16

D 162

*château*

**FONTEVRAUD**
**L'ABBAYE**

*abbey*

*Château du*
*Petit Thouars*

GR 3

*la Vienne*

*les Fontenils*

**CHINON**

D 147

Couziers

D 117

Thizay

D 751

GR 3

Faubourg St-Jacques

D 8

D 749

*Château*
*d'Eternes*

D 50

*Château de*
*Chavigny*

*Château de Vaugaudry*

D 117

*château*

*Parilly*

Lerné

D 24

D 117

D 23

*le Négron*

D 759

D 147

Roiffé

D 147

1724 west | 1724 east

*1723 west | 1723 east*

**Legend:**
- Route of Walk
- ⋯ GR
- Railway
- Vineyards
- Woodland
- 1623 1:25000 scale map grid and reference numbers

kilometres
0 — 4

miles
0 — 2

# BRIEFING

## THE LIE OF THE LAND

Of all the great rivers of France, only two – the Rhône and the Loire – have given their names to wine regions of equally great repute. As, at 1005 kilometres (625 miles) the Loire is the longer of the two by more than 160 kilometres (100 miles), so its 400 kilometres (250 miles) of vineyards situated more or less on the river are greatly superior as walking country to the 80 or 100 river kilometres (50 or 60 miles) where grapes are grown south of Lyon.

It is of fundamental significance to the topography of this region that until modern times the lands bordering the Loire were subject to frequent and disastrous flooding, and that therefore vineyards and villages were set back at what people hoped was a safe distance. On the right (north) bank the vineyards of Bourgueil and St Nicolas-de-Bourgueil occupy an alluvial terrace some 19 kilometres (12 miles) long and a kilometre and a half (one mile) or so wide, mostly at a distance of three to five kilometres (two or three miles) from the river. On the left (south) bank the vines of Saumur-Champigny are mostly up behind the villages, on the plateau. And of course the edge of the plateau is broken by little valleys running at right angles to the river, so that the way of the walker cannot for long be straight and level. Walking through the appellations of the north bank, therefore, is quite different from walking on the opposite bank.

Once it has left the Massif Central well behind it and united with the Allier just south of Nevers, the Loire has done with any chasms, canyons, gorges or ravines, indeed with hard country of any kind. From then on it flows mostly across the limestone, sands and clays of the edge of the Paris basin, along a valley floor that is seldom more than 100 metres (330 feet) below its neighbouring plateaux. There are no rugged uplands above the wide valley of the middle and lower Loire, which flows smoothly and peacefully, through gentle and fertile country, on its way to the Atlantic.

## WALK

The two essential pieces of equipment for any walker in the wine country of the Loire are a copy each of the *Topo-Guides* GR 3, '*Châteaux du Val de Loire: Orléans-Saumur*', and GR 3, '*Sentiers de la Loire, de l' Anjou à la Brière, de Saumur à Guérande*'. The first covers the walk from Saumur to the Vienne, en route for Chinon, as well as the important Touraine appellation of Montlouis, east of Tours. The second covers not far short of 160 kilometres (100 miles) of Anjou appellations to the borders of Muscadet country, just east of Nantes, not walking down

the rows of Chenin, Cabernet Franc, Gamay or other *cépages* all the way, of course, but with sufficient '*à travers les vignes*' and '*entre un pré et une vigne*' to be valuable.

**Saumur to Chinon** by way of Montsoreau and Fontevraud on the GR 3. About 40 kilometres/25 miles; allow 9–10 hours.

The path is that of the GR 3, but in the opposite direction (which is to say from west to east) to the detailed description given in the *Topo-Guide*. The route is therefore on the south bank of the Loire to Dampierre-sur-Loire, Souzay-Champigny, Turquant, Montsoreau, Candes-St-Martin, then south to Fontevraud. From Fontevraud the way is by a very old track through forest down to the D 751 and 500 metres along it to a paved way (the old Roman road), which after about a kilometre (just over half a mile) becomes a track running beside the Vienne all the way to Chinon.

| Maps | | | |
|---|---|---|---|
| 1:25,000 | 2021 | est | Blois |
| | 2022 | ouest | Montrichard |
| | 1922 | est | Amboise |
| | 1822 | est | Tours |
| | 1823 | ouest | Langeais |
| | 1723 | est | Chinon |
| | 1720 | ouest | Bourgueil, Fontevraud |
| | 1623 | est | Saumur |
| | 1623 | ouest | Saumur |
| | | | |
| 1:50,000 | 1922 | | Amboise |
| | 1823 | | Langeais |
| | 1723 | | Chinon |
| | 1623 | | Saumur |
| | | | |
| 1:100,000 | 25 | | Angers-Chinon |
| | 26 | | Tours |
| | | | |
| *Topo-Guides* | GR 3 | | *Châteaux du Val de Loire:* |
| | | | *Orléans-Saumur* |
| | | | *Sentiers de la Loire, de* |
| | | | *l'Anjou à la Brière, de* |
| | | | *Saumur à Guérande* |

# MAY IN
# THE LOIRE VALLEY

In the beautiful illustrations by the Limbourg brothers to the celebrated medieval book of hours, the *Très Riches Heures du Duc de Berry*, September is represented by a scene of grapes being harvested in vineyards close to the château of Saumur. Sadly, many of the exuberantly impressive architectural features to be seen in the painting have disappeared over the centuries – if indeed they were all ever there – but the château remains incontestably one of the most imposing historical monuments in France; a wondrously romantic place from which to set out on a perfect morning in May on a six-hour progress from one of the Loire valley's most attractive cities to the abbey of Fontevraud, burial place of Henry II of England, his Queen, Eleanor of Aquitaine, and their son, Richard Coeur de Lion.

In truth, I started from a campsite almost directly opposite the château, on the Ile d'Offard, in the middle of the great river itself. Sunrise and birdsong had woken me, and with coffee in one hand and yesterday's buttered bread in the other I had watched and listened to this *son et lumière* staged by nature with the château as its centrepiece. Then, hoisting a weighty pack, I crossed the bridge to the left bank of the Loire, bought a newly-baked baguette, verified the directions given in the GR 3 *Topo-Guide*, and set off along the D 145 with the sun on my face.

There are no vines beneath the walls of the château of Saumur today. They begin rather more than a kilometre (nearly a mile) to the east, in an area identified encouragingly on the map as St Vincent. There are no wide, rolling vistas of vines here above the Loire, such as are to be found in Champagne and Alsace, or on the Côte d'Or, or in the appellations of Bordeaux, but for the next ten kilometres (six miles) or so, the vineyards are constantly mentioned in the *Topo-Guide*'s directions: '*emprunter le chemin dans les vignobles*', '*obliquer à droite dans les vignes*', '*se diriger à travers les vignes*'. As for the wine itself, a walk of a few hundred metres down to the D 947 and the river brings one to *cave* after *cave* where the wines of Anjou are to be tasted, especially the red ones of the Saumur-Champigny appellation, of which Steven Spurrier and Michel Dovaz observe in their *Académie du Vin Wine Course*: 'The true *cru* of Saumur, with a dark ruby colour: it has a nose of violet and raspberry and is subtle on the palate. The great old vintages are outstanding'.

But wisteria blossom, not violets, provided the scent just then in Anjou and Touraine. In its pale-purple loveliness it cascaded over ancient tufa walls, filling the early summer air and abundantly decorating the terrace wall below what an almost apologetically unobtrusive, not easily legible plaque identified as the Château de Souzay. '*Ici mourut le vingt août 1482 Margarite d'Anjou, Reine d'Angleterre. Première héroïne de la Guerre des deux Roses. La plus malheureuse des Reines, des épouses, et des mères.*'

*The villages, with their weathered stone and wealth of unostentatious and often charming architectural detail, are characteristic of the central valley of the Loire. The romantic, medieval, viticultural past as illustrated in the* Très Riches Heures *seems as close here as anywhere in France.*

*Montsoreau marks the end of the Saumur-Champigny appellation. The fifteenth-century château was the home of the lovely comtesse who inspired Dumas' romantic tale* La Dame de Montsoreau.

*The Gothic Hôtel de Ville of Saumur was fortified at the beginning of the sixteenth century, when the River Loire almost lapped its walls. The town has long been famous not only for the school that trains the elite of the French cavalry, but also for sparkling wine made by the méthode champenoise.*

Margaret of Anjou, the reputedly beautiful daughter of René of Anjou and Provence, married at sixteen to Henry VI of England and subsequently imprisoned in the Tower of London, was reluctantly ransomed by Louis XI, before being rescued by François de la Vignolle, her father's old servant, to spend most of her remaining four years of life here in the glorious valley of the Loire. Did she ever sit in one of these corner turrets, gazing out over the river, looking back over her crowded, bloody, tragic career, thinking of her son, the Prince of Wales, slain on the distant field of Tewkesbury; her husband gone mad, and finally murdered; all that she had schemed and striven for horribly lost?

Frogs were croaking in the pools and lagoons of the Ile de Souzay, beside the D 947, as I braved thunderous traffic for a few metres before spotting the red-and-white GR bars and turning up a paved road to a handsome church with (as I could see) a Renaissance doorway and (as I could not see, because the door was locked) a Romanesque nave. Leading to the south, the GR 3 surveyed a wide expanse of vines undulating very gently towards distant forest. On its eastern side was an old and pretty house whose north-facing windows must have commanded a far view across the Loire to the slopes of Bourgueil and St Nicolas-de-Bourgueil, appellations of the Touraine vineyards, not of Saumur.

Taking a vineyard track, I paused to talk with a man standing beside a *camionette,* who told me that the vines I was walking through were Cabernet Franc and belonged to the Château de Targé in the commune of Parnay. The château's wine, he added, was exclusively the red Saumur-Champigny. Yes, he agreed, the soil was very sandy: river soil from countless centuries ago with some slate and a chalky base. Yes, I would be able to taste the wine and buy a bottle down at the château; there was still plenty of time before they closed for lunch.

Out of the vineyards I went and down between the houses of la Rue Valbrun, almost to the D 947 again, and back towards Targé. Up on my left, in its terraced grounds, the Château de Targé looked not at all the sort of place where a walker might be welcome to taste and buy, but my determination to have a good bottle of Saumur-Champigny for lunch within the appellation, or next door to it, overcame my inhibitions.

The south side of the courtyard at the top of the drive formed the north side of the high ground over which I had been walking: a cliff face. Just as I arrived, a dark, good-looking man in his thirties wearing blue jeans and a blue working shirt emerged from a doorway at the base of it. '*Monsieur*?': his manner was neither hostile nor especially *accueillant,* but unmistakably authoritative. Good morning, I replied; was he by any chance the proprietor? The property, a former hunting lodge, had been in his family since the seventeenth century, he later told me. His father and mother, Edouard Pisani and Fresnette Ferry, had completely renovated the château and restored the vineyards after the Second World War; now he, Edouard Pisani-Ferry, had taken over the wine side of things.

From the noonday heat of the courtyard he led me back into the welcome cool of the cellars deep inside the tufa cliff, where his wines were ageing in bottle or cask. Outside again, we went to see his ultra-modern vinification plant with its computer-controlled, thermo-regulated vats. Back in his *salle de dégustation* and elegant office, looking down into the courtyard and out over the Loire, we spent twenty minutes tasting a range of his wines – 'robes' of ruby; 'noses' of violets, raspberry and blackcurrant (I thought), and of geraniums (I felt sure) – interrupted only by the arrival of a couple from Switzerland who had bought wine at the Château de Targé before and wanted another case or two now to take away. Casual callers wanting seriously to taste and buy a bottle or two, said Pisani-Ferry, were always welcome.

Not a case, but a single, precious bottle of a five-year-old vintage was my own, careful purchase. Happy with expectation, I went down from the château, through the lower reaches of Turquant, past mushroom caves in the tufa cliffs, then up again into the vines. The sky was cloudless, the sun very hot. Beside the remains of the windmill of la Perruche I paused to study the map and the *Topo-Guide*. Though the site was not a hundred metres (330 feet) above sea level, a welcome breeze blew there. Under 500 metres away, in the valley just ahead, was Montsoreau, the end of the appellation of Saumur-Champigny, lying astride the boundaries of Anjou and Touraine. Each department has both red and white wines of distinction, but at that moment I was too thirsty for either. Down in Montsoreau, under the extended awnings of a café on the corner of the village square, close

*The* Très Riche's Heures du Duc de Berry *depicts a medieval* vendange *beneath the walls of the château at Saumur. Today the vines begin rather more than a kilometre to the east, at St Vincent.*

to the river road, I drank a delightfully cold *pression*; then – more slowly – another. 'Hot work on a day like this,' said the *patron*, giving a wipe to the table as he set down the second glass tankard, and nodding towards my pack propped against one of the legs.

Hot indeed. But I had come 16 kilometres (10 miles) and had under eight to go. Soon, I paid the reckoning and toiled on up the narrow village street, a little tired but contented with the day. The vineyards, unspectacularly and somewhat untidily scattered along the edge of a near-plateau, effectively remote from the river, might themselves have lacked the cohesive and impressive character of so much other wine country, but the villages, with their weathered stone and wealth of unostentatious and often charming architectural detail, so characteristic of the central valley of the Loire, more than compensated for any such imperfections. Somehow the romantic, medieval viticultural past as illustrated in the *Très Riches Heures* seemed as close here as anywhere in France.

That Margaret of Anjou and the wisteria had a lot to do with my elation I do not doubt. There was more to come. The château, poised on the cliff-edge of the village against a background of the river and the distant, wooded hills, made as pretty a picture as any tourist could wish for. Opposite, the sign of an appealing Logis de France – Le Bussy – and further on the name of another equally attractive Renaissance house – the Logis de la Dame de Montsoreau – were reminders of the romantic and tragic tale that was to inspire Alexandre Dumas' novel *La Dame de Montsoreau*.

*Built between 1513 and 1521, Chenonceaux was given by Henry II to his mistress, Diane de Poitiers, who financed additions by income from a tax on church bells instituted by her royal lover. 'The King has hung all the bells in the kingdom round the neck of his mare,' said Rabelais.*

The lady of the title was Françoise (though Dumas called her Diane), the lovely wife of the Comte de Montsoreau, governor of Saumur. She fell in love with, and yielded to (or rather invited, some said) the attentions of Louis de Bussy-d'Amboise, the swashbuckling and predatory governor of neighbouring Anjou. When rumours of the affair reached Henri III, he is supposed to have remarked of the cuckolded Count, 'Our Master of the Royal Hunt must be a very poor huntsman, for he has allowed his own game to fall into de Bussy's traps.' Much humiliated, the Count obliged his wife to write a letter of assignation to her lover, luring him to his country residence, the Château de la Coutancière. Here Bussy d'Amboise was duly done away with, thus enabling the Count and his wife to live happily ever after with their several subsequent children.

Encouraged by a sign proclaiming *Panorama* and pointing ahead, I went on up a dirt track at the far end of the village to reach as admirable a place for lunching and musing as I could have dared hope for, almost 90 metres (300 feet) above the beginning of the River Vienne at its confluence with the Loire at Candes-St Martin. Below the ruins of what I supposed to have been a mill was a grassy bank with a shady tree, may blossom and birdsong.

Here I settled myself with my back against the tree, poured myself a glass of the Château de Targé, and looked out over Candes-St Martin and its magnificent church to the river and forest and distant hills, and to blue sky and white clouds sailing eastwards towards Tours, Blois and Orléans.

*The abbey of Fontevraud, founded at the end of the eleventh century and burial place of Henry II, Eleanor of Aquitaine and Richard Coeur de Lion.*

*Casks in a cellar at Chinon appear to be almost as old as some of the fourteenth- and fifteenth-century half-timbered houses of the marvellously picturesque little town. Most of the wines of the appellation are red, made from the Cabernet Franc grape.*

Had I planned the walk with such a prospect in mind I could not better have contrived it. In a straight line on the map, not ten kilometres (six miles) away, just south of Brain-sur-Allonnes, was the notorious Château de la Coutancière, where a little more than a year ago I had started a walk through the appellations of St Nicolas-de-Bourgueil and Bourgueil itself, whose red wines are easily mistaken for those of Chinon.

Targé was the perfect complement to the pâté de campagne and cheese that I had bought in Parnay and the *baguette* that had travelled from Saumur under the straps of my pack. There are those who would say that it was a waste to drink so good a wine with so vulgar a menu, but they and I differ.

The next two kilometres (one and a quarter miles) were more or less level-going on a virtually unavoidable and very minor road southwards across the plateau towards Fontevraud, with vines here and there, before the hard-top road petered out with a gentle uphill inclination and I was among the chestnuts and slim young oaks of la Grande Forêt, which used to surround Fontevraud for thousands of square miles and which to a large extent closely borders it still. In places the path was hedged with yellow broom in full flower and with sweet-scented hawthorn blossom. Clearings in the trees were carpeted with long grass and bluebells. A breeze hardly louder than a thought stirred the new leaves. A cuckoo called. The path through the forest is wide and very ancient: over the centuries from the abbey's twelfth-century foundation to the Revolution countless pilgrims must have trodden it. Did Queen Eleanor, called to the deathbed of her son Richard Lionheart, hurry frantically this way?

Coming down out of the forest, the walker sees the abbey buildings rising beyond open ground below the steep edge of the trees before suddenly joining the road to climb the main street of Fontevraud. After a *citron-*Perrier at a pavement table in the shadow of picturesque old houses, I pitched my one-man tent not far from the abbey, in a corner of an orchard whose very obliging owner also offered me the use of a bathroom.

Dinner was another matter. '*La vie est un art*' is the motto on the cover of the menu at La Licorne in Fontevraud. It seemed to me no less than artistic to juxtapose a tent in the orchard with dinner at a restaurant of considerable repute, long distinguished in the Michelin guide. Sitting with a certain feeling of virtue in a charming room with windows open to the soft spring evening, I drank a half-bottle of Langlois Crémant, a sparkling Saumur, to preface *raviolis de langoustines*, followed by *carré d'agneau rôti au jus d'estragon*. I finished the Langlois with the raviolis and had a five-year-old Cabernet Franc of Touraine with the lamb.

Next day, as I was sampling the wines of the delightful Château du Petit Thouars, some six kilometres (nearly four miles) along the very ancient path from Fontevraud to the Vienne and Chinon, the Comtesse Marguerite du Petit Thouars, who writes about wine and to whom I had an introduction, chided me for not having invited myself to stay in one of her guest rooms; but as I explained to her, for a day and night or two at least I was strictly committed to the simple life.

# THE WINE

Two grape varieties predominate in Touraine: Chenin Blanc for the majority of white wines, and Cabernet Franc (a relative of the Cabernet Sauvignon of Bordeaux, and used there also) for red. But Chardonnay and Sauvignon (both white) are also grown, as are Cabernet Sauvignon and Gamay, both red. And there are others in minor roles.

Second, the appellations. Here is a selection of names to be found on the labels of wines made in the Saumur-Touraine area which I think are likely to be of the most interest.

**Still white**
Saumur (Chenin Blanc): dry.
Touraine (generally Sauvignon Blanc): dry (like Sancerre).
Touraine-Amboise (Chenin Blanc): dry.
Vouvray (Chenin Blanc): dry to sweet.

**Sparkling white, made by *méthode champenoise***
Crémant de Loire (Chenin Blanc, Sauvignon, Chardonnay): *brut*.
Saumur Mousseux (Chenin Blanc): *demi-sec* to *brut*.
Vouvray Mousseux (Chenin Blanc): sweet to *brut*.
Vouvray Pétillant (Chenin Blanc): sweet to *brut*.

**Red**
Bourgueil (Cabernet Franc): from the north bank of the Loire.
St Nicolas-de-Bourgueil: as above.
Saumur-Champigny (predominantly Cabernet Franc).
Chinon (Cabernet Franc): from the south bank of the Loire.
Touraine (Gamay, Cabernet Franc).

*Near Souzay-Champigny in the appellation of Saumur-Champigny, the vines are Cabernet Franc, a cousin of Cabernet Sauvignon. The wines are probably the best reds of Anjou.*

# MUSCADET

**MUSCADET**

Legend:
- Route of Walk
- ····· GR
- —— Railway
- Vineyards
- Woodland
- ▢ 1323 1:25000 scale map grid and reference numbers

kilometres 0 — 14
miles 0 — 7

# BRIEFING

## THE LIE OF THE LAND

Geographically, if Pouilly and Sancerre – far inland and upstream beyond Angers, Tours and Orléans – may together be considered the first wine country of the Loire, Muscadet might be called the last. All but a tiny part of the appellation lies in a very rough semicircle to the south of the river, with the great Atlantic port of Nantes at the middle of its northern boundary and mostly on the Loire's northern bank.

The land within the rough semicircle is part of a wide plateau based upon the geologically very ancient rocks of Armorica, its central zone, running north-west to south-east, bisected by the valley of the River Sèvre Nantaise. South and west of the Sèvre Nantaise is the lesser stream of the Sèvre itself. Both rivers, flowing from inland, converge upon a point near Vertou, where the Sèvre is lost in the larger stream for the last eight kilometres (five miles) of its journey to the Loire.

The vineyards of the general appellation of Muscadet lie on both sides of the rivers Sèvre and Sèvre Nantaise; those which start with a fairly narrow band west of the Sèvre, cover the land between the two streams and continue to almost the full extent of the general appellation north and east of the Sèvre Nantaise are those which constitute the supposedly superior viticultural territory of the appellation of Muscadet Sèvre-et-Maine. The immediate river valleys only excepted, this is level or gently undulating country, all meadows and woods and cultivated fields and lanes and hedgerows, with no hard walking at all.

## WALK

**Tiffauges to Clisson** along the River Sèvre Nantaise. 16 kilometres/10 miles; allow 4–5 hours.

Given the unspectacular topography of Muscadet country, pleasurable walks are largely in the vicinity of the river valleys. The one from Tiffauges to Clisson, though beginning well outside the viticultural area, comes within sight of scattered plots of vines in the area of Boussay, and arrives within the appellation boundaries 2 or 3 kilometres (1–2 miles) south-east of Clisson. After Clisson the vineyards stretch all the way to the Loire.

The walk leaves Tiffauges between the castle grounds and the south bank of the river, and briefly enters a narrow wood before joining a lane running roughly parallel to the river. Footpaths and virtually traffic-free narrow lanes alternate for the rest of the way, with some stretches of path running along the river bank. At Hucheloup the route crosses the Sèvre Nantaise to continue to Gétigné and Clisson on the north side of the stream. Away from the river the land is largely devoted to mixed farming with many dairy cattle, so that although flies cannot be said to constitute a special nuisance, in summertime insect repellent may be a useful thing to take along.

**Maps**

| 1:25,000 | 1324 est | Bouffière |
|---|---|---|
| | 1324 ouest | Clisson |
| | 1244 est | les Sorinières |
| 1:50,000 | 1324 | Clisson |
| | 1224 | St Philibert-de-Grand-Lieu |
| 1:100,000 | 33 | Cholet |

# BESIDE
# THE SEVRE NANTAISE

*'The river flowing slowly and secretly, bordered here by high, leafy banks, there by water-meadows, there by narrow woods where our path ran through welcome shade.'*

There were five of us on the walk: Philippe, the young president of the regional *association des randonneurs*; thirty-five-year-old Jean-Daniel and his wife Marie-Odile (he a doctor, she a radiologist) from Nantes; their friend and neighbour Françoise, an engaging physiotherapist of about the same age, and I. The three from Nantes were smartly dressed in well-cut shorts, tennis shirts and trainers: Françoise, to my concern given that we planned to walk 20 kilometres (12 miles) or more, was wearing no socks. We had met largely by chance in Tiffauges. Philippe and I had met by arrangement, admittedly, intending to walk together, but half an hour after the appointed time he had telephoned in great embarrassment. The local tourist office, he said, offered the public a variety of organized walks as part of a weekend package; one of them was from Tiffauges to Clisson, which he and I had arranged to do. The local man who ought to have conducted it had suddenly become unwell, so that three people from Nantes, who had paid for a package and were already in Tiffauges, now found themselves without a guide. Would I mind very much, asked Philippe, if they came with us?

By starting in Tiffauges, Philippe had told me, we would have an interesting route to Clisson along the valley of the Sèvre Nantaise, which would be a fair distance for an August day, and besides having a good hotel for the night I would also be able to visit Bluebeard's castle. Gils de Rais, 'Bluebeard', he reminded me, had been a companion in arms of Joan of Arc during her reconquest of the kingdom of France from the English. '*Mais pas du tout sympàthique*,' remarked Françoise *sotto voce*, as we stood in a meadow at Tiffauges below the massive castle walls.

There was little talking as we walked. Speaking no English, the weekenders were to begin with extremely reserved and almost painfully apologetic for their 'intrusion' (as they put it) upon my plans. It took some time for me to discover that they had been intimidated by a briefing that had presented me not only as a vastly important person, but also eccentrically solitary by inclination. 'We thought you looked very severe,' said Françoise.

All francophiles, I suppose, have their own images of quintessential France. Mine has always been of a supreme rurality, and in the valley of the Sèvre Nantaise were all the elements of my ideal. The river flowed slowly and secretly, bordered here by high, leafy banks, there by water-meadows; here by narrow woods where our path ran through welcome shade, there by steep slopes with very old farmhouses at the top and cattle swishing their tails in the summer heat. By ancient mills willows drooped, ducks paddled, and a line raised and recast by an angler constituted an exercise of such moment as to mark the very air.

At about one o'clock we lunched near an old mill in the half-shade of what my French companions said were *frênes*, or ash, but which were certainly not ash as the tree is known to me. A large common supply of bread had been bought that morning in Tiffauges before setting out; otherwise we offered one another whatever each of us happened to have brought by way of provisions, including wine. I had kept a bottle of good Muscadet cold by my customary means of wrapping it up in a goosedown 'body warmer'; a refinement much admired by the others. 'Ah, the English!' remarked Françoise mockingly. 'How fussy they are about their wine.'

After we had eaten, the sound of water over a distant weir and of the leaves rustling in the lightest of breezes stilled all chatter, and we lay on our backs, gazing up at a blue sky where a solitary, very high-flying jet ejected four perfect vapour trails. I wondered where it had come from and where it was going to and thought that there was nowhere in the world that I would rather be than where I already was.

When we started walking again my French acquaintances kept together at some distance behind Philippe and me. I was glad to leave the map-reading to him, to have no cares for time and distance. I was also glad in the heat of the summer afternoon to enjoy more pauses than I might have taken on my own; pauses when Marie-Odile and Françoise flopped down with a 'phew!' and a '*mon dieu, qu'il fait chaud!*' and drank deeply from water-bottles. Occasionally forced to abandon the riverside, our path would climb steeply enough for me to envy the three from Nantes their shorts and skimpy shirts and their super-lightweight footwear. While I plodded, they

*Le Pallet, some six kilometres (four miles) from Clisson, has three claims to attention: it produces good Muscadet Sèvres-et-Maine; it has a very interesting wine museum; and it is said to be the birthplace of Pierre d'Abelard, the twelfth-century theologian.*

seemed to step lightly as fawns. Françoise, it is true, was obliged at one point to confess that a sore place had developed where a shoe had chafed a heel, whereupon I had the undeniable satisfaction of supplying first aid.

We reached Clisson at half past five in the afternoon, and a more agreeable end to a 20-kilometre (12-mile) walk it would be hard to devise. At the approaches to the town our path took us close beside the river through a tiny park shaped roughly like an amphitheatre with an open green sward where the stage might be, and a steep tree-covered slope that long ago must have been the river bank occupying the auditorium: all shaded; all cool; all verdant. Ahead, high above the banks of the Sèvre Nantaise and its confluence with the Moine, rose a castle which, though at heart a ruin, looked as a medieval castle ought to: mighty, proud and forbidding. '*C'est très plaisant*,' remarked the undemonstrative Françoise, surveying the little park. '*C'est fabuleux*,' said Marie-Odile, looking up at the castle; and indeed, with the addition of a turret or two it could have been an illustration to a fairytale.

Hardly less pleasing in all our eyes were five tankards of cold draught beer, sitting under a parasol on a table outside the Café des Sports, in the town square. 'It's best to drink slowly when you're hot,' advised Philippe sagely. 'You're right,' said the rest of us as we sank the glorious golden stuff in almost the same breath and looked eagerly round again for the waiter.

Clisson was enchanting. It had been arranged that a local doctor, a medical analyst who is also a passionate historian, should take me on a tour of

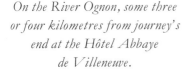

*On the River Ognon, some three or four kilometres from journey's end at the Hôtel Abbaye de Villeneuve.*

the town, but we walkers had arrived later than we ought to have done and had sat too long at the Café des Sports, so that when at last I presented myself at his house he suggested that rather than attempt a hurried tour at the end of a tiring day I might like to relax for a while with a drink. Built on the edge of a cliff close to the Sèvre Nantaise, the house seemed almost to be lodged among the tops of tall trees growing in the riverside park below, and was wholly delightful. The doctor's wife was truly beautiful and dressed with impeccable elegance, so that in my shabby old walking trousers, bush shirt and muddy boots, and with my face grimy from the exertions of the very warm day, I was hardly at my ease to begin with. Soon I was.

'Here,' said my host, filling my glass with a deliciously cool Muscadet for the third time, 'It's only eleven and a half degrees.' While I had been drinking, he had been telling me something of the history of Clisson, from its time as a colony in the Roman province of Aquitaine Secunda down to 1794 and the end of the Revolution, when the savagery of the republican Turreau and his infamous '*colonnes infernales*' had left it a fire-blackened ruin, 'abandoned to wolves and dogs'. The eventual rebuilding had been much influenced by the architect Lemot, who in the fashion of the times had studied in Italy.

The doctor and I joined Jean-Claude, Marie-Odile, Françoise and Philippe for dinner at the Auberge de la Cascade. We ate little oysters cooked with herbs, followed by sea bass with a *beurre blanc*, duck, cheese and *tarte aux pommes*. We drank a Muscadet de Sèvre-et-Maine with the oysters and the fish and a Chiroubles with the duck, then Philippe and a lady from the tourist organization left for Nantes, the doctor went home, and the rest of us walked up to the Café des Sports for *un petit digestif*. The night air was warm and soft and scented with hay, or with lawn grass cut but left lying all day in the hot sun.

The experience of walking alone again took a lot of getting used to next morning. The sun had gone, the sky was a uniform grey, the breeze was cold. I had an appointment in le Pallet, some eight kilometres (five miles) along the river towards Nantes, where I was to be shown the village's Musée Pierre Abelard, normally closed on Sunday. Part of the way was on a good, firm, pretty path, tree-shaded, separated from the river only by water-meadows and bordered by a wood, fields of maize, and vines. Perhaps a kilometre or two (a mile or so) of the way was on a minor road, but with no traffic to speak of. And the weather improved. After a while the rhythm of the exercise worked its usual therapy, so that my spirits rose a little and, having breakfasted lightly, I began to speculate on the prospect of dinner that evening at the Abbaye de Villeneuve, about 16 kilometres (10 miles) west of le Pallet, where both food and wine were reputedly good.

The collection of tools and many other artefacts associated with the centuries-old viticultural life of the region (a document of 1142 tells of the replanting of vines following spoliation first by neighbouring Bretons, then by Normans) was well worth seeing in the little museum, and in all sincerity I enthused over it. 'Ah,' said my guide, a leading member of the community, 'if only you could see everything we have to show you! A pity you can't visit Galisonnière and its arboretum. One member of the proprietor's family was the man who introduced the magnolia to Europe from North America. Another was the sailor who defeated your own Admiral Byng at Port Mahon in 1756. Poor Admiral Byng, victim of political incompetence and self-interest, shot on his own quarterdeck *'pour encourager les autres'*. A train of thought headed by Admiral Byng and including the sea, *fruits de mer* and Muscadet with shellfish from the coasts of Brittany was suddenly interrupted by an enquiry as to what I was proposing to do about lunch. 'Give me ten minutes,' said the man who had so kindly opened the museum for me, when I told him that I had no specific plans for what, considering the contents of my rucksack, I had privately feared would be an exceedingly modest occasion. In less than the time he had asked for he was back. He thought I ought to meet *'un vrai vigneron'* and had arranged for me to have a little tasting at a small property just down the road. The vigneron himself was away in Nantes, but his wife knew all about the business and would be pleased to see me.

Madame Mandat was handsome, rosy-cheeked, strongly built, cheerful and very capable. The business was, she explained, *'une petite exploitation familiale'*: perhaps twenty thousand bottles a year. The 'cellars' consisted of a barn-like building with a floor of beaten earth topped with fine gravel, two metres (six feet) or so below the level of the courtyard. There were a

*Typical Muscadet country may be flat and unexciting, but on such paths the going is good, especially on a fine early autumn day.*

few casks, but mostly glass-lined cement vats. We tasted two wines, both of which I swallowed unashamedly. Very good, I said. Very refreshing. Ah yes, said Madame Mandat She used to walk a lot the way I was walking, with a pack on her back. She was especially fond of the Pyrenees. A day on foot in the mountains: what a pleasure! Then one *really* appreciates a re-freshing glass of wine!

The invitation to lunch was casual and apologetic. If I would care to. Nothing special whatever. Only herself, her son, her son's *copain* and two *jeunes filles*. We sat down to a green salad, tomatoes stuffed with minced lamb, *haricots verts*, cheese and *tarte aux pommes*. We drank a Muscadet with the tomatoes and a light Gamay with the cheese. The food was delicious; the wine good. No, said Madame Mandat, they didn't make the Gamay commercially, just a few bottles for their private consumption. Yes, they were very fond of vegetables and they grew everything they wanted. They had quite a lot of fruit, too. And they kept rabbits for the table.

After lunch, said the girls and the young men, they were going rock-climbing at Châteauthébaud, about six kilometres away (four miles) in the direction in which I was walking. Why didn't I come too? We packed into a little Citroën. As we crossed the Sèvre Nantaise at le Port Domino, they told me that it used to be an important shipping point for wine going down to Nantes. Vines stretched all the way to the Maine, flat and unexciting, and it was clear from the map that I was unlikely to find better walking in Mus-cadet than I had had on the way from Tiffauges to le Pallet. '*Pas amusant,*'

*All francophiles have their own image of quintessential France. Mine has always been of a supreme rurality, and the valley of the Sèvre Nantaise has all the elements of my ideal.*

*In French,* Virginia creeper *is called* vigne vierge *– virgin vine. Its flaming autumn colours recall the grapevines in the surrounding vineyards.*

said Monique as rain began to fall. 'If it gets any worse we'll all go to the cinema in Nantes.'

It got worse, then better. Just the other side of the river, at the bottom of the cliff that forms part of the southern foundations of the hamlet of Châteauthébaud, the two girls and one of the men (the other went fishing) cast off their tracksuits and took to the rock. 'I'll watch you for a while,' I said, 'then I'll be on my way.'

It was almost eight o'clock in the evening when I presented myself at the imposing Abbaye de Villeneuve in its spacious grounds. 'Is that all the luggage you have?', asked the receptionist, eyeing my small and venerable day-pack, evidently surprised and hoping, I imagined, that against all appearances it might hold the means of my making a more or less respectable showing in the dining room. Alarm bells jangled in my mind. 'But hasn't the rest of my luggage arrived?', I asked anxiously.

'*Ah non!*', she replied, 'what were you expecting?'

'A much bigger rucksack, and a black holdall.' In other words, everything except the essential walking gear that I was either wearing or had in my small day-pack. 'It will be waiting for you when you get there,' the *patronne* of Auberge de la Cascade at Clisson had assured me. 'Never fear.'

An hour later, I lay propped up by pillows on my bed while the *maître d'hôtel* gave me his suggestions for dinner. Though I very much dislike eating in bed, that was where I was going to dine unless my belongings turned up very soon. As a little something to raise my morale, the head waiter had suggested a bottle of Muscadet Château de Cléray: 'a superb wine'. So it was, and I was enjoying a second glass when the telephone rang and the now jubilant receptionist announced that my luggage was on its way up. A lady had brought it and was waiting to see me, she added. A lady? The *patronne* of the Auberge de la Cascade had been particularly helpful, and now, I feared, she had felt obliged to bring my luggage in person. What a fuss I had unwittingly caused!

'I'm very sorry,' said Françoise as we sat at table in the dining room ten minutes later, with the waiter pouring the last of the Château de Cléray into our glasses while we waited for the *saumon rôti au basilic* to arrive. 'It was all my fault. I was thinking about you in Clisson this morning. Then, when we were leaving, I saw your luggage by the reception desk at the Cascade. They said a taxi was going to collect it later on and bring it over here, so I volunteered to do it instead after getting back to Nantes and picking up my own car. I would have been here earlier, only I had to look in at the hospital.'

I was in that light-headed, feet-not-quite-on-the-ground state that can be one of the rewards of a day's walk and a long bath and a glass or two of wine, and there was a moment's silence while I just looked at her happily. 'Still,' she went on, filling the hiatus, 'I did save you the cost of the taxi. I hope you're glad I arrived in time for dinner.' I said I was rather, and asked for two glasses of champagne.

# THE WINE

It is all too easy to entertain a lively aversion to Muscadet: Muscadet at office functions and office temperatures; Muscadet ordered by the unfortunate man to whom has fallen the job of choosing the wine at the not-too-expensive restaurant dinner after the drinks party: How one hates it! Thin, acid, or not infrequently repellently flabby from over-chaptalization, it can be the sort of stuff which, like Liebfraumilch, gives white wine a bad name.

Muscadet is all white (the red and rosé wines which are made in very small quantities in the region are of no more than passing interest). The name signifies the grape as well as the wine, though in most wine books the grape is called the Melon de Bourgogne. It ripens earlier than most varieties and has a low acidity, with a consequent tendency to oxidize quickly; even more than with other white wines, therefore, skill, care, and good technology (not to mention integrity) are of crucial importance in its vinification. Floods of Muscadet have been made, and one fears are still made, without such advantages.

The region has three appellations: Muscadet, Muscadet de Sèvre-et-Maine, and Muscadet des Coteaux de la Loire. The first comes from the most western of the Muscadet vineyards, reaching from Nantes to the Atlantic, a territory which it shares with another grape, the Gros Plant, which produces a very similar wine, the Gros Plant du Pays Nantais. The second comes from an area further to the east, astride the rivers Sèvre and Maine, which embraces more than three-quarters of all the Muscadet vineyards and is supposed to produce wine of a higher quality than Muscadet pure and simple. The third, Coteaux de la Loire, is produced in the smallest district of all, along the banks of the Loire to the east of Nantes.

There is also Muscadet *sur lie*. In theory, Muscadet *sur lie* is wine which instead of being racked or filtered after fermentation and before bottling is left in barrel, in contact with the sediment (*lie*) of fermentation until March or April, when it is then bottled straight from the cask. By this method it ought to acquire significantly greater nuances and depths of flavour than otherwise. (The principle is the same as Champagne's *récemment dégorgé*.) It ought also still to contain a touch of natural carbon dioxide, and thus possess freshness and a hint of sparkle. In practice, some producers, but not the very best, interpret *sur lie* in a less rigorous fashion. In the Muscadet region especially, all depends upon the strict integrity of the wine-maker. In seeking the best it helps to look for declarations such as '*mis en bouteille au domaine*' (or '*au château*', or '*par Jean Quelqu'un*') rather than the worthless '*mis en bouteille dans la région de production*'.

Generally speaking, Muscadet is best when drunk within two years or so of the harvest, but a well-made Muscadet *sur lie* might be excellent at twice that age or more.

On the south-eastern outskirts of Nantes, the commune of St Fiacre is home to some of the best wine-makers in the appellation of Muscadet Sèvre-et-Maine.

# BORDEAUX

## INTRODUCTION

The very large wine district that is invariably referred to as Bordeaux, occupies about half of the department of the Gironde, which with the Dordogne, Lot, Lot-et-Garonne and Landes (all sand dunes and pine forests) is in turn part of what for administrative purposes constitutes present day Aquitaine.

Just north of the city of Bordeaux the River Gironde divides to become the Dordogne and the Garonne, giving us four distinct geographical and viticultural areas. First, there is the territory north of the Gironde and the Dordogne, with all its appellations, which from west to east include the Côtes de Blaye, Côtes de Bourg, Fronsac, Pomerol, St Emilion and Côtes de Castillon: in short, the Blayais and the Libournais. Secondly, there is the large stretch of country between the Dordogne and the Garonne known as Entre-Deux-Mers, which includes Langoiran, the Premières Côtes de Bordeaux, Cadillac, Loupiac and Ste Croix-du-Mont. Thirdly, there is the narrow strip of land south of the Garonne and south-east of the city of Bordeaux which is the Graves, and which includes Langon, Sauternes and Barsac. Lastly, to the north-west of the city and reaching almost to the sea is the Médoc, beginning at Blanquefort. After Blanquefort, going north, is a succession of small villages with disproportionately great wine associations.

All in all, and in terms of quality and significant variety allied to quantity, Bordeaux is indisputably the greatest wine country in the world. The significant majority of the greatest wines of the region come from the Médoc. The proprietor of La Tupina in the Rue de la Monnaie, one of Bordeaux's cosiest restaurants and much frequented by wine-makers, is the organizer of walking tours of the Médoc and is scornful of those who say that the landscape is monotonous. 'Cantenac, Margaux, Listrac, Beychevelle, St Julien, Pauillac, St Estèphe: how can anywhere where the villages have names like that be boring?'

*Vineyards of Sauvignon or Sémillon, or both, in a landscape near Pujols that can fairly be described as 'bien accidenté'.*

# THE MÉDOC

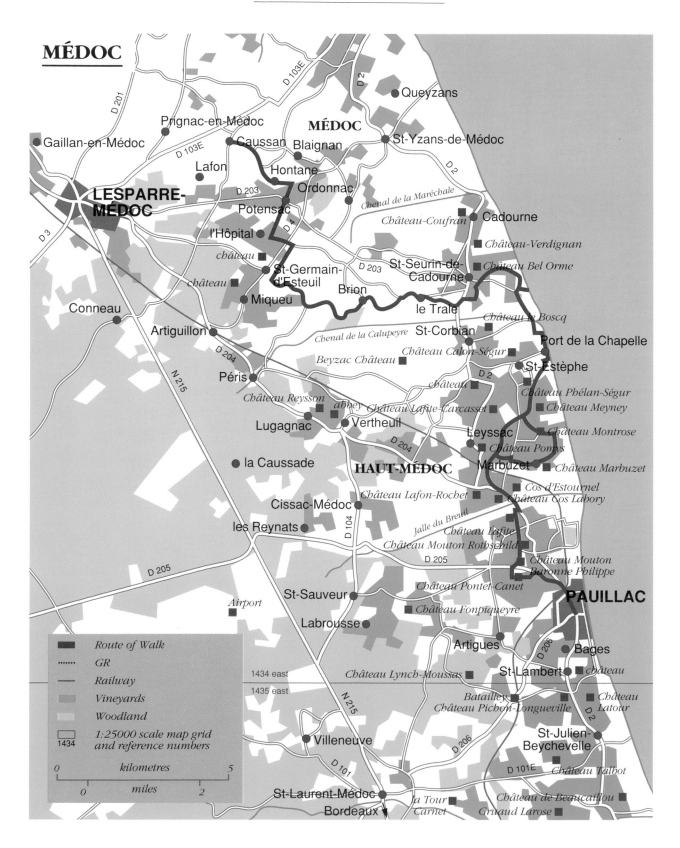

**MÉDOC**

Queyzans

**MÉDOC**

Prignac-en-Médoc

Gaillan-en-Médoc · Caussan · Blaignan · St-Yzans-de-Médoc

Lafon · Hontane

Ordonnac

D 201 · D 103E · D 103E · D 2 · D 2

*Chenal de la Maréchale*

Potensac

*Château-Coufran* · Cadourne

D 203

l'Hôpital

*Château-Verdignan*

*château* · St-Germain-d'Esteuil · D 203 · St-Seurin-de-Cadourne · *Château Bel Orme*

*château* · Brion

Miqueu · le Trale

Conneau · *Château le Boscq*

Artiguillon · *Chenal de la Calupeyre* · St-Corbian · Port de la Chapelle

D 204 · *Château Calon-Ségur* · St-Estèphe

Péris · *Beyzac Château*

*Château Phélan-Ségur*

*Château Reysson* · *château* · *Château Meyney*

*abbey* · *Château Lafite-Carcasset*

Lugagnac · Vertheuil · Leyssac · *Château Montrose*

D 204 · *Château Pomys*

la Caussade · Marbuzet · *Château Marbuzet*

**HAUT-MÉDOC**

*Cos d'Estournel*
*Château Cos Labory*

Cissac-Médoc · *Château Lafon-Rochet*

les Reynats · *Jalle du Breuil* · *Château Lafite*

D 104 · *Château Mouton Rothschild*

D 205

*Château Mouton*
*Baronne Philippe*

D 205

St-Sauveur · *Château Pontet-Canet*

Airport · *Château Fonpiqueyre* · **PAUILLAC**

Labrousse

Artigues · Bages

D 206

1434 east · *Château Lynch-Moussas* · St-Lambert · *château*

1435 east

N 215 · *Batailley* · *Château Latour*
*Château Pichon-Longueville*

St-Julien-Beychevelle

Villeneuve · D 206

D 101 · D 101E · *Château Talbot*

St-Laurent-Médoc · *la Tour Carnet* · *Château de Beaucaillou*

Bordeaux ▼ · *Gruaud Larose*

**Legend:**
- Route of Walk
- GR
- Railway
- Vineyards
- Woodland
- 1:25000 scale map grid and reference numbers (1434)

0 — kilometres — 5
0 — miles — 2

# BRIEFING

## THE LIE OF THE LAND

The broad-hilted Gironde stabs down into Aquitaine from the Atlantic, forking into the rivers Garonne and Dordogne before reaching the city of Bordeaux, which is on the southern prong, the Garonne. The Médoc (which means land in between, or land in the middle) stretches for some 65 kilometres (40 miles) northwards from the suburbs of Bordeaux towards the mouth of the Garonne and along its western bank, in a strip rarely more than ten kilometres (six miles) wide, and mostly under half that. Wine books tend to talk about 'hills' in the Médoc, since there may be a world of difference in drainage, and therefore in the character of their wines, between vineyards which are no more than a few metres apart in altitude, but they are not hills as the walker is accustomed to understand the term. The many mills that used to decorate the region depended upon winds, usually from the Atlantic, which were able to blow unimpeded across an at best very gently undulating land.

Of more significance for walkers are the small streams (*jalles*) and drainage channels which cross any path running from north to south, since they frequently interrupt progress by requiring diversions to bridges or causeways. A good pair of field-glasses may be especially helpful in these circumstances.

It is difficult to generalize, but guidebooks and other forms of travel literature which encourage casual visits to the well-known wine châteaux should be regarded with caution. 'Wine tourism' is now a recognized form of activity in the Bordeaux region, and some of the more famous wine estates accept visitors only by appointment. There may be little harm in trying to 'drop by' this or that château, but it is as well to be prepared for disappointment.

## WALK

**Caussan to Pauillac** by way of St Seurin-de-Cadourne and St Estèphe. 24 kilometres/15 miles; allow 6–7 hours.

Caussan straddles a minor road running south-east between the D 103 and the D 203, both of which roads fork out eastwards across the Médoc from Lesparre-Médoc. The Moulin de Courrian dominates the vineyards just south-east of Caussan. At Hontane a track goes east beside vines, then south to Potensac and on over arable fields and through vines to a minor road north of the Château de Castéra and St Germain-d'Esteuil, from where tracks and very minor roads lead eastwards to the Roman excavations (*fouilles archéologiques* on the 1:25,000 map) just west of Brion. A dirt track leads to a lane through le Trale to the north-south D 2,

and to St Seurin-de-Cadourne. The dirt track leading to the picnic place by the Gironde is under a kilometre (less than half a mile) out of St Seurin.

A very minor road now runs south to Port de la Chapelle, just east of St Estèphe and Château Phélan Ségur. Going south by vineyard paths of the D 2, Château Meyney, Château Montrose and Château Marbuzet, all surrounded by their vines, are the next points of reference. The road is unavoidable for the last few hundred metres north of Château Cos d'Estournel and on to Château Lafite-Rothschild. Vineyard tracks lead from Lafite-Rothschild to Mouton-Rothschild, and it is not inconceivable that the walker might use them. Estate roads and a minor public road run from Mouton-Rothschild to neighbouring Château Mouton Baronne Philippe. Château Pontet-Canet is just south of Mouton Baronne Philippe. A final stretch of D 2 is unavoidable into Pauillac, but verges and vineyard margins provide a certain relief.

### Maps

| Scale | Sheet | Name | Notes |
|---|---|---|---|
| 1:25,000 | 1434 est | Lesparre-Médoc-Pauillac | includes most of Bas-Médoc and the whole of the indicated walk |
| | 1435 est | St Laurent-et-Bénon | |
| | 1535 ouest | Blaye | includes west bank of Gironde and Margaux |
| 1:50,000 | 1434 | Lesparre-Médoc | |
| | 1435 | St Laurent-et-Bénon | |
| | 1535 | Blaye | |
| 1:100,000 | 46 | Royan | |

# WINDMILLS AND CHÂTEAUX IN THE GIRONDE

When I arrived at Philippe Courrian's place near Blaignan in the Médoc and saw the bread and ham and cheese on the top of the upturned barrel I thought it was a bit much, and not at all professional for a wine-tasting that I had not, in any case, expected. What sort of an amateur was I supposed to be? Only when Courrian and his son Fabien arrived and tucked into the victuals with what might fairly be called gusto, encouraging me to follow their example, did it dawn on me that they had been politely awaiting my arrival before having the *casse-croûte* they were accustomed to when working long hours in the *cuverie*. Though claret at half past nine in the morning was a novelty for me, and I had done nothing so far that day except drive the 80 kilometres (50 miles) from Bordeaux, I had no difficulty whatever in appreciating the *jambon de Bayonne* and the *fromage de brebis* (ewes' milk cheese) from the Pyrenees together with the Château Tour Haut-Caussan.

Though Courrian's labels quite properly and legitimately place Tour Haut-Caussan in the appellation of the Médoc, in geographical terms Blaignan is more precisely in the Bas-Médoc. The 'Bas' (low) has nothing to do with altitude, but signifies only that the area is nearer the Atlantic end of the Gironde than is the more prestigious Haut-Médoc, which lies further upstream towards the city of Bordeaux. It is because the term 'Bas' is so widely and mistakenly understood to suggest inferiority that no winemaker at the seaward end of the Médoc likes it, and the official wine literature of the department of the Gironde is at pains to avoid it. It may also be the reason why Philippe Courrian has been careful to include the word 'Haut' on his labels. The wine-makers of Bordeaux are by no means amateurs in such matters of marketing. Whatever the case, the windmill of the Haut-Caussan label stands on one of the very few hills in the appellation, and incidentally is in working order. The 'Château' implies no deception either, since in the Gironde this is merely the accepted term for a winemaking property possessing certain attributes, though the architectural or social status of the chief building on the domaine is not one of them.

While Fabien returned to the job of transferring grapes from a fermentation vat, where they had been macerating, into a horizontal press, and I fussed with maps and checked over my rucksack, Philippe Courrian went to put his boots on: a good sign in my eyes, since although I had been told that he had volunteered to show me something of the Médoc, I had privately feared that this might consist of a car tour of the tourist sights followed by lunch in a restaurant. Such misgivings were finally dispelled when he asked if there was room in my rucksack for 'a few odds and ends to eat and a bottle or two'. I stood like a patient pack-horse while he loaded me

*Winter pruning at Château Latour, Pauillac: one of the most famous of all Premiers Crus Classés and neighbour to Château Pichon-Longueville-Comtesse de Lalande. Owned since 1963 by the Pearson group of London, the estate has produced wine since the fourteenth century, when the fortress of 'la Tor' was built where the present chais now stands.*

up, the last item being a bag of walnuts from his garden, and then we set off down the road to his eighteenth-century mill, prominently marked on the 1:25,000 map as the Moulin de Courrian. His ancestors in the commune of Blaignan could be traced back to the seventeenth century, he said. One of them had been a baker before land and the mill had been acquired in 1877, which was one of the reasons why he, Philippe, had so much wanted to restore the mill to working order, and with master craftsmen had succeeded in doing so. When we reached it, he disappeared inside while I picked a few grapes from the many that had ripened since the harvest three weeks ago, and which were pleasant enough to eat if too acid for wine-making. Hearing a creaking overhead, I looked up to see that with their slats now unfolded the sails of the mill had begun to turn in a gentle wind coming from the Atlantic, some 24 kilometres (15 miles) away. Inside, the solid rumble of the hand-built machinery was a curiously pleasing sound from another age.

'There was only corn here at one time,' explained Courrian as we walked on southwards, still on the road for a while, 'and a hundred and eighty mills. The remains of them are still all over the place. Look: there's one over there. And another over there.' He pointed out low round stone towers, bereft of the sort of pointed superstructure with which his own mill was now equipped. 'There used to be forty-five thousand mills of one sort or another in France before the industrial revolution,' (which incidentally came much later in France than in Britain). It was the building of a dyke to prevent flooding by the Gironde at high tide, then the draining of the land – all done by Dutch engineers on the orders of Colbert, Louis xiv's great minister – that transformed the Médoc, continued Courrian. Looking eastwards to the river, I thought how indeed the light and the whole feel of the country reminded me of the polderlands of Holland and parts of Norfolk. The Dutch were employed in East Anglia as well as in Bordeaux.

Walking with Courrian was walking with a one-man information centre on the Médoc in general and the Bas-Médoc in particular. A spring from which we drank never failed, he told me, not even in the driest of weather. Between the Médoc and the Atlantic were the great forests of the Landes, which acted like a reservoir for the vineyards of the Médoc. See that rounded hill with the tree over there? It used to be an island and the site of one of the Médoc's many religious foundations. Like all too many such places, the abbey was destroyed in the Revolution, and its lands, including vineyards, were appropriated by the state, as were those of the feudal aristocracy. 'Cru Bourgeois' was an appropriate term. He talked of geological periods, primary, secondary and tertiary; of land and sea rising and falling; of 'plates' overlapping; of sedimentary deposits and soil formation. This area was *argilo-calcaire* (clayey-chalky); that, on the other hand, was '*très calcaire*: look!' He picked up what appeared to me to be a clod of *café-au-lait*-coloured, white-speckled mud and broke it open by banging it on a large stone. The inside revealed the texture of a confectioner's nut-crunch bar, the 'nuts' being tiny white sea-shells. Further along towards Bordeaux, where the really big estate names were, said Courrian, you got soil full of pebbles, such as you found on a beach, and in places a lot of sand. Tremendous variety; hence the infinite variations in style of wines between one property and another.

In Courrian's office at Blaignan I had been surprised to see two colourful posters depicting vineyards in the Corbières (Languedoc) on the wall. What, I now asked him, was the significance of them? Oh, he replied, laughing, he supposed it was really just '*pour provoquer un peu les gens*'; to tease people a bit. In 1987 he had bought an old wine domaine not far from Lagrasse and had set about rehabilitating it. A few weeks ago he had had his first harvest there. It would be hard, I thought, to find two more contrasting wine regions than the Médoc and the Corbières; the one topographically no more exciting than the East Anglia I had just been reminded of, wholly tamed and accessible, predictable, comparatively closely populated; the other still in large measure *sauvage*, not easy to know, given to extremes of mood and to a large extent territorially inhospitable. The Médoc with its long-established, self-confident (not to say arrogant) aristocracy and bourgeoisie of châteaux and 'growths'; the Corbières still mostly at the cheaper end of the supermarket wine shelves, unassuming, striving for quality and recognition, experimenting and innovating. Beside the dirt track we had taken to, on a little rise (a commanding eminence in these parts) near the hamlet of Potensac, was an old stone bench. 'I remember when I was a very young man', remarked middle-aged Courrian, talking of one of the elders of the Médoc, head of a famous château, 'how he used to sit here in the

*Fishermen's huts on the banks of the Gironde. Narrow, precarious walkways on spindly legs set in the river mud give access to these patchwork cabins high above the water, equipped with contraptions by which circular nets can be lowered on a pulley.*

evenings, giving advice to other vignerons who came to ask him about the best way to do this or that. He knew everything there was to know about the Médoc.' Again the contrast: here in the Médoc was a tradition of viticulture that was long-civilized and fundamentally little questioned; in the Corbières the elders of even twenty-five years ago were as likely as not to have had ideas about wine-making considered by the following generations to be disastrous, and anyway to sit at the feet of a sage such as Courrian was describing might have entailed an hour's travelling from one valley to the next.

Unspectacular topography notwithstanding, the Bas-Médoc exerted a certain charm. There was the light, the sort that Dutch and Flemish masters captured in their landscapes. There was autumn: dry leaves underfoot here and there; rich colours in the woods and the vines; the scent of woodsmoke; the feeling of all living things quietly submitting to the advances of winter. An hour or so south of the Moulin de Courrian was the Château de Castéra in the commune of St Germain-d'Esteuil, a property which not only produced a well-reputed Cru Bourgeois claret, but which was itself old and attractive with a piquant history, having been beseiged by England's infamous Black Prince during the appalling Hundred Years War. Though uninvited and without an appointment (I had to prevail upon my companion, who had proper inhibitions about such extempore calls), we were received in the *chais* without rancour or reluctance, and were generously given a brief tasting of what David Peppercorn has called 'a good

*Château Pichon-Longueville-Comtesse de Lalande, Pauillac. Built in the 1840s, the château used to be part of the same estate as the Château Pichon-Longueville-Baron. The wines are among the finest of the Médoc.*

solid enjoyable Médoc'. Castéra, says Peppercorn, is on 'a series of high, gravelly ridges'. Significantly, I was not aware of any change of altitude, our path having seemed to me more or less on the level, but I was later to see from the map that in continuing eastwards and slightly south for half an hour from St Germain we went from twelve to two metres (from forty feet to just over six) above sea level; in the Médoc, a giddy descent.

We moved on from associations with the Plantagenets to solidly tangible souvenirs of the Romans, who introduced wine to the Gironde as to so many other parts of France. 'This may surprise you,' remarked Courrian as we approached the hamlet of Brion, between St Germain and St Seurin-de-Cadourne, where once were only marshes and still is not very much. It did. It was an archeological site of fairly recent and intermittent activity, severely limited, Courrian informed me, by lack of funds. There in the middle of nowhere, wrapped in a silence so profound that we could quite literally hear the leaves falling from the tall oaks that distinguished the site, were the substantial remains of a Roman amphitheatre, dating, a modest noticeboard announced, from the first century AD. 'Two thousand five hundred seats,' said Courrian. 'Quite a size!' Some people, he said, himself included, were convinced that the principal Roman port on the Gironde must have been here or hereabouts. The amphitheatre and the foundations of a Gallo-Roman temple a little further on almost certainly represented no more than a very small part of a far larger complex of remains, most of which were still concealed. In what must have been the Roman arena stood

*Once, only cereals grew where now the mill of Haut-Caussan stands surrounded by the vines of this highly regarded Cru Bourgeois. In a region of few landmarks, so prominent a one as the mill can be a blessing for the walker trying to get his or her bearings.*

the four-square vestiges of an evidently medieval construction. In the thirteenth century, said the noticeboard, a certain Arnaud de Bourg, having been 'banished from society on account of his extortions', took refuge here in the marshes and built a stronghold, using stones from the Roman walls.

The site was on ground very slightly elevated above the surrounding land; from it a broad, raised path like a causeway led on eastwards to what, it was reasonable to conjecture, might well have been the waterfront of Roman times. It led us to paths and lanes positioned above lower ground so as to suggest the shore of a long-since drained and reclaimed inlet of the Gironde (here some four kilometres or two and a half miles wide), and eventually to a broad track that ended at the bank of the great river itself. We had come some 12 kilometres (7 miles) or more from Caussan and were ready for lunch. In a grove of young trees that in summer would be a blessing was a stone table of refectory size with benches to match: put there by the fishermen, said Courrian. From the grove a narrow and precarious timber walkway on tall spindly legs set in the river mud gave access to a patchwork cabin high above the water, and to a contraption by which a circular net could be raised or lowered on a pulley. There were several such constructions along the shore. 'Fishermen's huts,' explained Courrian. 'Not professionals, but enthusiasts all the same.'

Enthusiasm was what we now brought to the *jambon de Bayonne* that had not been finished back at the *cuverie* and to the various other items that Courrian had contributed from his kitchen, plus a bottle of Corbières and

*Stainless steel fermentation vats with heat exchange apparatus in the spotless* cuverie *of the Château Pichon-Longueville-Baron, close neighbour to Pichon-Longueville-Comtesse de Lalande, and once part of the same estate. The grapes macerate in steel for at least twenty-one days before 'seeing wood'.*

another of Tour Haut-Caussan, each of them only three years old. Courrian said he liked drinking his own wine when it was either young or fairly old, but not in between. Young, like this one, it had the appeal of youth and fruit. After six years or more, depending of course on the character of any particular vintage, it had the complex charms, including suppleness, that came with maturity. In between, the wine tended to be '*fermé*', its youthful freshness gone, while the tannins were still hard. He drank the Corbières; I kept to the claret and loved it. I doubt if I shall drink a young Cru Bourgeois of the Médoc in future without seeing in my mind's eye tall reeds by a river so wide that the far bank is barely discernible; and ships passing, as two substantial freighters passed our picnic place that day, going up to Bordeaux; and over the whole scene the luminosity of autumn sunshine lightly veiled by high, thin cloud above a wide land with far horizons. I shall also be likely to remember what Philippe Courrian said when I asked him if the harvest just over had been a good one and – not too seriously – whether one ought to be buying the wine in advance. His answer to the first question had been 'not too bad'; then he had laughed and said, 'When a wine-maker here tells you that the year's been a really good one you keep your money in your pocket. When he says that it hasn't been too bad you know he's expecting great things.'

At three o'clock Fabien Courrian arrived to drive his father back to Caussan, as I had said that I would walk on southwards to Paulliac. There were fewer footpaths and more tarmac than most walkers would like for the 12-kilometre (7-mile) march, but the minor road between St Seurin and St Estèphe, the most northerly and largest wine commune of the Haut-Médoc, gave a first half-hour of wholly traffic-free progress close to the river as far as Port de la Chapelle, than an even lesser road and an imperfect grid of vineyard paths occupied the best part of an hour to Château Marbuzet (Cru Grand Bourgeois Exceptionnel) by way of Château Meyney (also CGBE) and Château Montrose (Deuxième Cru Classé). Meyney, a beautifully maintained seventeenth-century priory, like Montrose isolated among its vines, might have been utterly deserted for all the activity I saw there. Montrose I skirted in favour of a curious grove of tall trees marking an evidently long-abandoned cavern, visible through an iron grill at ground level, which held rows of very large, mouldering casks. A mystery. The grove would offer welcome shade on a hot summer's day, I thought, as I marched on in a cool little breeze that held a tang of the ocean under a darkening November sky.

Cos d'Estournel, Lafite-Rothschild, Mouton-Rothschild, Mouton-Baronne-Philippe, Pontet-Canet: of the six kilometres (four miles) to Paulliac, four or five consisted of vines, and three or four of these lay almost unavoidably on the busy D 2 ('la route des Châteaux'): five of the most famous wines in the world, and at the end a rather drab little town. There was no denying a sneaking sense of anticlimax. Courrian picked me up from a telephone cabin opposite the post office and took me back to Caussan and Crus Bourgeois country. It was a bit like going home.

*Casks such as these represent a fortune in wood alone: new oak barrels can cost £350. The wine of Château Pichon-Longueville-Baron spends some two years in cask before bottling, at least one third of the casks being new each year. Only a big classic wine such as those of Pauillac could benefit from so long in the wood.*

# THE WINE

*Bordeaux, fourth city in France
and wine capital of the Gironde,
has no convincing rival anywhere.
'Take Versailles, add Antwerp,
and you have Bordeaux,' wrote
Victor Hugo.*

In the instance of the wines of Bordeaux in general, and those of the Médoc in particular, it would seem to be little short of an impertinence to do anything other than draw attention to the authoritative reference books and other sources of information on the subject. Short of a far wider enquiry, however, there are a few points which may be useful. Firstly, unlike Burgundy's Côte d'Or which produces great white wines as well as red, the Médoc is strictly and almost exclusively red wine country. Secondly, in further sharp contrast to that other world-famous region within a region, the red wines of the Médoc are derived from at least three major varieties of grape. The great red wines of Burgundy rely only upon the Pinot Noir; those of the Médoc derive from Cabernet Sauvignon, Merlot and Cabernet Franc.

Thirdly, there is the 'château' system. On Burgundy's Côte d'Or categorization and classification are first and foremost territorially based; one looks for – say – a Gevrey-Chambertin, which is a Premier Cru, or for a Chambertin-Clos de Bèze (which is a Grand Cru), from wine-makers of what one believes to be reliable reputations. In the Médoc one may prefer a Pauillac, say, to a St Julien, but thereafter, vintage considerations apart, one goes entirely by 'châteaux' (or wine-makers') names: Château Mouton-Rothschild in Pauillac, say, or Château Gruaud-Larose in St Julien.

The inverted commas around 'châteaux' indicate something which comes as a surprise to many first-time visitors to the Bordeaux region in general, and to the Médoc in particular. With pictures of Château Margaux or the delightful Gruaud-Larose in mind, they expect all the well-known names to be synonymous with more or less elegant or noble mansions, and are disappointed, if not shocked, to find a Château X or Y that might easily be mistaken for a modest farmhouse, with outbuildings more appropriate to light metal-working than the making of high-class wine. 'Château' in relation to a wine from the Gironde has no architectural connotations whatever, and if it has implications of anything other than an 'estate' it is difficult to discover what they are. Certainly it is nothing to do with the classification of the wine itself, since Château this or Château that are as likely to be Crus Bourgeois as Grands Crus; nor with volume of production, since this varies hugely from one wine-maker to another. '"Château": the term used in the Gironde to designate a vineyard of a certain size, owning the appropriate buildings for making wine. The terms domaine, "*clos*" and "*cru*" are also used,' explains the *Petit Guide des Vins*, published by the Conseil Interprofessionel du Vin de Bordeaux. Which leaves my understanding of the subject exactly where it was before.

The concept of a cellar also deserves special attention in the Médoc. Briefly, the cellar as popularly understood – an underground cavern of some sort or other – is very rare where 'hills' are measured in single figures of metres and the water table is high. Its place is commonly taken by the *chai*, a sort of shed, wholly or partly above ground and constructed so as to provide stable conditions for the vinification and storage of wine. In places such as the Châteaux Margaux, Mouton-Rothschild or Lafite, where great fortunes lie in long and perfectly ordered lines of oak barrels in no less perfect lighting, visitors to the *chais* might suppose that they had arrived at a permanent exhibition of the work of some avant-garde sculptor in a gallery.

Finally, categorization and classification are not nearly so difficult to understand as on the Côte d'Or, though whether it is any easier to know how to find a good inexpensive Bordeaux than it is to find a good inexpensive Burgundy is open to debate.

After categorization by territory (the appellations of Margaux, St Julien, Pauillac and so on) Médoc wines are classified in 'growths', or *crus*, numbered from the first to the fifth (*premier* to *cinquième*). Outside of these aristocrats of wines, ranging from major to minor, there are the Crus Bourgeois, which may in turn be Crus Grands Bourgeois Exceptionnels, Crus Grands Bourgeois or plain Crus Bourgeois. Naturally, the higher the classification the more expensive the wine, which does not of course mean that a very expensive wine will infallibly be a good one, or that a very good Cru Bourgeois cannot be found at a fraction of the price of a Premier Cru.

*Château de Pichon-Longueville Baron, in make-believe Gothic of 1851, in the appellation of Pauillac. 'Sturdy wines that repay keeping,' notes Steven Spurrier.*

# ST EMILION

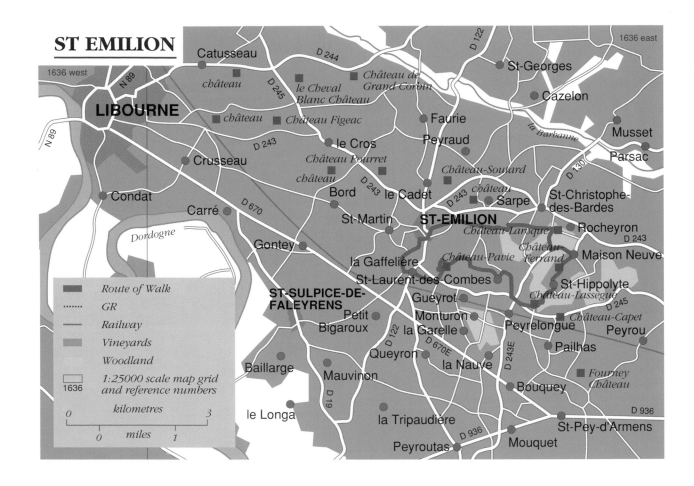

# BRIEFING

## THE LIE OF THE LAND

The town of St Emilion stands on the edge of a plateau a few kilometres to the north of the River Dordogne, about 40 kilometres (25 miles) from the centre of the city of Bordeaux. Though at an altitude of some 100 metres (330 feet) the wine country is higher than that of the Médoc and Graves, it shares the topographical lack of excitement that is characteristic of most of the Gironde. The vine here holds not merely the centre, but all of the stage.

St Emilion rivals Riquewihr in Alsace for its reputation as the most attractive wine town in France. Founded on the site of the grotto occupied by the hermit St Emilion in the eighth century, it was once ruled by the English before being besieged and gravely damaged by them during the Hundred Years War. Beneath it the limestone plateau is honeycombed with the cellars from which the stone to build the town was quarried. Picturesquely and poignantly rich in the architectural remains of its intensely religious and turbulent past, it is classified in its entirety as a historical monument, and deservedly so.

## WALK

**A Tour of the Grands Crus** 10 kilometres/6 miles; allow 3–4 hours.

This walk covers certainly the most interesting part of the St Emilion wine district topographically and most of the best viticulturally. Though it is almost unavoidably on metalled roads virtually all of the way, wide verges and vineyard margins are accessible and traffic is very rare.

The Rue des Fosses is just to the east of the Palais Cardinal and leads to la Clotte. Turning east, names to look for on the map are Bergat, Barde, le Barrail and Château Laroque. The route follows the road past Château Laroque and its park-like grounds, then turns south at the next junction to a three-pronged junction at Maison Neuve. Taking the middle prong, it traverses vines to Château Ferrand and on past an attractive church of the local limestone before descending the wooded escarpment to Château Lassègue. Here it turns right (west) for a few metres on the D 245, and crosses the north-south D 243 to a very minor road running from Roteboeuf north and uphill past Goudeau. Here a left (south-west) turn leads to the church of St Laurent-des-Combes. From a few metres north of the church a lane runs westwards past les Carrières, past a wood and on to a meeting of tracks, where the route takes the one going south to Château Pavie. The route now crosses the

D 245 to reach a track leading west to the *cave coopérative* on the D 122, just west of which is la Gaffelière. A perfectly straight few hundred metres of road leads north up the escarpment towards Berliquet; just before Berliquet the route goes right to Château Magdelaine, Château Belair and Château Ausone, and so back into St Emilion.

### Maps

| 1:25,000 | 1636 est | Castillon-la- | |
|---|---|---|---|
| | | Bataille– | |
| | | St Emilion | |
| 1:50,000 | 1636 | Libourne | includes St Emillon |
| 1:100,000 | 46 | Bordeaux, | |
| | 47 | Royan | |

# A TOUR OF
# THE GRANDS CRUS

*When attached to wine properties in the Gironde, the term* château *has no architectural significance whatever; it simply implies the existence of certain capabilities for the making and ageing of wine.*

All the previous day in all of Aquitaine the rain had persisted, so that I had huddled in my hotel room in St Emilion with the heating on, writing and hoping for better things, but finding no encouragement from any quarter. Nor did the November morning give the slightest hint of relief until, swathed in protective clothing from head to foot, I determined to make the best of a bad situation and set out to walk to St Hippolyte and back. Not two minutes after my leaving the hotel the rain stopped, and as I stood on the edge of the plateau at the end of the Rue des Fosses, close to the old fortified town gate of the Porte Brunet and the Tour du Guetteur (literally watchman's tower), the grey clouds broke and sun flooded the steep vine-covered slopes, the wooded hillsides and the plain reaching south to the Dordogne with theatrical brilliance, as if properly to illuminate for my reassurance and reward the whole lovely, autumn-coloured scene. Within a few hundred metres to my right and in front, on the high ground across the little valley which approaches the town from the south, were Château Ausone and Château Belair, two of the eleven Premiers Grand Crus Classés of the St Emilion appellation, the vines of the first all on the glacis to the plateau; those of Belair partly on the slope and partly on the level ground above. Immediately below me was part of the vineyard of la Clotte, a much-admired Grand Cru Classé.

No wine centre in France is more intimately associated with its vineyards than St Emilion. In the Palais Cardinal hotel, contiguous with the ruins of the thirteenth-century residence whose name it has taken, I had drunk what was truly the wine of the house, since it comes from the owners' own property. From the Rue des Fosses, which forms the western boundary of a number of Grand Cru vineyards, I had seen an enclosure of vines even within the ruined ramparts, literally a stone's throw away.

With the sun full on my face, I went on from la Clotte past the vines and handsome little white-shuttered house of Château la Serre and the vines of Château Couvent des Jacobins, both Grands Crus Classés, and past those of Château Trottevielle, Premier Grand Cru. On my right, the autumnal gold and amber acres of Troplong-Mondot, Grand Cru, swept up to 100 metres (330 feet) of altitude and a landmark water-tower. At the base of a bramble-covered wall beside the narrow lane were square-cut openings in the solid limestone which gave access to mysterious dark caverns deep beneath the precious rows of Merlot and Cabernet. There was no traffic at all, but for some of the way I walked on the wide grass margins of the lane or the vineyards, now and again helping myself to an ice-cold grape that would otherwise have known no better fate. At a crossroads a hand-painted sign bearing the outline of a scallop shell, with an arrow pointing back the way I had come, reminded me that one of the ancient routes to Santiago de Compostela comes down from the north through Pomerol and into the adjoining appellation of St Emilion, before crossing the Dordogne at Branne and so entering the wine country of Entre-Deux-Mers.

What did the pilgrims drink? The Romans had introduced the vine to the slopes overlooking the valley of the Dordogne (the rather ubiquitous Roman poet, Ausonius, is said to have had a villa there: hence Château Ausone), and in medieval times the wines of St Emilion were deemed worthy of royal patronage. One likes to suppose that after a long day on the road travellers who had not carried vows of self-denial and poverty too far were able to comfort themselves with a draught or two of the *vin du pays*. After St Emilion, then as now, there could hardly have been wines of equal distinction on the way to the burial place of St James in Spain.

No part of France – not even Alsace, where the forests of the lower Vosges may fairly be regarded as part of the wine country – is topographically so exclusively devoted to the vine as are St Emilion and Pomerol. Monoculture and a well-populated but seldom more than gently undulating terrain rarely make for a captivating landscape. As I continued eastwards the tall oaks and extensive, well-tended, park-like grounds of Château Laroque – an imposing, mainly eighteenth-century restoration with medieval beginnings on a limestone cliff above sylvan combes – came

*Protected as a historic monument, St Emilion is built on limestone honeycombed with miles of ancient quarries ideal for the storage of wine. The Jurade de St Emilion, instituted by King John of England and France in 1199, still regulates the wine business of the appellation.*

as a welcome surprise. The very tall, blue-painted gates with a gilded fleur-de-lis were open, but nobody was about. Ready with an apology and the excuse of making a '*reportage sur la région*' (an explanation almost always acceptable in promotion-conscious wine districts), but stonily observed only by two classical statues, I trespassed as far as a balustrade and a superb view far across the plain. Shuttered windows, non-resident owners, employees no doubt busy in the *cuverie* attending to another vintage of Grand Cru: not a footstep but my own sounded on the gravel, not a dog barked.

So intensively occupied and cultivated a territory is not greatly to be recommended to the walker who walks only for walking's sake. On the other hand, if adding a happily memorable dimension to an already familiar wine is the chief object of the exercise, the vineyards of St Emilion are not to be disregarded. Comparatively innocent of the arrogance of the Haut-Médoc, yet hectare for hectare producing more top-rank wines than anywhere else on earth, the best of the entire appellation, in terms both of wine and of walking, could be covered in a 20-kilometre (12-mile) day.

Less ambitious for what I feared could be no more than a short break in the foul weather, I turned south after Laroque to Château Ferrand in the commune of St Hippolyte, not with the intention of exploring its reputedly

*Topographically, the best walking near St Emilion is on the eastern edge of the plateau. The Grottes de Ferrand near St Hippolyte are a subterranean curiosity.*

prehistoric caves, nor yet of tasting its Grand Cru wines, though both are reputed to be rewarding experiences, but because it was on the minor road that would take me to the edge of the plateau and down to the plain. As at Laroque, a deep autumnal quiet (which I would not in any case have been so bold as to disturb unless by appointment) reigned there, broken only by the sound of shots from a little coppice nearby. But I saw nobody until the tiny cemetery beside the chapel a few hundred metres further on, where a man with dead flowers in a wheelbarrow gave me a '*Bonjour*' and remarked that it was not the best time of the year for walking, which was true, though just then the sun was still shining and I had no complaints.

No more than a kilometre (just over half a mile) after coming down to the plain, and seeing no other sensible way of avoiding the D 245 back to St Emilion, I took a lane up to the plateau again and to the church of St Laurent-des-Combes, which was locked. The cemetery was an extravagance of colour, mostly from the massive pots of chrysanthemums traditionally placed on the graves on All Saints' Day. Opposite, a dispiritingly drab dwelling in weather-worn grey stucco was called '*Mon Repos*'. Then the rain returned. I had taken off my pack and was putting on my protective clothing once more when a man in a smart raincoat appeared from a sort of hovel close to the lane. We exchanged *bonjours*. But not so good, he added, for walking. Thus I encountered Monsieur Faniest, an enterprising *négociant* from Libourne whose 'train' tour of some of the best of the wine domaines has been a resounding success. If I had the time and cared to shelter from the rain for a while I might like to see his own cellar, he suggested. Five minutes later I was marvelling not only at the sight of the roots of one of Monsieur Faniest's three hectares (seven and a half acres) of vines, which had reached more than five metres (16 feet) down through the limestone of the plateau just south-east of St Emilion, but also – and even more – at the technical accomplishment of the quarrying that had created so huge a warren of underground chambers so long ago. But this was nothing, Monsieur Faniest assured me; it was possible to walk underground from his property of Rochebelle, where we were standing, all the way to the cellars of St Emilion itself. Proudly he showed me his Grand Cru wine, ageing in oak, and we tasted a five-year-old, which we thought needed at least another two or three years in bottle, and a ten-year-old, with which I would have been happy to fill a niche or two in my own former coal-hole beneath the pavements of London. Within a kilometre or so of Rochebelle were Ausone, Magdelaine, Belair, la Gaffelière, Pavie and Trottevielle: all Premiers Grands Crus Classés. Rochebelle, claimed my host, was '*un petit parmi les grands*' – a little fellow among the giants.

Monsieur Faniest wanted to drive me back to the Palais Cardinal, but I managed to persuade him that I sincerely preferred to walk, in spite of the weather. Down I went again from the plateau, then up the main road into the heart of the town. Not knowing what the day would bring, I had taken a picnic with me four hours earlier; now, as the rain fell noisily, I had it in my room, taking care not to spill wine and to clear up every last crumb.

*Just below the edge of the plateau where the best vineyards of the St Emilion appellation are to be found, Château Lassègue is quite a modest property, typical of the 'châteaux' of the Gironde.*

# THE WINE

*Neighbouring Château Ausone,
the vineyards of Château Belair –
Premier Grand Cru Classé B –
are partly on the sides of the valley
(*les côtes*) and partly on the
plateau outside of St Emilion.*

*A vigneron, his wife and his gun
near Branne, on the Dordogne.
There is little enough to shoot
nowadays, but* le droit de chasse
*has been cherished by French
countrymen since the Revolution.
Walkers are not threatened.*

It used to be commonplace for the wines of 'the hill' (as opposed to the lowlands of the Médoc and Graves) to be called 'the burgundies of Bordeaux', by reason of their supposedly rounder, slightly less complex and more alcoholic character. 'The wines of St Emilion are less of a puzzle when young and mature faster,' notes Hugh Johnson with the telling simplicity that tends to distinguish his work. Rounder, fuller and softer are the epithets heard most often when St Emilion (and Pomerol) wines are being compared with those of the Médoc. There would seem to be two main reasons for this. First, whereas the Cabernet Sauvignon predominates in the Médoc it is the Merlot which rules the roost in the St Emilion vineyards of the Libournais, though Cabernet Sauvignon or Cabernet Franc may rival Merlot in the blends of wine-makers who are seeking to produce long-keeping wines. Merlot produces wines which are less tannic, more supple, more alcoholic and quicker maturing that those yielded by the Cabernet Sauvignon: to paraphrase Hugh Johnson, wines that are easier to understand. Second, the limestone soils of the plateau and its *côtes* are inclined to contain rather more clay and less real gravel than those of the Médoc, a further contribution to simplicity in the wines when young.

The classification of St Emilion wines is also simpler than that of the Médoc. First come two categories of Premiers Grands Crus Classés: A and B. Very roughly, the Bs occupy about the same level in the market for St Emilion wines as the second and third growths occupy in the Médoc. Next in the hierarchy come the Grands Crus Classés, without the 'Premier'. Last comes St Emilion AOC.

# ENTRE–DEUX–MERS

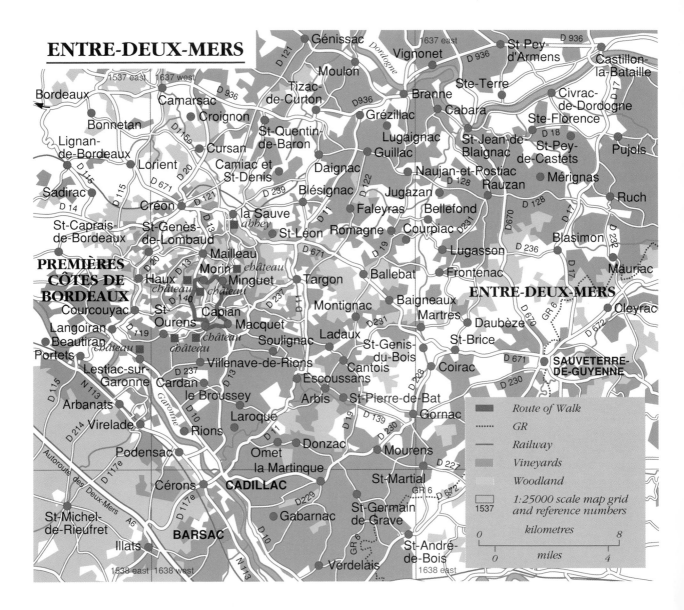

**ENTRE-DEUX-MERS**

Bordeaux

Génissac
1637 east
St-Pey-d'Armens
D 936
Castillon-la-Bataille
D 121
Moulon
Vignonet
D 936
D 936
Camarsac
Tizac-de-Curton
Branne
Ste-Terre
Civrac-de-Dordogne
D 217
Croignon
D 936
Cabara
Ste-Florence
D 18
St-Quentin-de-Baron
Grézillac
St-Jean-de-Blaignac
St-Pey-de-Castets
Pujols
Bonnetan
Lignan-de-Bordeaux
D 115e
Cursan
Lugaignac
Guillac
Lorient
Camiac et St-Denis
Daignac
Naujan-et-Postiac
D 128
Mérignas
D 20
D 122
Rauzan
D 115
D 671
Blésignac
Jugazan
D 128
Sadirac
Créon
D 239
Faleyras
Bellefond
Ruch
D 14
Romagne
D 670
D 217
D 121
la Sauve
abbey
St-Léon
Courpiac
D 231
Blasimon
D 232
St-Caprais-de-Bordeaux
St-Genès-de-Lombaud
D 13
D 11
D 19
Lugasson
D 236
Mailleau
D 671
Frontenac
D 17
Mauriac
**PREMIÈRES CÔTES DE BORDEAUX**
D 20
Morin
château
Ballebat
**ENTRE-DEUX-MERS**
Haux
château
Minguet
château
Targon
Montignac
Baigneaux
Martres
GR 6
Cleyrac
Courcouyac
St-Ourens
D 140
D 231
Capian
Macquet
Soulignac
Ladaux
St-Genis-du-Bois
Daubèze
St-Brice
D 670
D 672
Langoiran
D 719
château
château
Villenave-de-Rions
Cantois
Coirac
D 671
**SAUVETERRE-DE-GUYENNE**
Beautiran
Portets
Lestiac-sur-Garonne
Cardan
D 237
Escoussans
D 228
D 230
D 115
N 113
D 13
le Broussey
Arbis
St-Pierre-de-Bat
Arbanats
Garonne
Laroque
D 10
Gornac
D 139
D 214
Virelade
Rions
D 11
D 19
D 230
Podensac
Donzac
Mourens
Omet
D 227
la Martinique
St-Martial
GR 6
D 672
Cérons
**CADILLAC**
D 229
St-Germain de Grave
St-Michel-de-Rieufret
A6
D 117e
Gabarnac
GR 6
Illats
**BARSAC**
D 10
St-André-de-Bois
1538 east 1638 west
N 113
Verdelais
1638 east

| | Route of Walk |
| --- | --- |
| | GR |
| | Railway |
| | Vineyards |
| | Woodland |
| 1537 | 1:25000 scale map grid and reference numbers |

kilometres

0                  8

0          miles        4

# BRIEFING

## THE LIE OF THE LAND

Entre-Deux-Mers means between two seas, but the 'Mers' here are the tidal rivers Dordogne and Garonne. The northern boundary of the region is the Dordogne; the southern boundary is the Garonne.

It is mostly very pleasant, deeply rural country, at best pretty rather than spectacularly beautiful, with a wealth of abbeys, churches, castles in one condition or another, and very old, often picturesque villages. Dominating the Landes south of Bordeaux, Entre-Deux-Mers is considered *haut pays* – high country – in relation to the rest of the Bordelais. There are little valleys where streams run and the ruins of mills are welcome features of an otherwise unremarkable landscape, to be sure, and the walker who traverses the region from modestly elevated plateau to plateau (never more than 100 metres or 330 feet above sea level) may honestly report going 'uphill', but as with all of the Bordeaux viticultural area south of the Dordogne, a relief map shows ground that only with a touch of hyperbole can be described as hilly. Especially in the southern part of the appellation, horizons tend to be limited by woods that for all their number and extent are merely tokens of the great forest that once covered the entire region. In winter they give colour to the landscape; in high summer walkers can only be grateful for their shade.

## WALK

**Capian: heart of the Premières Côtes de Bordeaux circuit**
About 9 kilometres/5.5 miles; allow about 3 hours.

In theory, this route is way-marked with yellow-painted bars, but it is easy for these to become concealed by new growths of trees and bushes. Leave Capian to the east on the D 13, in the direction of Targon. After a kilometre (just over half a mile) turn left at a Y-junction and continue for about 400 metres to Macquet, then turn left past the buildings and into the woods, past the picturesque ruined mill of Lacroy and on down to meet a hard-top lane. Turn right. Cross the Lavergne stream and the D 140, then carry on straight up past vines and along the edge of a wood. About 800 metres from the D 140, take a track on the right to Montagne.

After a few hundred metres, turn left (that is north, under the word *télégraphe* on the 1:25,000 map). Turn left again through the woods and down, and cross a ford in the Patrouilleau stream to reach Minguet and the D 120. Here a track heads west into the Pins de Minguet, down to the Buchon stream and across it to hard-top lane and the hamlet of Morin. The lane continues to and through Bretagne, where a track passes vines, then enters woods again to reach German. A hard-top road crosses the Lavergne stream and the D 140 again. On the other side of the D 140, a path climbs into a wood, in which it meanders, to emerge in less than a kilometre (about half a mile) to vines again, and then the D 13. A path through vines on the other side of the road leads to the cemetery, from which a lane returns to Capian.

**Maps**

| 1:25,000 | 1637 est | Podensac |
|---|---|---|
| | 1637 ouest | Sauveterre-de-Guyenne |
| 1:50,000 | 1637 | Podensac |
| 1:100,000 | 56 | Marmande |
| *Topo-Guide* | 46 | Bordeaux, Royan |

*In the Premières Côtes de
Bordeaux, where the already
superior red wines are constantly
improving, a woodland path
through hornbeams – charmes –
provide a sylvan idyll.
Hornbeam is also a very good
wood for burning.*

# FROM THE DORDOGNE
# TO THE GARONNE

Early in my enquiries into walking possibilities in the whole great viticultural region of south-west France, it was suggested to me in a telephone conversation with the Conseil Interprofessionnel du Vin de Bordeaux that I might like to begin my field experience in the largest Bordeaux wine district of all, that of Entre-Deux-Mers. The Conseil would be glad to suggest an itinerary. It was a kind thought, I replied, but I feared that Entre-Deux-Mers, like the Médoc and Graves, might be a trifle too flat for the sort of walking that I most liked to do. Also (thinking only to offer a tactful excuse for declining the helpful suggestion), I happened not to be fond of semi-sweet wines.

There was a split-second of silence, than a half-strangled exclamation of incredulous outrage. 'But Entre-Deux-Mers is nothing like the Médoc,' cried the lady in Bordeaux in a torrent of protest. 'It is quite hilly (*bien accidenté*), and there are many rivers and streams; also proper castles (*des vrais châteaux-forts*), not just smart aristocratic houses like the ones in the Médoc; and many other things of interest, especially for an Englishman. And Entre-Deux-Mers is not semi-sweet white wine: the appellation is exclusively for completely dry wines. Have you never heard the saying "*Entre deux huitres* (between two oysters), Entre-Deux-Mers"? And anyway, Entre-Deux-Mers produces some excellent red Bordeaux Supérieur. And....'

Quite hilly? She could have fooled me, I thought a few weeks later as I trudged south from Castillon-la-Bataille for kilometre after kilometre on the busy D 17 at the giddy and virtually unvarying height of nine metres (30 feet) above sea level. 'It's not very exciting to begin with,' Baron Jean-Louis de Fontenoy had warned me as I was about to set off from his delightful wine domaine of Château Castegens, on the northern bank of the Dordogne, on my intended journey to Sauveterre-de-Guyenne. 'Better to let me drive you as far as Pujols. After that it's more interesting.' But after St Emilion I had the picture of pilgrims on the road to Santiago de Compostela in my mind's eye, and rather fancied myself as a hard traveller in an ancient tradition. Declining the Baron's kind offer, I made the best of a boring start by taking to a track and minor roads as soon as practicable. It was not until I stood by the Romanesque church of Pujols, on a terrace with a far view down and back the way I had come, that I began to believe the 'hilly' story. An hour later and some two and a half kilometres (one and a half miles) further, having descended into the valley of the Escouach stream then toiled up the other side to the isolated Hôtel Château Lardier, near Ruch, I needed no more convincing. Entre-Deux-Mers was *bien accidenté*, and no mistake.

So it continued for about half of the 14 kilometres (nine miles) to Sauveterre, by way of Ruch and the wondrous fourteenth-century fortified watermill at Labarthe, with its fifteenth-century tower. Like so much of France's architectural heritage the mill was built by Benedictine monks, the ruins of whose abbey stand below the village of Blasimon, for long in the hands of the English. At an artificial lake fed by several streams I had a picnic and cut myself a hazel staff, before going on up to Blasimon itself with its Romanesque and Gothic church. I saw none of the 'many rivers' that the lady in the CIVB had talked about on the telephone, except for the Dordogne at the start. But I saw the Courbut stream and the Ste Catherine stream and the Treynem stream and the Gamage stream (though it *was* called 'Gamage Riv' on the map) and the Pontet stream and the Fontasse stream. Nor did I come across any castles that day, but if I had made a five-kilometre (three-mile) detour to Rauzan I would have seen the romantic ruins of the fourteenth-century Château de Duras. In spite of what the books had led me to suppose, the land appeared to have as many woods as vines and a lot more clay than gravel, and I might easily have imagined myself somewhere in the English home counties. Drainage, say the experts nowadays, is at least as important to the vine as soil content, so perhaps all those streams play a significant part in the viticulture of the Entre-Deux-Mers. Most of the wine in the northern two-thirds of the region is produced by *coopératives*, and I came across no private wine-makers' houses, aristocratic or otherwise. Though at times I walked through vineyards as neatly tended as any well-kept municipal park, moreover, I tasted not only no 'completely dry' wine but no wine at all, except for the red Bordeaux Su-

*From the Romanesque church in the white wine appellation of Pujols there are fine views over the valley of the Dordogne to Castillon-la-Bataille. Entre-Deux-Mers has a wealth of abbeys, churches and castles in varying states of preservation.*

périeur Côtes de Castillon that I had brought with me all the way from the scene of the defeat and death in 1453 of 'Old John' Talbot, Earl of Shrewsbury, and his son in the last battle of the Hundred Years War.

Now and then shots sounded from the woods where pigeon hides in tall oaks gave me ideas about shelter for the night in an emergency, but otherwise peace reigned as I walked where the English must once have roamed, hunting and looting and murdering in the age-old manner of armies of occupation. At the approaches to Sauveterre-de-Guyenne a sign proudly proclaiming '*Bastide du* XIIIème *siècle*' was grotesquely offset by another advertising '*Snack bar Chez Tony*', a huge panel listing shops and services, and the monumentally vulgar SUPER U supermarket. All the same, the little town that was founded by Edward I of England seemed to me to be well worth walking to, with its fortified gateways, its ancient houses and alleys, its arcaded square and its view of the surrounding vineyards, let alone its wine museum and smart new tourist office.

'Nothing nearer than Langon, I'm afraid,' replied the deputy mayor when I asked about the possibility of a taxi to Langoiran, some 25 or more kilometres (15 miles) away, where I was due for dinner. 'But never mind,' he continued, 'I'll drive you.' Thus, with the briefest of glances in the fast-fading light of the autumn afternoon at the marvellous Romanesque doorway of the church in nearby Castelviel, I was transported as no self-respecting pilgrim ought to be from the dry white wine country of the appellation of Entre-Deux-Mers into the predominantly red wine country of the Premières Côtes de Bordeaux.

I wished then and I wish now that I had had the time to walk there. Wood-smoke scented the near-dark when we arrived at Château Lamothe, and a log fire burned cleanly and brightly in the drawing room. A rather more expensive, no less delightful scent belonging to my hostess, Madame Néel ('Nayelle'), preceded me as she showed me up to my room (I had left my boots in the hall along with a collection of green wellingtons and shooting sticks) in the eighteenth-century mansion. 'Very fat colour. Impeccably

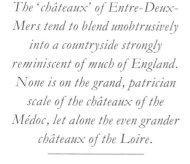

*The 'châteaux' of Entre-Deux-Mers tend to blend unobtrusively into a countryside strongly reminiscent of much of England. None is on the grand, patrician scale of the châteaux of the Médoc, let alone the even grander châteaux of the Loire.*

rich nose. Excellent on palate, fruity soft and round. Excellent balance and will keep. Very good,' was the judgement of Master of Wine Christopher Tatham on the Château Lamothe AC Premières Côtes de Bordeaux 1985 in a tasting carried out for *Decanter* magazine. Made from 60% Merlot, 30% Cabernet Sauvignon and 10% Cabernet Franc, the wine was all of those things and went quite perfectly with the common but completely delicious wood pigeon that we had for dinner. With dessert we had a delectable Loupiac from the sweet white wine appellation of that name, 12 kilometres (seven miles) or so south-east along the river, next door to Cadillac. (The Roman poet Ausonius, they say, had a villa there.) With coffee in front of the fire there was a very old cognac. Talking of my walk, Fabrice Néel told me to my great satisfaction that Château Lamothe had been a stopping place for pilgrims to Compostela. The vines that the Romans planted on the slopes of what was now the Premières Côtes de Bordeaux appellation, he added, were the beginnings of the whole vineyard of the Gironde, so I had come to the right place for historical associations. Tomorrow he would show me something of the five kilometres (three miles) of caves formed by the quarrying of the limestone used for the building of the present mansion. Very useful, he remarked, for storing wine.

*The ruins of the twelfth-century Benedictine abbey and the church of St Pierre dominate the village of la Sauve, near Créon.*

Boots resumed, hazel staff in hand, I left that most engaging domaine after an early sight of the cellars and a tasting of Château Lamothe white (40% Sauvignon, 30% Sémillon, 30% Muscadelle) and made my way by wood and stream and vines and lanes to Capian, where Anatole France is said to have stayed at the beginning of the nineteenth century. Here a re-tired army officer of public spirit who was concerned to promote the attrac-tions of the district, and who had been alerted by Madame Néel, gave me a hand-drawn map of a walk that he had surveyed and that would lead by lunchtime to a certain Château Plaisance. It was a heavenly morning. The sun was shining, the sky was blue. Within a few hundred metres from the centre of the village I was taking a wide track through a wood where my feet swished through the fallen leaves and an ancient windmill with a grey pointed roof like a witch's hat was sadly in need of salvation. Once it must have stood clear and proud against the Atlantic breezes above the Lavergne stream. A glance at my IGN map showed the sites of at least four more windmills within a mile radius of where I stood.

How quintessentially rural it all was. So lovely were the autumn colours of a grove of sweet chestnut trees that I wasted a lot of time trying to photograph them artistically against the blue sky, then felt it necessary to step out more briskly. '*Il fait beaucoup chaud pour la saison,*' remarked a woman in the hamlet of Minguet who came out to see why a chained dog was barking.

'*Beaucoup*!', I agreed, mopping my face.

'Are you German?', the woman asked cautiously, looking me up and down.

'No Madame, English.' She seemed relieved. Then,

'Ah, English! We don't see many English here.' I wondered if a cot-

*In summer, the woods offer welcome shade to the walker.*

tager in those parts seven centuries ago could have said the same. Further on another dog had its say, this time bringing out a much younger woman.

'Don't mind him,' she apologised. 'It's just that we don't see many strangers here.' From an outbuilding a young man appeared. Reassured, he offered me a glass of beer. Set into the roughly plastered wall of the kitchen and clearly no part of the original fabric of the place was a massive block of limestone. Out of it had been hollowed a perfectly arched recess above a circular basin hollowed from its base: the sort of things one might see for the washing of hands and sacramental vessels in the chancel of a church. No, they had no idea where it came from. A very old couple native to the hamlet said it had always been there. She offered me chestnuts from the adjacent wood, pickled in white rum, and more beer. Declining both, but as touched as I was refreshed by the hospitality, I went on through the wood along a path closely hedged by tinder-dry, exquisitely patterned bracken, down to a stream where a ford, clear, fast-running water and dappled shade made an appropriate setting for a sylvan idyll. The stream was called le Bouchon – the cork. Another happy name.

In the course of the next twenty-four hours I was to walk in other woods and other vineyards there on the southern margins of Entre-Deux-Mers, and to visit other domaines. At Château Bréthous in Camblanes I met François Verdier, a soft-spoken man who clearly lived for his wine-making and who had worked under the world-renowned Professor Emile Peynaud of Bordeaux, who enjoys a reputation not far short of god-like among knowledgeable vignerons. Tasting Monsieur Verdier's wine, I thought that the professor must be proud of his one-time pupil. At the sixteenth-century *gentilhommière* of Château le Chèze, close to Capian, having emerged without an appointment from the trees, I was entertained to drinks on the lawn by the charming seventeen-year-old daughter of the house, her parents being away on business. It was hard afterwards to know whether I had made a truly dispassionate judgement of the wines: I only knew that they seemed to me to have been worth walking any distance for.

Looking back, all those happy experiences in the Premières Côtes seem to be summed up by the aptly-named Château Plaisance and my hosts, Sabine and Patrice Bayle. Their exclusively red wine (Cabernet Sauvignon and Merlot), some of it aged in new oak, was impressive ('Dark red. Good rich nose; spice and cedar. Good length, with fruit and soft tannin. Warm. For keeping. Very good,' commented another member of the *Decanter* tasting team of the 1985 vintage). Patrice Bayle is the founder of a group of wine-makers dedicated to raising the quality of red wines of the Premières Côtes de Bordeaux to the highest level, and there can be little doubt that great things have yet to come from these wooded hills overlooking the Garonne. But what I remember most affectionately was wine on the terrace before lunch in that extraordinary Indian-summer weather, looking far away over vines and woods to the river, the light-hearted talk at table, the courtesy and solicitude of civilized people in a civilized occupation, the log fire again in the evening, and the deep silence of the night.

# THE WINE

Today, the appellation Entre-Deux-Mers is exclusively for dry white wines; the crisper, drier ones mostly relying on Sauvignon (the same grape as in Sancerre), but with Sémillon of high importance. Appellations for the – now – commercially rather less important sweet and semi-sweet wines are Ste Foy-Bordeaux, in the extreme northeast corner of the region; Côtes de Bordeaux-St Macaire, down on the Garonne; and Cadillac, Loupiac and Ste Croix-du-Mont, enclaves within the far larger red wine territory of Premières Côtes de Bordeaux.

In general the better red wines are found in the appellation of Premières Côtes de Bordeaux. Even twenty years ago most of the district's production was of mediocre quality, and even when better was mostly sold to *négociants*. Now the owners of numerous private estates are devoted to raising the already greatly improved standards still higher.

*The ruins of the Benedictine abbey of Blasimon lie below the village of the same name in the valley of the Gamage stream. The monks who built it were also responsible for the wondrous fortified watermill at nearby Labarthe.*

# SAVOY

## INTRODUCTION

From north to south, and naming only some of the most prominent localities, the wine country of Savoy starts on the southern shore of Lake Geneva with Ripaille, Marignan and Crépy; continues with Seyssel and Chautagne to the north of the Lac du Bourget and Jongieux and Monthoux to the west; and has its focal point in the city of Chambéry. In spite of severe damage during the Second World War and a later fire, the former capital of the Dukes of Savoy has great dignity and no little charm. Dominated by the heights of the Grande Chartreuse to the south and those of the Massif des Bauges to the north-east, its atmosphere is unmistakably that of a city of the mountains.

South of Chambéry are the Apremont and Abymes appellations. Round the corner, in the valley of the Isère, is the town of Montmélian together with the appellations of Arbin and Cruet.

Of all the wine regions of France visited in this book, Savoy is probably the one that is least represented outside of France in wine merchants' racks or on the supermarket shelves. This is not because the wine trade does not want its wine, but because Savoy does not make enough of the best of its wine to support a steady export business as well as supplying a loyal home market. Nor are the widely perceived virtues of Savoy wines so unusual or so great as to give them any significant advantage in competition with other red, white or rosé wines. Here, then, are the classic circumstances for making the most of the wine of the country on the spot. And nothing could be more delightful than the enjoyment of the wines of Savoy, either in winter or summer, in this, one of the most delightful parts of France.

*The vineyards of the Combe de Savoie, the deep valley of the River Isère, lie on the lower slopes of the escarpment of the Massif de Bauges. Here a newly harvested crop of maize is overlooked by the Château de Miolans.*

# BRIEFING

## THE LIE OF THE LAND

We are concerned here with piedmont country. The ground covered in the ramble around Apremont lies almost in the shadow of Mont Granier, at the northern end of the Massif de la Chartreuse, which is itself part of the pre-Alps. It is an area of vineyards (mostly), meadows, woods on the higher ground and small streams in sometimes stony, scrub-bordered little ravines. The scene of the walk in the Combe de Savoie described in the following pages is at the foot of the escarpment to the Massif des Bauges in the Val d'Isère. The walk outlined below climbs the escarpment to a plateau which is itself broken by hills and valleys. There is, then, no flat and level walking whatever. On the other hand, though many paths may be steep, none of the vineyards is in what might remotely be called 'wild' country.

## WALK

**Montmélian: 'mountains and vines circuit', Combe de Savoie** About 18 kilometres/11 miles; allow 7–9 hours.

This walk is fundamentally the walk called 'La Savoyarde' in the excellent leaflet *Itinéraires de promenades autour de Montmélian*, published by the Office National des Forêts and obtainable through the Savoy Tourist Office. The greater part is well under 1000 metres (3300 feet) of altitude; nevertheless, the rule of all mountain country ought to be respected – no excursion should be undertaken in doubtful weather. In good conditions the walk is richly rewarding and offers a superb experience of Savoy at its best: far views of mountains and valleys; exhilarating air; and freedom from so much as a suspicion of a crowd, even in high summer. Though not difficult in the sense of there being any obstacles to negotiate or any particular hazards to be faced, it does require stamina. Almost a quarter of the distance is through the vineyards.

Convenient departure points are Montmélian railway station or the *cave coopérative* on the north side of the tracks. Almost immediately a path skirts vines and traverses acacia, laburnum and pines to climb the escarpment to les Calloudes, then zig-zags steeply up to the ridge and the Rocher de Manettaz. There is a moderate descent to the Col du Mont and on down to le Mont, where the route meets the GR 96, which it now stays with all the way to Chignin. From le Mont the track undulates west and south to Montfruitier, with successively the Rocher de Manet, the Roche du Guet, le Tapin, la Savoyarde and the Roc de Tormery high above. From Monfruitier the path descends steeply, at first fairly

straight then in tight hairpins, to Chignin. Tracks now head south-east through the vines to Tormery and all the way back to the *cave coopérative*.

**Maps**

| | | | |
|---|---|---|---|
| 1:25,000 | 3333 est | Montmélian | includes Apremont |
| | 3332 ouest | Chambéry | |
| | 3332 est | Challés | |
| TOP 25 | 3432 OT | Massif des Bauges | includes Montmélian and all the 'mountains and vines' walk |
| 1:50,000 | 3333 | Montmélian | includes above-mentioned walk |
| 1:100,000 | 53 | Grenoble–Albertville–Mont Blanc | |
| Topo-Guide GR 91 | | Hauts plateaux de Vercors–Fontaine-de-Vaucluse | |

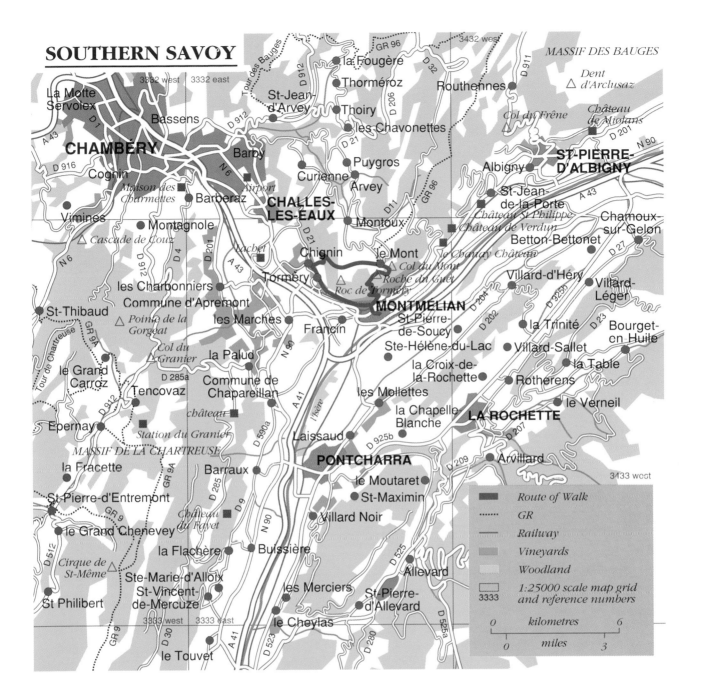

# SOUTHERN SAVOY

*MASSIF DES BAUGES*

la Fougère

Thorméroz

Routhennes

△ *Dent d'Arclusaz*

*Château de Miolans*

La Motte Servolex

St-Jean- d'Arvey

Thoiry

*Col du Frêne* △

Bassens

les Chavonettes

N 90

**CHAMBÉRY**

Barby

Puygros

Albigny

St-Jean- de-la-Porte

**ST-PIERRE- D'ALBIGNY**

Cognin

Curienne

Arvey

*Château St Philippe*

Chamoux- sur-Gelon

*Maison des Charmettes*

Barberaz

**CHALLES- LES-EAUX**

*Château de Verdun*

Vimines

Montagnole

Montoux

le Mont

Betton-Bettonet

△ *Cascade de Couz*

Chignin

*le Chantay Château*

Villard-d'Héry

Villard- Léger

les Charbonniers

Tormery

*Col du Mont*

*Roche du Guet*

△ *Roc de Tormery*

**MONTMÉLIAN**

la Trinité

Bourget- en Huile

Commune d'Apremont

les Marches

Francin

St-Pierre- de-Soucy

Villard-Sallet

St-Thibaud

△ *Pointe de la Gorgeat*

Ste-Hélène-du-Lac

la Table

le Grand Carroz

*Col du Granier* △

la Palud

la Croix-de- la-Rochette

Rotherens

Tencovaz

Commune de Chapareillan

les Mollettes

le Verneil

Epernay

*château*

la Chapelle Blanche

**LA ROCHETTE**

*Station du Granier*

Laissaud

*MASSIF DE LA CHARTREUSE*

la Fracette

Barraux

**PONTCHARRA**

Arvillard

St-Pierre-d'Entremont

le Moutaret

St-Maximin

*Château du Fayet*

le Grand Chenevey

Villard Noir

la Flachère

Buissière

Allevard

*Cirque de St-Même* △

Ste-Marie-d'Alloix

St-Vincent- de-Mercuze

les Merciers

St-Pierre- d'Allevard

St Philibert

le Cheylas

le Touvet

| | Route of Walk |
|---|---|
| | GR |
| | Railway |
| | Vineyards |
| | Woodland |
| 3333 | 1:25000 scale map grid and reference numbers |

kilometres 0 — 6

miles 0 — 3

# LATE SPRING IN THE ALPS

Méribel, les Trois Vallées, the Savoy Alps: a group of skiers sits on the terrace of a hotel-restaurant beside the *piste*, their skis stuck points up in the snow not twenty paces away. It is lunchtime. Before even glancing at the menu thrust into their hands by an impossibly over-worked waiter they have asked for a carafe of white wine. Now they sink it eagerly, happily, admiring its greeny-gold colour, delighting in the sort of qualities which, when enunciated rather than merely felt, provide the stuff of winespeak mockery: 'unassuming, unpretentious, charming, vivacious, frank, uncomplicated. . . .' And refreshing: exactly suited to that particular happiness which is compounded of the exhilaration of a long, clear downhill run, the warm spring sun on one's face as one sits at table, and good company. Why on earth did they not ask for two carafes while they were about it? Try to catch the waiter's eye again.

Apremont, near Chambéry, Savoy: I was sitting on the ground with my back against a drystone wall, overlooked by the towering mass of Mont Granier, and overlooking in turn the valley of the River Isère. It was lunchtime in late May, and since it was my birthday, I raised a glass to those who might be raising theirs to me if I were at home in England rather than about 30 kilometres (18 miles) east of les Trois Vallées. The wine was an Apremont, made from the Jacquère grape which predominates locally and acquired not half an hour before from the man who made it, up near la Torne. Leaving the car at le Mollard, just clear of the southern suburbs of Chambéry, I had followed a hillside lane past vineyards to St Baldoph, up again quite steeply to more vines above St Pierre, on down and round by vineyard tracks and lanes to Apremont village, then up to le Villard, and on, this way and that as opportunity offered, until I reached the chalet-

*Vineyards of the Jacquère grape near Myans in the appellations of Abymes and Apremont. Early to mature, the wines may have a 'nose' of honeysuckle and a hint of gun-flint on the palate.*

restaurant called Le Devin. Ah, they said, they were very sorry, but the restaurant was not open for lunch today. That was quite all right, I assured them; I had not come in the expectation of lunch, but in the hope that they would give me the name of a wine-maker I might visit.

So it was that I came to meet Monsieur Teppaz, who was working on the foundations of a new *cuverie* that he was constructing with his son, where chickens scratched in a yard and there were rabbits in a hutch. They could sell a lot more wine these days than they had the capacity to make, they said. There would be a new stainless-steel, temperature-controlled fermentation vat in the extension. They made only Apremont, from the Jacquère grape, of course. Many of their vines were fifty years old. But it was time we tasted what we were talking about. The last year's vintage had only just been bottled and Monsieur Teppaz said it really needed a week or two '*pour se reposer un peu*'. With an enthusiasm born of exercise and circumstances, I drank the wine of the year before and thought it delightful; there were acacias in full flower near the cellars and it seemed to me that there were hints of acacia, and perhaps vine blossom, in the wine. As a general rule, said Monsieur Teppaz, Apremont was a wine to be drunk young. Amen to that, I thought.

After leaving him, I had followed what the 1:25,000 map showed as a good, wide path up into the woods, walking off the one map sheet that I possessed, and thinking that I would simply follow my nose so as eventually to swing round and down again into the vines. Thus had I effectively lost myself, been obliged to climb into and out of a moderately deep ravine in order not to go back on my own tracks (though that is what I ought to have done), and so added two or three kilometres (a mile or two) to the half dozen I had already covered. When I did at last emerge it was into a meadow of buttercups and daisies, and meadowsweet and pink vetch, which Monsieur Teppaz had said was called Saint Foin: literally, holy grass. Below, reaching two kilometres (over a mile) or more into the valley in the

*A view south-eastwards to the high mountains of Savoy, where Méribel, Courchevel and Val d'Isère are among the ski resorts in which so much of the wine produced by the vineyards of the slopes below the Col du Granier is enjoyed.*

direction of Myans and les Marches, was a descending chaos of tormented ground. Planted with vineyards wherever vines might sensibly be grown, it was otherwise criss-crossed with a maze of lanes and minor roads and strewn with a variety of dwellings, barns and other buildings, many of them modern and unlovely. I was looking at the curiosity of les Abîmes.

*Abîme* may be translated as abyss, gulf or chasm; in this context and in the plural it may be taken to mean debris: the great mass of rubble that resulted from the collapse in 1248 of part of Mont Granier, a catastrophe said to have killed some five thousand people. In time, the limestone rock slide was found to provide an excellent *terroir* for the Jacquère grape. Just as the vignerons of Pouilly-sur-Loire are inclined to insist upon the differences between their wines and those of neighbouring Sancerre, so the producers of AOC Abymes claim distinguishing characteristics between theirs and those of Apremont. Most of the rest of us are likely very easily to confuse the two. No such niceties concerned me as I lunched there that May afternoon. *Apre*, meaning harsh or raw, was a fitting epithet for the mountain that had been the cause of so great a disaster, perhaps, but the Apremont that I was drinking suggested only meadow flowers, clear alpine air, youth, zest and happiness: the perfect spring skiing wine; the perfect summer walking wine. I almost fancied I could hear cowbells on distant slopes.

'The favourable orientation of all these vine varieties allows them to ripen perfectly and gives white, rosé and red wines the most pleasant taste,' says a leaflet published by the Comité Interprofessionel des Vins de Savoie,

*Dominating the vineyards of the Combe de Savoie, the Château de Miolans occupies a site that has been fortified for at least 1500 years. Now a prime tourist attraction, for more than two hundred years before the French Revolution it was a state prison: a sort of Bastille of Savoy.*

prettily. The leaflet is about the vineyards of the Combe de Savoie, the deep valley of the Isère, running north-eastwards from Montmélian (which itself lies south-east of Chambéry) to Albertville. The vineyards are on the lower slopes of the 1500-metre-high (5000-foot) escarpment of the Bauges mountains, parallel to the Isère. To the north and west the Bauges look towards the lakes of Annecy and le Bourget. To the east and south they face the winter sports country of the Val d'Isère: this is the orientation which the leaflet describes as favourable.

Walking, like wine, is taken very seriously in Savoy. Hearing in his office in Chambéry that I intended walking in his territory, the head of the organization responsible for the department's footpaths had suggested that he might accompany me for at least half the day; but when we met the following day at the little wine village of Arbin, close to Montmélian, we were three, not two. He hoped I didn't mind, but he had brought his daughter Gayle along; she was on holiday and very much liked walking.

At the cellars of Louis Magnin in Arbin, where both fermentation and ageing are in wood, we tasted a very distinguished white Chignin de Bergeron made from Roussanne, the chief grape of white Hermitage of the Rhône, white Roussette and the charmingly named Altesse. No less impressive was the red Mondeuse, a grape peculiar to Savoy and neighbouring Bugey in France. Here was a wine-maker as devoted to his art as any I had met. The wine is not at its best when young: I have a bottle of Monsieur Magnin's Mondeuse which he says I may safely keep for ten years or more.

*The church spire of Châteauneuf, Combe de Savoie, seen briefly from St Pierre-d'Albigny on the north side of the valley: circumstances in which to be thankful for a compass.*

*A roadside chapel near the
Col du Granier.*

From Arbin we climbed steeply up above the vines to find views of Montmélian (once a Celtic stronghold and in modern times more attractive before hideous industrial and commercial building threatened to ruin the ancient place) and out over the river valley to distant, snow-capped peaks. In tangled hanging woods there were sometimes vines growing wild like clematis, and masses of acacia blossom, which my guide said was good to eat if deep-fried. Was he serious? Absolutely: 'Where you see acacia like that,' he added, 'you are often looking at ground which was once planted with vines: being a very hard wood, acacia is widely used by the vignerons for supporting stakes. Before phylloxera, he went on, the mountainside used to be planted higher up than it is today. Now some of the abandoned slopes were being cleared and planted again. Wild flowers were everywhere. The alpine air was scented with summer. Near Cruet, some four kilometres (just over two miles) along the valley from Arbin, we saw a paraglider with a bright scarlet parachute floating down towards the meadows; Gayle said that if we looked into the far distance, just to the left of where the paraglider had been a moment ago, we would see Mont Blanc.

At Cruet, where the church is surrounded by vines, we spent half an hour at the *coopérative*, where they have twenty-eight fermentation vats that revolve like cement mixers: the only place in Europe with so many, the director told me proudly. Tasting was free and people were arriving with twenty-litre plastic containers to buy wine at prices which varied between six and fifteen francs a litre, and which was dispensed from what looked like miniature petrol pumps. Most of their wine, said the director, was sold to private customers, of whom they had no fewer than twenty-three thousand of all nationalities on the continent of Europe. The trouble was, he said, that he simply couldn't supply all that he was asked for. England had just requested sixty thousand bottles of Chardonnay. 'Very fashionable,' I remarked, adding sardonically that I hoped it tasted nicely of new oak. Not on your life, he replied. Their Chardonnay saw no wood at all. I thought it was very drinkable indeed; but in the mood I was in that morning I would have found it difficult to dislike any of the *coopérative's* wines. The last one I tasted was a rosé de Gamay, which I drank outside, looking out across the valley to fold after fold of mountains. There were roses growing over a wire fence: the colour of some of them exactly matched the Gamay and I thought about English gardens, and summer, and lunch.

We had a late picnic near the Château de Miolans, beyond pretty St Pierre-d'Albigny, from where there are views to uplift the soul. We ate excellent Beaufort, a high-Alpine cheese. I thought it went superbly well with the Gamay rosé we had brought from Cruet. Gayle, remarking on the snow-covered heights of the Massif de la Grande Chartreuse to the south, asked if I liked to ski. Truthfully, I said I did, though I had never been very good at it. But anyway, winter was a long way off: there was plenty of good walking time before then.

# THE WINE

Whte, simple and fresh, the three most widely used descriptions of the wines of Savoy, are far from being the whole truth, but embrace enough of the truth to be useful. Roughly two-thirds of Savoy wine is white, and most of it is the product of grape varieties and methods of vinification which give wines that in general (but there are exceptions) gain nothing or little with age, and which are intended to be drunk young. The rosé and red wines of Savoy are mostly based on Gamay, but Pinot Noir and Mondeuse are also not uncommon. The rosés are not for keeping, of course, but some of the reds are much more 'serious' than Savoy wines are in general believed to be, and increasingly so. Very little Savoy wine is drunk outside France, which is why it remains for the great majority of foreigners essentially a holiday wine, and in particular a 'skiing' wine.

Though the wines themselves tend to simplicity (any hint of conde-scension is much resented by wine-makers who know what can be done with the red Mondeuse grape), the Savoy appellations are relatively com-plicated. The main appellation, Vin de Savoie, contains some sixteen indiv-idual *crus*. A wine might therefore be identified only as 'Vin de Savoie' and be made from several varieties of grape, or it might have a place name such as Ripaille or Marignan added, together with the name of the principal grape used – as likely as not Jacquère. Roussette de Savoie is another appel-ation likely to be found on wine lists. Without any additional identification it will have been made from the Roussette grape – also called Altesse together with other white varieties; but it may also be labelled as having been made exclusively with Roussette, and in a specific commune.

*The lake of St André, below the Col du Granier, looking towards the Massif des Bauges. People say that the bones of some of the five thousand victims of the landslide of 1248 are hereabouts.*

# THE SOUTHERN RHÔNE

## INTRODUCTION

Like Bordeaux, the region loosely called 'the Rhône' produces some of the best wines in the world, such as Condrieu, Côte Rôtie, Hermitage and Châteauneuf-du-Pape. But as in Bordeaux, the part of the Rhône which produces the most famous wines – the narrow, northern part – is not one that offers the best walking. We are largely concerned here with the eastern half of the spectacularly beautiful department of the Vaucluse, which embraces not only Orange, but also Gordes and Fontaine-de-Vaucluse. It is country that almost ideally meets our established criteria for inclusion.

Gigondas is at the feet of the Dentelles de Montmirail. Eastwards of the Dentelles, marked by the town of Malaucène, is Mont Ventoux, the northern tip of the crescent of mountains which curves southwards for some 24 kilometres (15 miles) to Venasque, holding Bédoin and Mormoiron between its westward-pointing horns. On the slopes of the foothills of the crescent, and on those of the lesser hills between the mountains and Carpentras, are some of the best vineyards of the AC Côtes du Ventoux.

And this is virtually all admirable walking country. The GR 91 follows the foothills of the crescent from Malaucène by way of Flassan and Méthamis to Fontaine-de-Vaucluse, but walkers equipped with the appropriate maps should have little difficulty in devising their own itineraries, which most rewardingly, if rather demandingly, might lead to the southern side of the Plateau de Vaucluse: to Fontaine-de-Vaucluse, Gordes, Joucas, Roussillon and Apt, and to Ménerbes and Bonnieux and over the Montagne du Lubéron into the appellation of Coteaux d'Aix-en-Provence. All in all, for the walker it is some of the best wine country in the world.

*The Dentelles de Montmirail represent one of the most popular rendezvous for climbers of all ages and both sexes.*

# BRIEFING

## THE LIE OF THE LAND

To the west of the lower valley of the Rhône is the high *garrigue* country of the Ardèche. To the east are the western extremities of the mountain folds of Ventoux and the Lubéron. Some of Châteauneuf-du-Pape country is gently undulating and pleasant enough, and the hills of les Alpilles, St Rémy-de-Provence, also provide good walking, but as a very general rule the further west one goes, that is the closer to the River Rhône itself, and the further south towards the Bouches-du-Rhône (a triangle with its base on a line drawn from Montpellier to Aix-en-Provence and its apex at about Orange), the less satisfactory the walking. The closer one is to the mountains, too, the more varied are the terrain and scenery: both factors of prime significance for the walker. The country bordered by a crescent-shaped line running from north to south through Bédoin, Mormoiron and Venasque, on the northern fringes of the Plateau de Vaucluse, for example, represents virtually ideal wine-country walking.

## WALK

**Séguret to Beaumes-de-Venise** by way of Sablet, Gigondas and the Dentelles de Montmirail. 14 kilometres/9 miles; allow 4–5 hours.

The suggested route leaves due south from under the walls of Séguret on a short stretch of metalled road, crosses a little ravine and stream, and at a Y-junction of tracks ignores the left-hand one running immediately at the feet of the woods of the Cheval Long, taking instead the more prominent middle one going south-west along the edge of vines past the mound of les Destrets. More metalled, very minor road then continues south-west for about 1.5 kilometres (1 mile) to meet the D7 500 metres south of Sablet.

Less than a kilometre on the D7 leads to a minor crossroads among the vines at point 178. The suggested way turns left (east) here on the minor road, passes Fazende and goes on up to bend south and east with a strip of woods to the right and a wide expanse of vines to the left just south and west of la Pallière. On the bend, immediately before the entrance to la Pallière, a track goes off south below a steep slope of vines into the woods of the Plaine du Diablet, crosses a little saddle, and descends to the bottom of the shallow Ravin du Pourra at a small stone ruin called Dufrêne on the map. Then it continues climbing through the woods to old olive trees at the edge of a field of vines and a view to the west over the minor D229 to the chapel of St Côme, just north of Gigondas, though the village is out of sight.

From this viewpoint the track descends to the D229, crosses it and turns immediately right along the bottom of steep woods with vines down to the right in order to enter Gigondas village. At the south-western edge of Gigondas a lane goes south-east below the castle ruins up on the left, the hill of St Jean (313 m/1027 ft) being steeply up on the walker's right. About 150 metres from the bend below the castle ruins there is a T-junction. Here, the path goes left (south-east) and climbs on up for about 300 metres, past a dwelling on the right, then turns south off the metalled lane to continue with woods on the left and vines on the right for a short distance, before entering pinewoods and continuing on a wide, terraced, level dirt road through the trees, at first south, then east and up to the Col d'Alsau.

From the col, a track leads down into the valley between the Dentelles Sarrasines and le Grand Montmirail, a valley planted entirely with vines and giving far views to the east. This is not the suggested path. The latter is shown as no more than a minor track (thin broken line) on the 1:25,000 map, running very slightly south of due east through brush, then open scree, with the rocky ridge of le Grand Montmirail up to the

| Maps | | | | |
|------|------|------|------|------|
| 1:25,000 | 3039 est | Valréas | includes Visan | |
| | 3040 est | Beaumes-de-Venise | includes Rasteau, Sablet, Séguret | |
| | 3140 ouest | Vaison-la-Romaine | includes eastern edge of Dentelles de Montmirail and Malaucène | |
| | 3041 ouest | Rouquemaure | includes Châteauneuf-du-Pape | |
| | 3141 ouest | St Saturnin-d'Apt | includes Murs | |
| | 3141 est | Carpentras | includes Mormoiron | |
| 1:50,000 | 3039 | Valréas | | |
| | 3040 | Orange | | |
| | 3041 | Avignon | | |
| | 3140 | Vaison-la-Romaine | | |
| | 3141 | Carpentras | | |
| | 3142 | Cavaillon | | |
| 1:50,000 | Editions Didier & Richard. *Itinéraires pédestres et équestres: Provence. Du Mont Ventoux à la Montagne de Lure: Monts du Vaucluse + Dentelles de Montmirail.* Based on IGN surveys and distributed by IGN. | | | |
| 1:100,000 | 60 | Cavaillon-Digne | parc naturel régional du Lubéron (nord) | |
| *Topo-Guide* | GR 91 | Hauts Plateaux de Vercors–Fontaine-de-Vaucluse | | |

right and the cliff face of la Salle, much used by climbers, over to the left front. This path goes steeply down through high brushwood to meet a very minor road which goes south, south-west and south-east again, alternately past vines and woods to the wooded hill of the Roque Rascasse. Tracks go over this high ground, but the easier way is to continue by the minor road, which eventually turns due east before a sharp turn down and west to join a lower road coming from the north down into Beaumes-de-Venise.

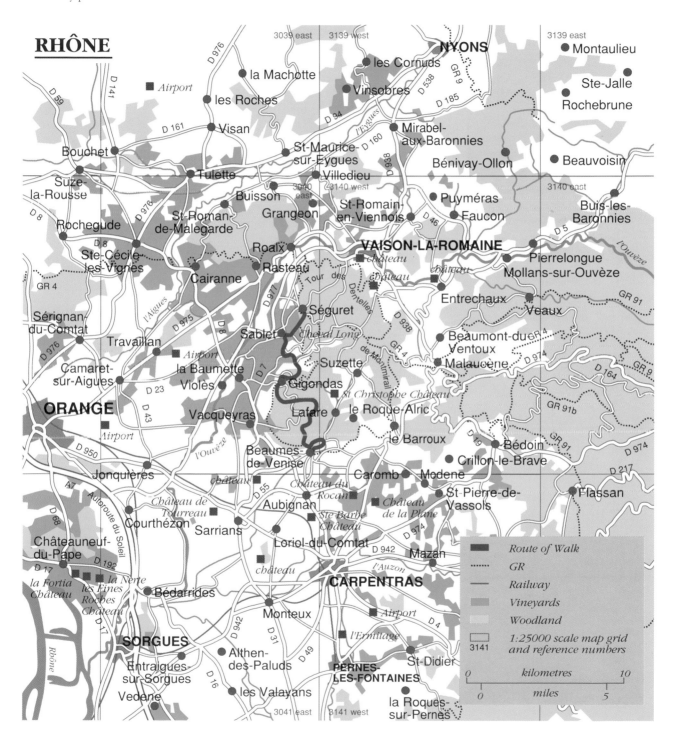

*Fields of sunflowers, all turning
their great heads towards the sun,
are a familiar sight in southern
France in summer. The seeds are
left to ripen, then harvested
to make oil.*

# HIGH ROADS
# AND GIGONDAS

I ought to have known better than to allow myself to be disheartened by two bad days among so many good ones, but that night, going to bed in the Hôtel du Domaine de Cabasse at Séguret, the pessimistic axiom '*Jamais deux sans trois*' was nagging at me, and I was apprehensive. Behind me were car problems, failed appointments, torrential rains, a walk from Visan that had inevitably been far more on hard-top road than off it, and to cap it all a thoroughly unsatisfactory dinner at a well-known restaurant in Séguret, instead of the good one that the reputation of the place had led me to expect and that I might have had if I had dined where I was sleeping. Now I intended to walk south to Gigondas, then over the hills to Beaumes-de-Venise, but as a result of yesterday's troubles I was ill-prepared. Also, the weather forecast for the next twenty-four hours was not good.

Séguret village clings improbably to the abrupt edge of what are really the foothills of the pre-Alps, which form the eastern limit of the vines of the southern Côtes du Rhône. These stretch for 16 kilometres (10 miles) or more westwards towards the Autoroute du Soleil, interrupted only by the shallow River Aigues. Below Séguret and a few hundred metres towards the plain, the Domaine de Cabasse is not only a most comfortable, quiet, restful hotel, but also a well-respected vineyard. Next morning, with recently harvested Grenache, Syrah, Mourvèdre and Cinsault fermenting in the vats, I spent rather too much time tasting last year's wines, so that it was almost eleven o'clock before I was walking along tracks and lanes to the *boulangerie* and the *alimentation* in Sablet. Measured by the scale on the edge of my compass, Séguret to Beaumes-de-Venise was ten kilometres (some six and a quarter miles) as the crow might fly, but rather more on the ground. Between the two soared the 734-metre (1800-foot) high Dentelles de Montmirail, and although I was not intending to *climb* the famous crags, I did all the same want to reach Beaumes-de-Venise well before dusk, and I had a lot of uphill work in front of me. There was also the matter of wine.

Though, with the possible exception of Châteauneuf-du-Pape, I had never known much about the wines of the southern Rhône, I had long been very fond of Gigondas, and my intention this day had been to visit the village's *cave de dégustation* on the way to Beaumes-de-Venise, in order to sample several of the many offerings of the appellation before buying one of them to take on my way. This, I calculated, would represent the best use of such little time as I could spare from the walk itself; but as I walked down the D 7 out of Sablet, then along a minor road leading towards the hills, I was more or less resigned to the fact that the *cave* would be closed before I could get there. Gloomily, I consulted the map so as not to miss the track that would take me off the hard-top lane. Further ahead, a substantial group of buildings lay back from the road at the end of an inelegant tree-lined drive, and a not unreasonable hope dawned.

Consider that at that moment, lacking as I did the sort of knowledge that is the stock in trade of John Livingstone-Learmonth, Hubrecht Duijker and Robert Parker, none of the names of the Gigondas domaines meant anything to me. The map indentified the place as 'Paillère', but of prime significance to me was the fact that the buildings of the domaine simply looked as if they had been there for a very long time, and that they were surrounded by vines. Nothing ventured, nothing gained. At noon I walked along the drive, hoping as always that the dogs were well chained. Almost an hour later I walked back again, richer for a thoroughly civil reception by Monsieur Pierre Roux, a look round the old cellars with their great oak *foudres*, a tasting of several vintages and a bottle of Domaine les Pallières in my pack (spelling on the map by no means always concurs with current usage), and above all with my affection for Gigondas elevated to new heights.

And now the hard-top was thankfully left behind as the track climbed towards the woods. It was very quiet there and I felt the approach of winter. Suddenly a cock pheasant rose from undergrowth, complaining loudly as it hurtled out over a steep slope of vines, but otherwise the only noise was my own steady tread as I climbed on up to a saddle where blue sky and the autumn gold of more vines beckoned. At the edge of the vineyard were very old olive trees, survivors from the not-so-distant time when they, not vines, constituted the chief wealth of Gigondas. It was the great freeze of

*On the northern face of the Montagne du Lubéron, Bonnieux looks out to the southern side of the Plateau de Vaucluse, beyond which are the heights of Mont Ventoux. Here the regions known to guidebooks as the 'southern Rhône' and 'Provence' tend to become confused.*

1956 that finished off the already declining olive industry, but only in 1971 was the wine of Gigondas promoted from Appellation Côtes du Rhône Contrôlée to Appellation Gigondas Contrôlée, thus becoming an AOC in its own right.

In Gigondas village at a quarter to two my earlier misgivings were proved justified: the *cave de dégustation* had been closed since half past twelve. Mockingly, the ever-open mouth of a Bacchus on a fountain across the square spouted cold, clear water into a stone basin prettily lined with drowned autumn leaves from the plane trees. Only a bar crowded with men in working clothes showed any sign of life. There was no reason for lingering, and no time for it either. From the village a lane climbed steeply up past the ruins of the castle to end in a wide track that led gently on and up before following the contours of the mountain side, giving far views westwards to Orange and beyond. Hidden away up here were yet more vineyards in what might have been thought inaccessible places, one of them occupying a tiny bowl among the pines in the romantically named Combe Sauvage, literally, 'wild little valley'. Another, a magnificent sweep of impeccably ordered rows a kilometre in length and almost 500 metres across at its widest point, was walled in by the high limestone ridges of the Dentelles Sarrazines to the north and the Dentelles de Montmirail to the south.

From this vantage point and on a clear day the eastern Pyrenees are in sight and the Mediterranean seems as close as a stone's throw away. Standing about 420 or 460 metres (1400 or 1500 feet) up in these hills to the south of Vaison-la-Romaine and north of Carpentras, the walker can look eastwards to the River Durance and the Alps and westwards to the Rhône and the Cévennes. Facing eastwards from the Col d'Aslau, which marks the end of the uphill track from Gigondas, a track no better than a goat path ran across a rocky slope at right angles to the cliff face of le Grand Montmirail. A few metres up from the path, to the right and on an almost level narrow terrace, the sparse, under-privileged vegetation included a very small tree

*Roads such as this one, near Bédoin, between the Dentelles de Montmirail and the foothills of Mont Ventoux and looking south to the Plateau de Vaucluse, feature in the walking literature available at local Syndicats d'Initiative in the Vaucluse.*

which might conceivably have been an evergreen oak and which, being roughly hedged in by box and other plants of the patchy *garrigue*, was partly sheltered from the keen little breeze which, at half past two on this autumn afternoon, defied a blue sky and an unclouded sun. Breaking away a few dead branches and removing a stone or two from the light brown, loamy soil, I contrived a seat with the curving trunk of the tree as a backrest. The air was scented with box and wild thyme that I had crushed beneath my feet. Practised in the art of deriving maximum pleasure from such moments, I arranged within arm's length a half *baguette*, a small packet of butter, *une belle tranche* of *terrine de canard* and a chunk of hard cheese on one side, and the Domaine les Pallières and glass on the other.

Before drawing the cork, I paused to admire the view. The sky was azure, with a few decorative white clouds. In the near and middle ground vines in all their variety – Carignan, Cinsault, Grenache, Syrah, Mourvèdre – formed patchworks of autumn colours: gold, amber, russet and red. Beyond the lower slopes of the Dentelles de Montmirail, to the east and north of Carpentras, was the Vaucluse plain (the most easterly part of the Comtat Venaissan), bounded by the crescent of mountains formed by the western reaches of Mont Ventoux and the Plateau de Vaucluse. The highest ridges of Mont Ventoux, their bare limestone reflecting the afternoon sun, gleamed white as snow. Beyond, in fold upon fold vanishing into the blue-grey distance, rose the Montagne d'Albion and the Montagne de Lure; and far beyond the hidden valley of the Durance lay the pre-Alps of Haute Provence, and beyond them again the Alpes-Maritimes.

'Gigondas is never a shy or subtle wine. Its appeal is its robust, frank, generous character . . . ,' says Robert Parker. 'A typical Gigondas has great profundity of flavour,' notes John Livingstone-Learmonth. Frank, generous and profound the Domaine les Pallières most certainly was. At the start it poured a suspicion too cold, but then I put the bottle under my down-filled waistcoat, over which I was wearing a bush-vest and – to cheat the

*Vineyards of Côtes de Ventoux, the village of Suzette and the Dentelles de Montmirail, seen from the east near Malaucène in the Vaucluse: virtually ideal walking country.*

*The Domaine de la Mavette is owned by Meffre, one of the largest firms in the appellation of Gigondas. Smaller growers may lack the sophisticated tasting facilities but are no less welcoming. The wines of many producers are found in the communal tasting* caveau *in Gigondas village.*

breeze – my Gore-tex jacket, and nursed the glass that I had already half-filled in the palms of my hands, drinking very slowly while I watched climbers whom I had just noticed on the formidable rock face of le Grand Montmirail. I was witness to a drama, for one of the climbers, a girl of perhaps nineteen or twenty, became stuck three-quarters of the way up the 30-metre (100-foot) cliff and had to be rescued. When I took the Gigondas out again it was significantly warmer. Whereas the first glass had been good, the second was a marvel of red berries and spice and (I thought) truffles: everything a lover of Gigondas might hope for. With the third glass I wanted frankly and generously to shout my praises of les Pallières to the whole world.

Half an hour later, the breeze was much colder than the bottle, and there were noticeably fewer climbers on the rock face. It was time to leave; *past* time, indeed, for the limestone ridge of Mont Ventoux, which for a few minutes had been pale pink in the setting sun, was now grey. Stiffly I collected myself and set off down one of the most beautiful trails I had ever followed. In places mists were forming and the colours in the vines seemed richer than before. Hips on wild rose bushes and a few lingering sprays of yellow broom were unreally bright.

I was becoming a little anxious now about direction-finding because I had failed to bring a flashlight. Dusk had fallen and the moon, when it rose, would be only in its first quarter. I quickened my pace. On a small patch of open ground, at a point where several tracks crossed, was a gipsy encampment with a fire scenting the air with wood-smoke, provoking the incipient dark. Lines from *Lavengro* came into my head: 'There's night and day, brother, both sweet things; sun, moon, and stars, brother, all sweet things; there's likewise a wind on the heath.'

At last I was almost loping down a steep, twisting minor road. Then there were houses with pink oleander in their gardens. Under the first street-light I unzipped an inside pocket so as to take out my wallet, in which was a note of the name and address of the wine-maker I had arranged to call on. The wallet was not there.

*Jamais deux sans trois.* The medieval streets of Beaumes-de-Venise were devoid of life. At last I found a café and successfully enquired about a telephone cabin that would take coins, of which I had a few. The friend who three days before had given me the name of the wine-maker in Beaumes-de-Venise, and who was now my most likely source of immediate help, was at home. 'They found your wallet at the supermarket in Sablet. The bill you'd paid at the Domaine de Cabasse was with the money, so they rang the Domaine, who collected the wallet and found my card in it and telephoned me a couple of hours ago. Everybody behaved incredibly kindly and intelligently. It must be your lucky day.'

# THE WINE

The southern Rhône is often wrongly called 'Côtes du Rhône', wrongly because Côtes du Rhône is the basic appellation covering all wines of the entire Rhône region – north as well as south – which are not more specifically categorized. But the region south of Montélimar in general, and especially the region to the east of the Rhône, is nevertheless by far the largest supplier of wines categorized as Côtes du Rhône. Here, too, are all but two of the seventeen districts entitled to the appellation Côte du Rhône-Villages, notionally all superior to the generic Côtes du Rhône. Yet higher in the scale come the four appellations of Gigondas, Vaqueyras, Rasteau and Beaumes-de-Venise.

There are red, white and rosé wines, but in spite of a considerable increase in white wines of recent years, the red still predominates overwhelmingly. Of the few sweet wines, Beaumes-de-Venise is internationally the best-known of the sweet ones (but Beaumes-de-Venise increasingly produces dry wines as well).

As so often in France today, generalizing about grape varieties in the region can be hazardous. Grenache is the mainstay of the southern Rhône, as Syrah largely rules to the north of Montélimar. But Syrah is used in the south, too, as are Cinsault, Mourvèdre, Carignan, Gamay and Pinot Noir, all for red and rosé wines. For the dry white wines of the southern Rhône there are Clairette, Bourboulenc, Marsanne, Ugni Blanc and Viognier. Muscat is the grape of the sweet Beaumes-de-Venise.

Most of the wine of the region is produced by *coopératives*, whose standards have greatly improved during the last decade or two. More and more wine is being produced and bottled by individual wine-makers, however, and their standards, too, have been steadily rising. As elsewhere in southern France, there is much innovation, and no doubt with luck and judgement many a happy discovery to be made.

*Near Châteauneuf-du-Pape, the Hostellerie-Château des Fines Roches has a very good restaurant and fine views. Its vineyards clearly illustrate the chief characteristic of the terroir of the appellation, with ground that is covered with large cailloux (pebbles) which act as night-storage heaters for the vines.*

# PROVENCE

## INTRODUCTION

What is meant by the area we loosely term 'Provence'? French officialdom sees it as embracing the departments of the Var, the Bouches-du-Rhône and the Vaucluse, but not the Côte d'Azur or its hinterland of the Alpes-Maritimes. Contemporary wine literature is inclined to regard Provence as anywhere that is not listed under Languedoc or the Rhône. Most helpful to us is the definition given by Food and Wine from France: 'The wines of Provence cover three departments in full: Alpes-de-Haute-Provence, Alpes-Maritimes and Var; and two in part: Bouches-du-Rhône and Vaucluse; the latter belonging also to the Côtes du Rhône region.'

No other region in this book has given me greater pleasure, none has involved greater difficulties: principally, how to convey something approaching a fair idea of so vast and varied a territory. Look at it, first, in terms of appellations, of which there are no fewer than seven Appellations Contrôlées: roughly from west to east, Coteaux des Baux de Provence, Coteaux d'Aix en Provence, Palette, Cassis, Bandol and Bellet; and overall, since territorially the appellation is fragmented, Côtes de Provence. There are also three VDQS appellations: Côtes du Lubéron, Coteaux de Pierrevert and Coteaux Varois.

Then in terms of actual localities and specific places, consider only those most obviously associated with the appellations: les Baux-de-Provence, Aix-en-Provence, Cassis, Bandol and its hinterland, Nice, Apt, and the interesting old town of Brignoles. They constitute no more than a tiny selection of the scores of names that are highlighted in any decent guidebook to a region that includes Cézanne, Van Gogh and Marcel Pagnol country.

I am all too uncomfortably aware that, as far as the land itself and places are concerned, I have been able to offer little more than a few fragments from a uniquely rich feast of potential pleasures, and with them no more than a few sips from a whole, ever-increasing cornucopia of some of the most pleasing and interesting wines in France.

*With la Cadière-d'Azur in the distance, the calcareous soil of Bandol reflects some of the 3000 annual hours of sunshine claimed by the appellation.*

# BRIEFING

## THE LIE OF THE LAND

A territory that reaches from the Bouches-du-Rhône in the west to the Italian frontier in the east, and from the Mediterranean coast in the south to the Alps in the north, and which includes six distinct Appellations d'Origine Contrôlées, clearly allows of few useful topographical generalizations. There is nevertheless one notable characteristic which is of prime significance for the walker: in Provence there is virtually no open wine country, or none of much interest to the wine-lover, resembling those classic models of Alsace and Champagne.

Most of the most interesting wine areas of Provence are in hard, hilly or mountainous, often fairly wild country where one wine estate is quite likely to be separated from another by terrain that is at best not particularly inviting for the walker, or that by reason of its topography or vegetation, or both, may well be forbidding. Easily identifiable paths and tracks lending themselves to a fairly steady pace on a reasonably uninterrupted line of march for a few hours are uncommon. All too often, the domaine that may be worth a visit for its own sake is one that also threatens a dead end. In other parts of France direction-finding may require little more than the sight of the spires or towers of village churches; in Provence, walkers are well-advised not to stray far from familiar paths unless armed with the appropriate 1:25,000 maps.

## WALKS

**St Baillon to Gonfaron, south of le Luc** by way of Flassans sur-Issole and the Commanderie de Peyrassol. About 18 kilometres/11.5 miles; allow 5–6 hours.

St Baillon is roughly 8 kilometres (5 miles) east of Brignoles, and north of the N 7 to le Luc. From the domaine, head east towards la Gariasse on the 1:25,000 map, by way of 'R*nes*' (ruins of a dwelling), then south towards la Grande Bastide. Cross to the east bank of the Issole stream, and so to Flassans. Leave Flassans on the D 38, in the direction of Gonfaron, but leave the road after about 750 metres for a choice of paths to Peyrassol. Aim for la Rouvière, not les Esparvins.

From Peyrassol, take the tarred road eastwards for a little over a kilometre (about three-quarters of a mile), then south to Vaulonge. Continue southwards on a way-marked path for about 3 kilometres (nearly 2 miles) to point 315, east of la Clémente, where a path marked in blue on the 1:50,000 Didier & Richard map, but not shown on the 1:25,000 sheet, climbs steeply down an escarpment to the N 97 and the railway line, about 3 kilometres (nearly 2 miles) north of Gonfaron. Alternatively, a track from point 315 south-westwards via la Clémente leads to the D 39, and so down to Gonfaron.

**Notre Dame-des-Anges to Bormes-les-Mimosas** on the GR 90. About 24 kilometres/15 miles; allow 11–12 hours. (Distance very approximate, since the route is sinuous and varies frequently in altitude. The GR markings were moderately good at time of author's walk, but very careful map-reading is necessary over the last 5–6 kilometres/3–4 miles. Facilities only at Collobrières.)

This is a walk which except for the village of Collobrières is wholly and beautifully rural. As the *Topo-Guide* suggests, it embraces high paths along mountain crests, deep valleys with clear running streams, woods distinguished by some of the largest and oldest sweet chestnut trees in existence, scented *garrigue* and magnificent views. An excursion of four or five hours from the GR 90 takes the walker to the romantically situated Chartreuse de la Verne and back to the described path. In the heart of the forest, the former Carthusian monastery, partly restored, offers food and drink and in future possibly simple accommodation.

Though strictly speaking not indispensable, the *Topo-Guide* GR 9: 98-90 is very much to be recommended. The route covered in detail by the guide, and followed in our narrative, is shown on the IGN 1:25,000 maps and summarized as follows:

Notre Dame-des-Anges. South to the Crête des Martels in the Forêt Domaniale de Pignans. West along the Crête to the fire defence heliport and reservoir at point 536, then south-east along the Vaucanes valley to Collobrières, where there are vineyards and a wine *coopérative*. From Collobrières the route climbs into the forest again, rises and falls, and eventually attains the Plateau de Lambert, indicated on the map with a red star. It then winds across the Montagne du Fauçon before descending to the Baraque de Bargean in the valley of the Bargean stream.

Col du Pommier, Femme Morte, Col de Labade and Col de Landon are successively the next points of reference to look for on the map, followed by the Pré de Roustan, the overhead electricity power line and la Pierre d'Avenon. Here, the Bormes-Canadel minor road and fine views of the sea are reached (Canadel is on the coast east of le Lavandou), and the path goes north-west, then west and south down into Bormes-les-Mimosas.

**Short walks from la Cadière-d'Azur** These suggestions take la Cadière-d'Azur as base and various domaines of repute as objectives. The tourist office in the village has local walking and wine information.

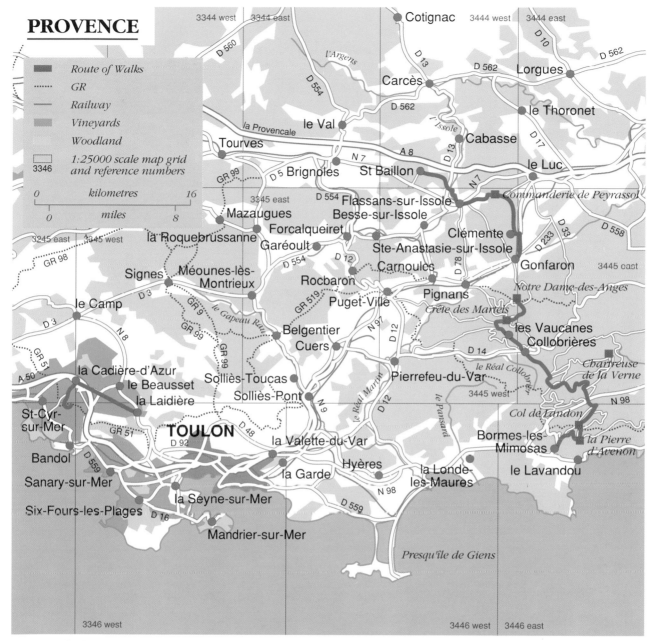

## PROVENCE

**Route of Walks**
...... *GR*
—— *Railway*
*Vineyards*
*Woodland*
*1:25000 scale map grid and reference numbers*

3346

0 — kilometres — 16
0 — miles — 8

**Pibarnon** high in the hills about 3.5 kilometres (2 miles) almost due south of the la Cadière: allow 1½–2 hours.

For the easy, minor road route with infrequent motor traffic, start off on the D 266 to the south-west, then – just past the roadside oratory marked on the 1:25,000 map west of St Jean – fork left towards les Costes. The road runs south, then west of south towards la Roquette, then south again to climb round eastwards and up towards Pibarnon. Footpaths are shown on the 1:25,000 map as running south from the oratory at the sharp bend of the D 266 immediately below la Cadière, just east of St Jean, and on south and up through vineyards marked 'le Moutin' and so on up towards Pibarnon. In the last 500 metres unmarked vineyards are involved.

**Moulin des Costes** in the hills about 2.5 kilometres (1.5 miles) south of la Cadière, about 1 kilometre (just over half a mile) of le Plan-du-Castellet, near Veyrole on the map. 1½ hours.

For the start of the minor road look for the oratory at the bend of the D 266 immediately below la Laidière. From here the narrow, tarmac road goes clearly south and slightly east towards the property marked on the 1:25,000 map as Veyrole. At a fork at point 102 on the map, about 1.25 kilometres from the oratory, the eastward-left-turn should be ignored in favour of the track continuing south and up to the Moulin des Costes domaine.

**La Laidière** near Ste Anne-d'Evenos, 7.5 kilometres (4–5 miles) south-east in a straight line, say 10 kilometres (6 miles) on foot; 6–8 hours.

On the map, rule a line between 'orat', la Cadière and la Laidière (prominently identified on map) to find appropriate tracks and minor roads. This route involves a lot of hill work and difficult path-finding, and is very strictly only for experienced, confident walkers good at map-reading. Weather conditions are also crucial.

The circuit of le Point du Cerveau and le Gros Cerveau is shown on the Didier & Richard 1:50,000 map (use in conjunction with the 1:25,000). The renowned Domaine Terrebrune is near la Tourelle, about 600 metres south of the route and same distance west of Ollioules.

*Among the delights of Provence are its fruit and vegetable markets. In the Massif des Maures, the terrain calls for good footwear.*

### Maps

| 1:25,000 | 3042 ouest | Châteaurenard–St Rémy-de-Provence |
|---|---|---|
| | 3245 est | Aubagne–le Ciotat |
| | 3345 ouest | le Castellet |
| | 3444 ouest | Cotignac |
| | 3445 est | Collobrières: Notre Dame-des-Anges is less than 1 km off this sheet to west, on 3445 ouest |
| | 3446 est | Hyères |
| 1:50,000 | 24 | Collines et Montagnes Provençales: Marseille to Hyères IGN, Didier & Richard |
| | 3042 | Châteaurenard |
| | 3245 | Aubagne |
| 1:100,000 | 66 | Avignon |
| | 67 | Marseille–Carpentras |
| | 68 | Toulon–Nice |
| *Topo-Guide* | GR 9:98–90 | Massifs Provençaux: Sentier Jura Côte-d'Azur |
| | PR | Sentiers de Petite Randonnée sur le Littoral Meditérranéen |

# MAY ON
# THE MASSIF DES MAURES

*Exuberant bloom on the plateau de Lambert.*

*In a valley of the Massif des Maures, young trees that have so far escaped the ravages of forest fires illustrate the sort of landscape that the* Topo-Guide *means by* la partie la plus verdoyante de l'itinéraire.

It began in wine country, near Pignans, in the valley of the Réal Martin stream, between le Luc and Toulon. It ended in wine country, at the Domaine du Galoupet, on the coast near la Londe-les-Maures. In between was the Massif des Maures where, except for those in the valley of the Collobrière, vineyards are rare, though I thought I saw one across a high valley, and certainly people are today planting vines in many a place where none grew before. Geologically and climatically, however, the Massif des Maures is of considerable significance in the viticulture of the Côtes de Provence, the largest appellation of the entire region. Moreover the forests of the Massif provide not only cork, but Liégeois oak for barrel-making. Besides, it was one of the best walks of my life.

I could claim, to stretch a point, that I began at the Domaine Gavoty and the Commanderie de Peyrassol, up near Flassans-sur-Issole. I had been there in November, when the white Rolle and Ugni Blanc were still in the vats at le Grand Campdumy ('*Entendez; comme il chante!*', remarked Roselyne Gavoty poetically as we listened to the sound of fermentation), and when the red Cabernet, Grenache and Syrah were softly bubbling away at the Commanderie de Peyrassol. I was there again in May, after the bottling *chez* Gavoty, and when the wine for the special *cuvées* was beginning its time in wood at the Commanderie. I had had my daydreams about walking to the coast at le Lavandon from the lovely thirteenth-century Commanderie, once the property of the Knights of St John of Malta, but had been defeated by circumstances. 'Never mind,' said Françoise Rigord, *châtelaine* and *vigneronne* of the Commanderie, 'I'll drive you to Notre Dame-des-Anges and you can start with a more powerful blessing than mine; but you'd better take a bottle of rosé with you for nourishment.' I raised a glass of the lovely wine to her next day near a spring in the heart of the Massif.

On the afternoon when I left the Commanderie, Françoise Rigord dropped me some 20 kilometres (12 miles) further south at the Domaine Rimauresque, twenty minutes' walk from Pignans, looking up at the television transmission masts of Notre Dame-des-Anges. Recently acquired by a Scottish businessman and managed by an enthusiastic young Frenchman, Rimauresque was the scene of great works and good wine. 'Why not let me drive you?' asked the manager, when we had looked round vines and cellars and tasted new vintages. 'Romance and pride,' I replied. 'I want to tread the path that pilgrims trod and I want to do it the hard way.' It was a two-hour climb to a superb view of the country I had come from and the hills I would be going through, and to an early bed in the *gîte d'étape* at Notre Dame-des-Anges. In the morning I made a quick breakfast at five o'clock. Just over three hours later, already enchanted with the trail, I was buying bread and a croissant in Collobrières. At nine, on a sort of alp above the village, I was

sitting on a well-sited park bench admiring a prospect of mountains before decisively entering the trees, celebrating such virtuous progress with a second breakfast among the spring flowers, accompanied by birdsong, the sun on my face and the scent of broom.

Fifty minutes from Collobrières, according to the *Topo-Guide*, the walker should reach a ruined mill with distant views back to Notre Dame-des-Anges. I saw no ruins, but was indeed able to look back to the start of the trail and down to the chestnut woods of the valley of la Mallière, and ahead and down again to the Destéou ravine, just as the guide said. There were chestnut trees here on the high path, too: enormous, very ancient ones, the largest and oldest I had ever seen. 'Collobrières, in the Massif des Maures', says one of my reference books, 'is famous for *marrons glacés*'. It also claims, as do all the guidebooks, that the word 'Maures' derives not from the Moors, the dreaded north African invaders of the ninth and tenth centuries, but from the Provençal *mauro*, meaning dark forest. This I take with a pinch of salt, for certainly the Moors established themselves hereabouts until driven out by Comte Guillaume de Provence in AD 973, after which they continued to ravage the coast at intervals for a further seven centuries. And the Moors were very dark. There was nothing dark about the Massif now, except perhaps the pines and the evergreen oaks and the deepest shade. To me, the rest seemed all sunshine, all light and life and new beginnings. Eastward the view appeared to be for ever, and I felt that in such air, under so blue a sky, I could go the distance without tiring. In a lush little valley, high up still on the edge of the plateau, was a spring of clear, cold water where I drank from cupped hands and laved my face and was profoundly grateful for such a place and such a moment. Up on the Plateau de Lambert, at 474 metres (1555 feet), the *garrigue* was in exuberant bloom in shades of yellow and pink, purple and white and crimson. *Arbusiers* were in blossom, and I remembered eating handfuls of the sweet berries in the fire-ravaged hills above le Galoupet and in the Corbières one autumn, and finding them not unlike wild strawberries.

Before long this trail was to pass through acre upon acre of the charred coal-black, grotesquely tormented skeletons of forest lost to criminals or fools. Forest degraded by excessive felling or prolonged neglect may before long become the *garrigue* (ironically, the beautiful asphodel, so prolific here, is one of the signs of such deterioration) that so delights the innocent walker in these hills of the Midi. Contrary to popular belief, forest killed by the fire does not regenerate itself with its strength renewed, but is lost for many generations, if not for ever. Knowing by report what lay ahead, I treasured every idyllic, unspoilt mile. At about noon, in a grassy valley, I came across a woman and three small children with a picnic spread in the shade of an immense and very ancient chestnut. '*Bonjour Monsieur*,' the children chorused, unprompted.

Soon, on a slope commanding a view of hills folding into a hazy blue distance, in the shade not of a chestnut but of an evergreen oak, I was admiring the Peyrassol rosé as I held it up to the blue sky, then drinking and conjecturing that together with Hervé Goudard's it must be one of the best rosé wines in France. I had climbed down a rocky path extravagantly and improbably hedged by cistus, wild roses, white daisies and honeysuckle, and the air seemed scented with all of them. I closed my eyes and heard only a breeze that ventured, and retreated, and returned shyly to stay, and I was drunk with pleasure; in an ecstasy of happiness.

All this was to the north of the Bargean stream and the valley of the les Campeaux river, which both run more or less parallel to the N 98 Toulon to St Tropez road at the point where it is crossed from north to south by the GR 9. South of the narrow valley the country changed: much of it was pleasing enough, but it lacked the distant views of the morning. The *Topo-Guide* judged it '*la partie la plus verdoyante de l'itinéraire*', but I thought it a touch too jungly. Some of the way ran through the burned forest, then there was a steep climb above the stream with the sinister name of la Femme Morte up to the Col de Landon at 382 metres (1254 feet) and the plateau of the Pré de Roustan. Here, says the guide, the rocky outcrop of the Pierre d'Avenon is a reminder that in times not long past the plateau was mainly given over to the growing of oats (*avoine*).

And here I got lost. I do not know why, though I am inclined to blame it, as walkers sometimes do, on ambiguous directions in the guide. I only know that I wasted a lot of time in trying to get my bearings, and that in the end I was obliged to take a very long way round and down into Bormes-les-Mimosas, with my pleasure in the view somewhat impaired. Strictly speaking, my walk did not end at the Domaine du Galoupet, since the process of putting one foot in front of the other along the paths of the Massif des Maures ended with that exquisite moment when I dumped my pack beside a chair on the terrace of a café in Bormes-les-Mimosas, just up behind le Lavandou, sat down and asked for two *citron*-Perriers. Having drunk both, I telephoned to le Galoupet so that they could come and fetch me in time for dinner. I doubt if even a million francs could have had me walking the 24 kilometres (15 miles) to la Londe. Anyway, it was well after eight o'clock and it would soon be dark.

The *citron*-Perriers were life-savers; now I badly needed rehabilitation. Fortunately, my host at the Domaine du Galoupet understood the sort of treatment that anyone who has walked from half past five in the morning until after eight in the evening likes to think he has deserved, and sent up champagne for me to drink in my bath.

# BANDOL, CASSIS AND LES ALPILLES

*For the walker, views over the Mediterranean, a certain escape from traffic and many a discovery in wine are to be enjoyed in the hills.*

*Vines grow almost to the walls of le Castellet, the Roman Castelletum, centre of one of the oldest and most important wine-making communes of the whole region of Bandol.*

I t was one of those occasions when the most painful part of being on one's own is not so much an awareness of loneliness, but an acute sense of injustice and waste. It is not fair that such perfection should be for one person alone. It is not right when others would appreciate everything just as much and deserve it more, but cannot share the pleasure. It is so sad when the food is plenty for two but the waiter has removed the second place-setting and helpfully drawn attention to the existence of several half-bottles on the list of wines.

Dinner at the Hostellerie Bérard in la Cadière-d'Azur, with a view of the heart of the wine country of Bandol, was just that sort of occasion. The Hostellerie has one of the best views from any restaurant in France, if not in the world, surveying valleys and vines, woods and hills and scattered red-roofed farmhouses which are as likely as not to be wine domaines. As a souvenir of the occasion I have kept a scholarly brochure in French on the subject of Bandol, entitled 'Where an exceptional soil and the most demanding of grape varieties meet'. On the back I made some rough notes about the wines that accompanied the admirable food. The Cagueloup was 'simply delicious: a lovely light golden colour; big but not brutish; perfumed (broom? thyme?) but dry'; the Ray-Jane, a ten-year-old red made mostly from Mourvèdre, I supposed, was superb: 'lots of red berries and herbs again, I think'. From my table I could identify the charming cluster of buildings which made up Château Romassan, belonging to Domaines Ott, the most famous of all wine firms in Provence. Further off, mostly hidden by trees, was the Domaine Tempier, of almost legendary repute in the world of wine. Some five or six kilometres (three or four miles) to the south-east, hiding the coast, were the 3 or 400-metre (1000 or 1300-foot) heights of le Gros Cerveau and the Pointe de Cerveau, on the far side of which, I knew, lay the very highly regarded domaine of Terrebrune.

I knew because for the better part of a week at the end of May I had walked here and there in the appellation of Bandol, and during that time I had studied my maps almost as much as I had walked. At the suggestion of the Bérards, whose wine list is a very good one, I had taken a path to wine-maker A, who had suggested that I ought to go and see wine-maker B, who had driven me over to the domaine of wine-maker C, from where I had walked to wine-maker D, and so forth. Bandol, it seems to me, is eminently suited to the sort of expeditions that are best undertaken from a comfortable base such as la Cadière-d'Azur and the Hostellerie Bérard provide: down the hill after breakfast; half a dozen kilometres (four miles or so) to this or that domaine, most probably known to and telephoned from the Hostellerie; see the cellars, taste the wine; buy a bottle and tell yourself that one day you will return to buy a dozen; picnic where the fancy takes you; later (much later if it is summer) walk to another domaine on the way back

*In the viticultural appellation of Bandol, hilltop le Castellet, like la Cadière-d'Azur across the valley, has one of the best restaurants in the region with some of the finest views.*

to la Cadière; back at the Hostellerie, cool off in the pool; at dinner, drink a wine from a cellar you have visited that day or plan to visit the following day. Choose from Comte Henri de Saint-Victor's Pibardon, wonderfully placed in the hills just south of la Cadière; the Bunan brothers' Moulin des Costes, less than an hour's walk eastwards; Domaine Tempier and Château Romassan down in the valley; or, some four or five hours' careful map-reading away, the delightful la Laidière, which half a century ago used to send thousands of baskets of spring flowers to England and now hopes to send wine.

They are not chauvinistic at the Hostellerie Bérard. One evening, scanning the wine list for a half-bottle of something white to go with a fishy first course, I noticed a Cassis Clos Ste-Magdeleine. 'A lovely wine,' confirmed Danièle Berard enthusiastically, which it was. Next day I made the half-hour drive out of the appellation of Bandol and into that of Cassis, to the cliff-top vineyards of Clos Ste-Magdeleine and the domaines of la Ferme Blanche and Fontblanche to the north of the boutique-ridden little town. Then I walked for three or four kilometres (a couple of miles or more) on and up to the top of the limestone ridge which overlooks valleys and vines, cliffs and sea, and lunched lightly up there among the rocks and the wild thyme, with the sun, a breeze and a cold bottle of Cassis, perfect for the circumstances. Back at la Cadière there was plenty of time for a long bath and a short sleep before dinner.

Another morning I followed five kilometres (three miles) of pine-shaded minor roads to St Cyr-sur-Mer and Château Pradeaux, which is said to have the oldest vines in all Bandol and has evidently known better days, but whose best wines still command respect. Dogs held me at bay for an unconscionable length of time before a sleepy son of the house appeared and kindly let me taste big, complex reds derived from 98% Mourvèdre with 2% Grenache, aged three or four years in oak. Then I fled the dogs and the hideous, inexorable spoliation of all that bay of les Lecques to reach neighbouring la Madrague and a coastal path leading eastwards. It is a path that touches few vineyards but is as pleasing as it is surprising. Here, though close to some of the most densely and disastrously urbanized acres of one of the most crowded littorals of the Mediterranean, it is possible to be quite alone on a tiny beach in a rocky cove, with only the noise of the cicadas to complain about. The *Topo-Guide* says that the 11 kilometres (seven miles) ought to take three hours and twenty minutes, but they took me almost two hours more, for I found a place in the sun close to the water and did not hurry over lunch before continuing to Bandol and a taxi back to the village on the hill.

Entertained, *faute de mieux*, by my own thoughts, I sat long there over dinner in the Hostellerie Bérard, remembering a November when I had stayed at the Hôtel la Régalido in Fontvieille, near Arles. After a walk that had included the château of Montmajour, I had arrived quite late at Font-vieille to find the hotel open but the Michelin one-star restaurant closed, as it was perfectly entitled to be on a Monday. Never mind, said *chef-patron* Mi-

*Wild flowers in the garrigue are an additional draw to the walker.*

*The renowned Calanques on the coast between Marseille and Toulon are towering limestone cliffs, sometimes over 400 metres in height. The limestone that underlies the vineyards is ideal for the white wine that goes so well with the local fish.*

chel, he would get me a little something. I was one of only two guests in the place that night, the other having gone out to dinner. When I came down from my bath I found a place laid at a low table in front of a log fire. The little something was a truffled omelette, an especially delicious Parma ham and several kinds of cheeses. Michel joined me. We drank a marvellously good Ferraton white Hermitage to begin with. Halfway through the bottle Michel went away and came back with a white Beaucastel Châteauneuf-du-Pape, another wine I had not met before. It seemed to me one of the best white wines I had ever encountered. Michel went off to get yet another bottle, which he opened and stood on the hearth – but not in the full heat of the flames – while we were on the lower half of the Beaucastel. The new-comer was another Châteauneuf, but a red one, also quite unknown to me. 'Jacques Reynaud,' explained Michel. 'Very good wine-maker.' It was a Pignan '81. We drank it with the cheese and I went into ecstasies. The other guest arrived back from his dinner and remarked on the joy of the log fire. What about a little *marc* for a cold evening, suggested Michel? It, too, was made by Ferraton in Tain l'Hermitage, and it was a revelation. The fire had burned low before we noticed that it was nearly one o'clock. As I started up the stairs to my room, Michel remarked it might interest me to know that *The Lion in Winter* was filmed in the area of Fontvieille and that Audrey Hepburn stayed at the Régalido.

From Fontvieille I had walked to les Baux, and from les Baux on over les Alpilles to St Etienne-du-Grès, some eight kilometres (five miles) west of St Rémy-de-Provence, where Eloi Durbach produces some of the most interesting and best wines ever made. We had met before. On this occasion, I asked if I might take him out to dinner. We tasted one or two of his extraordinary reds and much more recent whites, then went to a restaurant of his choosing, the modest Vaccarès in Arles. I asked him to choose the wine, too, and after some demur he did, saying that it was a favourite of his and that I would like it. It was superb. The label, which I kept, identifies it as Châteauneuf-du-Pape, Pignan, 1981, made by J. Reynaud.

I have several labels from Bandol, too, but they are still on bottles which are tucked away in the old coal cellar. I hope to draw a cork or two about 1997 or 1998 – in carefully chosen company, of course.

# T R U F F L E S   A N D   T A S T I N G S
# I N   C Ô T E S   D E   P R O V E N C E

Anyone coming upon Hervé Goudard and me without warning or explanation might easily have supposed us to have taken leave of our senses. We were both crouched on our haunches facing one another in a patch of grass under an oak tree at the edge of some of his vines. His head was hard over to one side, so that his ear was on his right shoulder, while his left hand was describing small circles a foot or two above the ground and parallel to it. We must have looked as if we were miming the antics of two fighting cocks, or engaged in some mysterious ritual.

'They're not easy to see,' Goudard was saying. 'You need to get down like this, with your eyes as close as possible to the ground and the flies between you and the sun. You can spot them much better then because the sunlight is reflected from their wings. Even though the truffle is buried it gives off a scent that we humans can't detect but that other creatures, like pigs and dogs, and these particular flies, can. Anyway, you watch carefully to see where they're circling, and you mark the place with a piece of stick or something, before using a large knife or a small trowel to dig round the mark in a bigger circle than indicated by the flies. You dig *very* carefully, bit by bit, not only so as not to damage the truffle when you come to it, but also so as not to destroy more of the spores than you can possibly help. And there you are!'

There I was that early November morning at Hervé Goudard's Domaine de St Baillon, hidden away among the woods between the N 7 and the A 8 about 16 kilometres (10 miles) east of Brignoles. 'You'll like Hervé,' his neighbour, Roselyne Gavoty of the Domaine Grand-Campdumy, had said to me. 'He makes very good wine and is crazy about horses.' A horse had watched me amiably over the half-door of a loose-box on my arrival on foot from the Grand-Campdumy. No dog had barked. Hervé Goudard, a tall man in his forties wearing breeches and riding boots, who looked more like the popular idea of a polo player than a vigneron, quickly revealed himself as being no playboy when it came to wine-making. After a walk down into the little valley enclosed by woods and *garrigue*, and up among the vines on the south-west-facing slopes on the other side, we returned to his impeccably clean cellars, with their brick floor and new-looking oak barrels, and talked (at my instigation) a little about himself, and (with no persuasion necessary) a lot about wine.

The son of an exceedingly rich industrialist, qualified as a lawyer, Monsieur le Docteur Goudard had spent three years globe-trotting in international business, devoting most of his spare time to training thoroughbred racehorses at Chantilly, before deciding to become a wine-maker. 'It seemed to me the only other thing that gave the opportunity of creating a truly personalized product.' He studied in Burgundy, the Loire and Bordeaux, took the best advice available, made careful plans and projections and settled on Provence: 'With such a poor image, and therefore without the need for high investment in land, yet with the right soil and climate, it represented a great opportunity.'

Keeping a few of the peach trees that used to be the domaine's principal source of income, Goudard landscaped for vines and introduced 'improving' varieties, so that now he had Cabernet Sauvignon and Syrah as well as Grenache and Cinsault for red wine, as well as Rolle and Ugni Blanc for white. He built a new four-level cellar into the hillside, thus avoiding the necessity of any pumping in his vinification process, which was a combination of the relatively modern *macération carbonique* and long-established, classic methods. In his little tasting cellar, where he keeps his own private stock of wines, I noticed a case of Trevallon '85, and remarked on it enviously. Goudard asked if I knew Eloi Durbach, and when I replied that I did he spoke of the other man with warm, unfeigned admiration. Such imagination! Such vision! Such courage! Such integrity! Clearly the vigneron in the appellation of Coteaux d'Aix-en-Provence had informed, inspired and encouraged his colleague in Côtes de Provence.

It was when we were tasting Goudard's special Cuvée du Roudaï, the

*The grapes may be gathered in plastic buckets and taken to the pressoirs in steel trailers, but the law still requires harvesting by hand – not by machine – in the appellation of Bandol. Red wines must also by law age for at least eighteen months in oak casks.*

'86 I think, made with Cabernet Sauvignon and Syrah, that the matter of truffles came up. We were talking about the 'nose' of the wine. Strawberries, blackberries, leather and *sous-bois* (undergrowth) had been mentioned when I said rather diffidently that I thought perhaps there were truffles as well 'You're right!', said Goudard, enthusiastically. 'You're absolutely right! And there's a reason for it. I'll show you later.'

When it was time for me to go, Goudard wanted me to take something for the picnic that I had said I would have somewhere on my way to the Commanderie de Peyrassol, so I put a cold bottle of his rosé in my pack. Instead of saying goodbye there and then, he said that he would like to walk with me for a bit, if I didn't mind, since my way would take me past something he would like to show me. Thus we set off together and five minutes later were crouching at the edge of a spread of Cabernet Sauvignon like men out of their minds.

The lesson in truffle-hunting over, Goudard set me on a path into the wood, where the trees were mostly young oak. Here and there, rocks smoothed by millennia of erosion showed above the earth. Jays called. Autumn was in the air and there was the sighing of a little wind in the trees. By a quarter past one I had emerged from the trees on to a wide track which ran beside an acre or two of vines growing in a shallow depression surrounded by the woods and smooth outcrops of rock. It seemed both the time and place for lunch. Away from the track, on the very edge of the vines, I found a corner formed by two half-ruined drystone walls. The sun was shining but heavily veiled by high cloud, and the light breeze was cool. The rosé was still cellar-cold and delightful; pretty to look at, too, with a hint of lavender to my eye. It was made from half-and-half Grenache and Cinsault, Goudard had told me. 'Suggestions of strawberry, raspberry and grenadine,' I was to read later, in a more or less technical appraisal of the wines of the domaine.

I was halfway through the bottle when a Citroën *deux-chevaux* appeared from the wood and stopped on the track. Out got a tall, stooping figure in *bleus de travail* and a peaked cap. '*Le patron!*' I thought. 'Has he spotted me? Is he going to come and tell me I have no business to be in his vineyard?' Sure enough, he came slowly towards me between the first two rows of vines, carrying what I feared at first was a gun, but which proved to be a pair of long-handled pruning shears. '*Bonjour Monsieur*,' I called boldly when he came within hailing distance. 'I hope I'm not bothering you by trespassing in your *vignoble*.'

'*Pas du tout. Pas du tout*,' he replied affably, then with a little nod, and referring as much to the bottle beside me as to my comfortable position in the lee of the wall, 'You look as though you're nicely settled (*bien installé*) there. And you're lucky with the weather, after so much rain.'

We chatted for a while. The vines, he said, were Cinsault which he sold to a local *coopérative*. He used to make a little wine for himself, but for some years now had found it too much trouble. Anyway, he had only about half a hectare, so it wasn't a big *affaire*. Well, he said, he must be getting on with what he came to do. '*Bon appétit.*' And with that, working his way back along the ranks of Cinsault, he returned to his car. When the sound of it had died away the silence of the woods seemed very deep.

Soon I too was on the move, much encouraged by the St Baillon, and by a quarter past two I had reached the D 13, a tortuous minor road running to the west of Flassans-sur-Issole. Within a few hundred metres I left it again by a bridge over the clear, fast-running, shallow river below what the 1:25,000 map calls la Grande Bastide. Here a wide, firm, stone-based track ran parallel with the Issole and across a little plain, where weathered mounds of stones among the juniper and the great carpets of wild thyme stood as monuments to a traditional husbandry abandoned long ago. High up on the hill were the ruins of what according to the map was the Château de Pontèves and further on stood what I supposed to be the nunnery of Notre Dame-de-la-Consolation. Shrivelled foliage on vines beside the Issole told of recent night frosts. The sweet, sad scent of wood-smoke hung in the air. Suddenly, winter seemed very near.

It was almost three o'clock now, and just as well that the doors of the ancient church with its Romanesque portal in Flassans were locked, for in view of what was to happen within the hour I could ill have afforded the time to go inside. By the route I intended taking, the Commanderie de Peyrassol was perhaps five kilometres (three miles) further to the north-east: say one and a half hours' walking at most. The way ran along the D 39 for about a kilometre (less than a mile), then along tracks through vines and woods almost all the way to the Commanderie's private drive. It was perfectly clear and unequivocal on the 1:25,000 map and I expected to reach the end of the journey comfortably before dark. But I had reckoned without the sort of contretemps with which few walkers can be unfamiliar. A path which the map said ought to exist was not identifiable on the ground. A path which looked promising on the ground did not appear on the map. I took it all the same, but after ten minutes came to a dead end at the edge of the forest. Tired now, I was starting to feel myself the victim of a hostile conspiracy. And it was now half past four. Back I was obliged to go to the D 39, taking a short-cut through the vines of la Bastide Neuve, where grapes missed during the harvest, or more likely ripened since, remained in plenty, and where a red-legged partridge exploded from under my feet when I went to pick a handful. On the road again, I quickened my step and lengthened my stride as much to counter frustration as to race the dark.

It almost caught me, all the same. By the time I reached the drive leading up to the Commanderie de Peyrassol I could no longer read the map. 'We thought you must be lost,' said Françoise Rigord. 'I don't suppose you really want to see the cellars and have a tasting now, do you? What about a little drink by the fire before your bath?' With apologies, regrets and heartfelt gratitude, I accepted the suggestion. There are occasions when a whisky and soda is the only drink in the world.

# THE WINE

W hen I mentioned to a friend whom most people would consider to be quite knowledgeable about wine that Provence had proved far from easy to write about, he replied, 'Well at least you don't have to dwell too much on the wine aspect of it, do you? I mean, what is there apart from a lot of rosé and maybe one or two fairly decent Bandols?'

To serious students of wine, or to anyone well acquainted with the wines of Provence, the remark must seem almost unbelievable. Had the man never heard of Cassis, or Palette, or Ott's Clos Mireille, or the Commanderie de Peyrassol, or Eloi Durbach and his Domaine de Trévallon in the Coteaux des Baux, to pluck no more than an almost derisory few from a score or more of names unquestionably entitled to better than patronising respect? Regrettably, it was all too typical of the remarkable lack of popular awareness of the viticultural revolution that has taken place during the past

The Château de Mille, just south of the Montagne du Lubéron, dates from at least the thirteenth century and is mentioned in the archives of Avignon of 1238 as belonging to Pope Clement V. Subsequently, it became the property of the bishops of nearby Apt.

two or three decades in the wine regions of the south. With Provence we are talking about an area which for serious endeavour and development in wine-making rivals any in France. As in neighbouring Languedoc, it has been the old, not-to-be-taken-seriously image of the region's wines that has proved one of the most powerful motivations to a new generation of native vignerons, as well as to newcomers to the region and to the wine business as a whole.

It is not easy to think of a single 'noble' variety of grape that is not nowadays to be found somewhere or other in Provence. Bold and enthusiastic wine-makers, women as well as men, are experimenting all the time. Rosé may still be the most popular of Provençal wines, and the one made in the largest quantity. A lot of it is excellent. But with the technical advances of the past few years, the quality of white wines has improved hugely and impressive results have been achieved. Bandol has long been highly regarded for its red wines, and there too the quality is ever improving. Perhaps the most useful thing to know about the wines of Provence is that they are eminently deserving of being far better known.

*The view from the Château de Mille is quintessentially Provençal. The vines grow on chalky clay with surface pebbles, all underlaid by sandstone: fine country for the hardy walker able to use a 1:25,000 map.*

# LANGUEDOC

## INTRODUCTION

It is no easier to define Languedoc than it is to define Provence, but for most practical purposes it is very roughly a 50 to 60-kilometre (30 to 40-mile) wide, 160 to 240-kilometre (100 to 150-mile) long curve of territory between the Pyrenees and the southern reaches of the Rhône: an amphitheatre between the Mediterranean and the foothills of the Cévennes. From north-east to south-west, a line drawn through Montpellier, Béziers, Narbonne and Perpignan traces the Mediterrancan littoral. Inland, Carcassonne guards the passage from Languedoc to the region of Tarn et Garonne; while north of Carcassonne and reaching to about Alès, north of Nîmes, the curve of the Montagne Noire more or less marks the northern limit of the vines of Bas Languedoc, the heartland of the region, and the start of the forests of Haut Languedoc.

Put another way, and going east to west, Languedoc embraces the departments of the Gard, Hérault and Aude, all of which can claim landscapes of very great attraction, no large towns with the exception of those cities of the coast already mentioned (a coast which in summer is hard to recommend to those who find it difficult to love mankind in the mass) and many villages of great character. Languedoc also includes the Cirque de Navacelles, the Gorges de l'Hérault near St Guilhem-le-Désert, the Pic de St Loup, the Grotte des Demoiselles and the Grotte de Clamouse, among a host of subterranean or other natural wonders and beauties. In the Canal du Midi it possesses, by contrast, one of the greatest achievements of civil engineering known to man.

Viticulturally, Languedoc's appellations are the well-known ones of Minervois, Corbières, Fitou and Blanquette de Limoux, the fairly well-known Faugères and St Chinian, and numerous others not yet familiar to international markets. It is hard to think of a shade or style of wine, from sweet and white to dry and deep red, that Languedoc does not produce.

---

*There is more red wine than white wine in the Minervois,*
*and much more sun than rain, and many more small proprietors*
*than large ones.*

---

# THE MINERVOIS

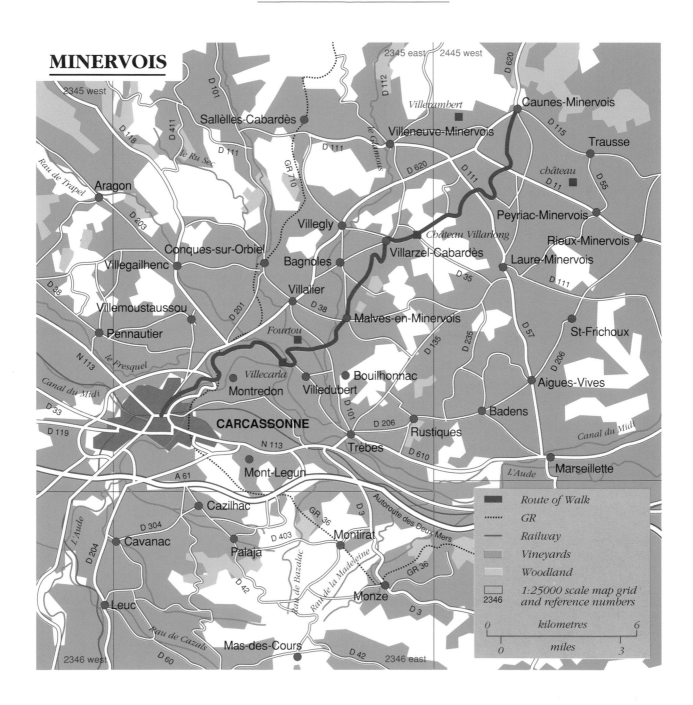

**MINERVOIS**

# BRIEFING

## THE LIE OF THE LAND

The heart of the Minervois is to be found within a quadrilateral formed by Carcassonne, Caunes–Minervois, Minerve and Canet (about halfway between Lézignan-Corbières and Narbonne). To the south are the Canal du Midi and the River Aude, and to the north are the foothills of the Montagne Noire, themselves roughly the southernmost reach of the Cévennes. Though seldom featureless, a large part of this country is more or less flat or only gently undulating. The highest of its few hills – Mont Ségonne, near Oupia, between Pouzols-Minervois and Olonzac – is no more than 293 metres (962 feet) above sea level.

The tamest, easiest parts for walking are closest to the Aude and the canal. Naturally, the closer one gets to the foothills of the Montagne Noire, the more hilly and broken the landscape, the deeper the gullies and ravines. In general, all ground too high and too poor even for the vine and the olive is left to a mostly Mediterranean type of growth. The higher one goes, the more one is likely to find oneself in *garrigue*, that thorny vegetation of rich variety and many definitions, which in spring can be very beautiful but which tends to be unforgiving to the careless or ill-equipped walker.

In general again, as the vines tend to yield better quality on higher ground than in the plain, most of the more interesting wine domaines and villages are to be found in the northern half of the quadrilateral. And naturally there are exceptions to this rule of thumb, such as Paraza.

## WALK

**Carcassonne to Caunes** About 24 kilometres/15 miles; allow 6–7 hours.

Exactly opposite Carcassonne station, a bridge over the Canal du Midi and steps down to the towpath give a point of departure. The towpath on the north bank of the canal is then followed wherever possible, but unless repairs have been carried out recently there is likely to be at least one unavoidable detour where the canal bank and path have been impassably eroded. At the Ecluse St Jean the path switches to the south bank and remains there all the way to la Mijane, a little more than 4 kilometres (2.5 miles). There, instead of crossing again to the north bank, as the author did, the map clearly suggests that it would be better to stay with the towpath for almost 2 kilometres (1.25 miles) more, as far as the Ecluse de l'Evêque, before crossing to the D 201, turning north-west along it for about 300 metres, then right along a track and so on to the Chemin des Romains.

The bridge over the Orbiel stream is reached after about a kilometre (just over half a mile) on the Chemin des Romains, then almost immediately take the D 101 at la Mée, and almost at once again the D 37, running north to Malves-en-Minervois. Under a kilometre north of Malves the D 735 forks north-eastwards off the D 37. Readers are advised not to leave the D 735 shortly after Malves, but to stay with it until about a kilometre south of Villarzel-Cabardès, where a track and a lane lead up to a cemetery and a Y-junction on the eastern edge of the village. Here the D 335 goes east and north towards Villeneuve-Minervois and the D 35 goes east.

A kilometre and a half (a mile) along the D 35 is the château of Villarlong and the start of tracks and paths which with very careful navigation ought to lead across to the D 111 at the site of excavations of a Gallo-Roman cemetery, then on across to the D 11 at the Château Rivière, from where tracks and minor roads lead into Caunes.

| Maps | | | | |
|---|---|---|---|---|
| 1:25,000 | 2345 est | Carcassonne | | |
| | 2445 ouest | Peyriac–Minervois | includes | |
| | | | Caunes- | |
| | | | Minervois | |
| | 2445 est | Lézignan–Corbières | includes | |
| | | | Minerve | |
| 1:50,000 | 2345 | Carcassonne | | |
| | 2445 | Lézignan–Corbières | | |
| 1:100,000 | 72 | Béziers–Perpignan | includes | |
| | | | Corbières | |

# CARCASSONNE, CAUNES AND THE CANAL DU MIDI

*The old city of Carcassonne, so extensively and controversially 'restored' by Viollet-le-Duc in the nineteenth century, is one of the prime attractions for visitors to southern France. Wines from the vineyards that grow close to its famous walls are classified as Vins de Pays – Coteaux de la Cité de Carcassonne.*

On the towpath of the Canal du Midi, 500 metres from the railway station and the neighbouring Pont Neuf in Carcassonne, puddles and soggy patches of ground obliged me to stop to change into the boots that I had not had time to put on before leaving the Hôtel Domaine d'Auriac. After breakfast, the *chef-patron* Bernard Rigaudis had unexpectedly offered me a lift for the five kilometres (three miles) into town. Hastily gathering my belongings, I had left the fine tuning until later. Besides the boots, this included buying bread in Carcassonne, but not wine, which I thought to acquire somewhere along my way to Caunes-Minervois. It was a miscalculation that I was to regret.

I had chosen to walk to Caunes because it was about halfway to the village of Minerve, my ultimate goal, and because Bernard Rigaudis had told me that I would like both the place and the Hôtel d'Alibert. Also, at some 19 kilometres (12 miles) in a straight line on the map, probably nearer 24 kilometres (15 miles) on the ground, it represented a sensible distance for a day's walk in unfamiliar territory. The towpath of the Canal du Midi was certainly the best way to start; afterwards I would simply keep as closely as practicable to the lines that I had ruled between Carcassonne, Caunes and Minerve on the 1:25,000 sheet. Soon after the puddles I came to a spot where the towpath had been eroded, so that I was obliged to take a track up into the trees and undergrowth, stepping over roots, ducking under brambles. Not until the Ecluse St Jean did I feel that I had got into my stride.

At the Domaine d'Auriac both the sky and the weather forecast had been unpromising, but now there were gleams of sun and patches of blue to be glimpsed through the overhanging plane trees. Blackbirds sang and doves cooed in competition with the traffic on the very busy road bordering the canal. Things were getting better by the minute. At the Ecluse du Fresquel the sun shone brilliantly and honeysuckle, gorse and a profusion of dog roses bloomed along the towpath. Approaching the Pont Rouge, nearly a kilometre (half a mile) further on, there were white daisies and blood-red poppies, tall cypresses lined the canal and I thought I heard nightingales. The road was further away now (it seldom hugs the canal quite so closely as in those first three kilometres, or two miles, out of Carcassonne), and I was able to admire a large area of well-tended vineyards, well ploughed and harrowed and free of weeds, with the vines not yet in full leaf.

Started in 1666, the year of the Great Fire of London, Pierre-Paul Riquet's Canal du Midi was the greatest civil engineering achievement since the end of the Roman Empire; *mutantis mutandis*, it is at least as impressive as the astounding Pont du Gard. In the 1660s France was at the height of its power. Colbert, Louis XIV's great Controller General of Finance, a

man of indefatigable purpose and ruthless resolve, was determined to increase that power yet further by every sort of expansion in the fields of industry, commerce and overseas trade. To further his designs, improvement
in the country's internal communications was vital. In seventeenth-century
Languedoc, where the hazards of dreadful roads were compounded by an
especially active brigandage, communications were appalling. To move
goods from one side of France to the other by land was thus both danger-
ous and tedious. To move them by sea through the Straits of Gibraltar and
around a hostile Spanish peninsula was hardly less so. When Riquet wrote
to Colbert in 1662, confidently outlining his scheme for what, if successful,
would be of inestimable benefit to the entire kingdom, his letter was therefore both timely and historic. Four years later, after a host of obstacles of
every conceivable kind had been surmounted, the digging of the canal
began.

By January 1667 two thousand labourers were at work. By mid-March
there were four thousand. A few years later their numbers had increased to
twelve thousand, of whom some six hundred were women, mostly moving
vast quantities of earth and stone in baskets balanced on their heads. A
great dam – an engineering marvel in itself – had to be raised at St Ferréol,
which in all its three hundred years of existence has never needed major re-
pair. Two hundred and forty kilometres (149 miles) of ditch were dug; 103
locks and scores of bridges were built; numerous tunnels and several
aqueducts had to be constructed; and to provide shade and consolidate the

*The Canal du Midi near
Marseillette, some 15 kilometres
from Carcassonne. On the
towpaths of the canal the walker
might travel almost 100
kilometres, from Carcassonne to
the Mediterranean near Béziers,
without losing sight of the vines.*

*A far view to the foothills of the Montagne Noire from near Peyriac-Minervois. The wines of the district may be Minervois AOC, or Vins de Pays des Coteaux de Peyriac. More than two hundred owners in the area belong to the local* cave coopérative.

*Marble from the quarries that are still called 'les Carrières du Roi Soleil', near Caunes-Minervois, was used in the building of the palace of Versailles and the Paris Opéra. Fragments of the same pink marble are to be seen in the outcroppings of 'schist' in which some of the vines of the nearby Château Villerambert grow.*

bank, 45,000 trees – originally elms, oaks and limes – were planted. On 16 May 1681 (just six months after the death of Riquet, who had exhausted himself both physically and financially with the project), the canal was ceremonially opened and a dream of centuries was realized. Walking along the canal towpath – with its dappled shade, its banks of yellow broom and irises, its tall umbrella pines and plane trees, its birdsong and cooling breezes – was a delight. Beside a footbridge made out of railway sleepers opposite the farm of la Mijane, a path led down to the ruins of a watermill under some huge plane trees. Massive pieces of finely dressed stone, like sections of a Roman pillar, lay mysteriously beside them.

At the ancient and imposing farm of la Mijane, swifts (or were they martins or swallows?) wheeled about the picturesque courtyard, but there was no other sign of life. I ought to have bought wine in Carcassonne, but had not only been eager to start walking, but also reluctant to buy supermarket wine when I hoped that more interesting, more romantic circumstances would present themselves. A few minutes more with the map would have shown me that there was no wine domaine that I was likely to reach before noon. A braver man than I might not hesitate at the prospect of interrupting a French family at table in order to ask for a single bottle from the cellars, and even a face at an open window at la Mijane might have emboldened me to the intrusion. As it was, hoping for once – but in vain – that a dog might bark and attract someone's attention, I carried on down the avenue of tall, spreading pines in the fear (fast developing into certainty) that on that perfect spring day in wine country I would have only water to drink with my *casse-croûte*.

At the end of the avenue were the D 620 and the Prade du Fraysse, a huge expanse of vines. A kilometre (just over half a mile) towards Villalier brought me to a junction with the D 201 and le Trapel, another wine domaine, I did not doubt, but at half past noon as seemingly lifeless and inaccessible as la Mijane. Now only a miracle could save me from a wineless picnic. Bitterly regretting my improvidence in Carcassonne, I went on along the D 201, looking for the track marked on the map variously as 'Chemin des Romains' and 'Voie Romaine Secondaire'. Then fortune smiled.

I had left the road in favour of what I believed to be the old Roman track, and was checking with the map and drinking from my water-bottle, when a *moto* appeared as if from nowhere and stopped beside me. The rider was wearing a white helmet, heavy-duty goggles, *bleus de travail* and green wellington boots. '*Vous cherchez quelquechose, Monsieur?*' he asked. No, I replied, not really: I was just making sure I was on the right road. '*Ici, c'est le Chemang des Romangs,*' he said in an accent of the south. '*Vous allez où?*'

'*À Caunes,*' I responded.

'*Caunes! Oh là là! C'est loin, vous savez.*' It was 13 or 14 kilometres (eight or nine miles) at most and I said well, it wasn't really so very far. '*Eh! Vous êtes courageux, Monsieur. Mais c'est assez compliqué, le chemang.*' Removing his helmet and taking his goggles off over his head, he revealed himself to be – I

*Marcel Julien is the fifth generation of the family to make wine at the Château Villerambert-Julien, a sixteenth-century Languedoc* bastide *near Caunes-Minervois. Some of the soil is* argilo-calcaire *(clay and limestone); some schist. The grapes are mostly Carignan, Syrah and Cinsault.*

judged – into his seventies. '*Eh bien! Vous continuez sur ce chemang jusqu'à la Mie, où vous tournez à droite, et puis toute de suite à gauche. Vous continuez . . .*'

There was no stopping him. Village by village – Malves, Bagnoles, Villégly, turning by turning, he charted what seemed to him the obvious course; a course that ended with some eight kilometres (five miles) on the almost dead-straight main road between Caunes and Carcassonne. I thanked him. There was a slightly awkward silence. Then – 'Warm weather!' he said, nodding at the neck of the bottle protruding from the side pocket of my pack. 'Thirsty work, walking.' I said that I would like to thank him for his kindness by offering him a drink, but unfortunately had only water. 'Only water! *Oh là là!*' So far he had stayed seated astride his *moto*, crash helmet and goggles hanging from the handlebars. Now he eased himself forward and off his bike, then turned to the pillion and the box with the leather strap. Out of this he took a bottle swaddled in newspaper and tied round with black baling twine fastened in a bow. Carefully closing the lid of the box, he held the wrapped bottle in one very brown old hand while he pulled at the string with the other, then unwound the newspaper wrappings to reveal an unlabelled litre bottle. The miracle had occurred.

He would accept nothing for it, and on the grounds that he had already eaten and was on his way to visit his sister in Trèbes, declined my suggestion that he take a glass with me there and then. He had been taking his sister a couple of bottles, but she didn't drink much, and there was plenty more where these came from. No; he wasn't himself a vigneron any longer. He used to have his own '*petit hectare*' of vines, but had sold them a few years ago to a neighbour, who now supplied as much wine as my benefactor needed. It was not '*grand' chose*', he said, but it wasn't bad either. It was made by the *coopérative* in Malves, which he used to belong to, as his '*voisang*' still did, so in a way it was still his own wine.

It may not have been *grand' chose*, but half an hour later, in the welcome shade of pines at the corner of a vineyard in the Fourtou domaine, I drank it with intense pleasure – a decent, honest wine, made with a predominance of the locally ubiquitous, high-yielding Carignan grape, together with Grenache, perhaps, and conceivably some Syrah. The last two were guesses on my part, and as likely wrong as right. It did not matter. What mattered was that the afternoon and the country were glorious, and I had a whole litre of what was truly *vin du pays* to go with my picnic. There were also the sun; the heavenly sound of a breeze in the pines; the chatter of cicadas and the song of the cuckoo; acacia in full blossom (unmistakably recognizable sometimes in the better wines of the Languedoc), hedge-roses and honeysuckle, daisies and poppies and wild thyme, with its pale mauve flowers and one of the most evocative of all scents; and there was the view down through the trees to the valley of the Orbiel stream and great vistas of vines and scattered villages and rocky *garrigue* rolling away to the harsh foothills and blue-grey, forested heights of the Montagne Noire.

The old Roman road took me down to a hump-backed bridge across the stream (a feeder to the Canal du Midi and a tributary of the Aude) where trees shaded the banks and a fisherman with a very long rod was casting into the improbably clear, fast-flowing water, not eight kilometres (five miles) from a city of fifty thousand inhabitants. A little further on, past the very venerable domaine of la Mée, with its avenue of noble plane trees and a lesser stream, the Clamoux, flowing down from Bagnoles past Malves, I was obliged to admit that for a while the only sensible way was indeed the one my benefactor on the *moto* had specified: the D 37 to Malves-en-Minervois, quiet enough, but hot, and the start of some eight kilometres (five miles) of steadily rising country.

In Malves I sat for a few minutes drinking mineral water on the edge of a horse trough opposite the very *coopérative* from which my picnic wine had come, before carrying on northwards out of the village to wider views of the vines and hills I had glimpsed through the pines an hour earlier.

At a junction nearly a kilometre (half a mile) out of Malves the D 735 forks right off the D 37 to reach Villarzel-Cabardès, to the north-east. Classified by the IGN maps as 'narrow and regularly maintained', these minor roads are inevitably less appealing to the walker than footpaths and other unmetalled tracks; few could be more agreeable, however, than the D 735 on a fine day in May. At first there were only vineyards and distant, lovely views. Then there were vineyards and outcroppings of the sandstone that at no great depth constitutes much of the basic structure of this land. In the grass of the verges, and at the edges of the vines, there were the ubiquitous white daisies and bright red poppies, great carpets of wild

*In the harsh limestone foothills of the Cévennes, at the confluence of the Cesse and the Briant streams, Minerve has given its name to the whole region whose wines are now so promising. Stronghold of the Cathars during the Albigensian crusade, Minerve surrendered to Simon de Montfort in 1210, whereupon some one hundred and forty of its defenders were burned at the stake.*

*In many progressive parts of the Minervois, old vineyards of the formerly ubiquitous Carignan grape are being replanted with more 'noble' varieties, such as Syrah.*

thyme in flower, and thickets of the startlingly yellow broom, with the added delight now of lovely tall pink orchids, like wild gladioli.

It really *was* hot now and I could feel that my face had caught the sun. Just beyond the hamlet of Villarzel water was running from a tall stand-pipe. *Potable*? I did not care to experiment, but put my head beneath the flow and felt greatly refreshed in the light breeze. By my very rough calculations I had some six kilometres (four miles) still to go to Caunes. It was already five-thirty, and although I had come only about 13 kilometres (eight miles) from Carcassonne there was no denying that I was a little tired. Three more kilometres uphill, then two less demanding ones but undulating and by sinuous tracks, meant hardly less than two more hours on the march, and my water-bottle was almost empty.

And now, having abandoned the road, I made trouble for myself by careless map-reading, and so found myself floundering about in prickly, knee-high vegetation and little gullies. It was half an hour before I knew exactly where I was, on a satisfactory path. In celebration I climbed up a few yards through juniper and thyme to a vantage point, and there drank my last drop of water and looked about me, both at the way I had come and the way ahead, and at the profusion of pink cistus in the *garrigue*, the mass of brilliant blue borage, and the clouds of butterflies. Rejoicing in the breeze, which was stronger now, I thought that I had never seen lovelier country, and that if it were true that '*le vin, c'est le terroir*', then indeed a good wine of the Minervois ought to be a delight.

Not twenty minutes later, thinking of a long, cool drink and a luxurious bath, I heard the unmistakable sound of a Citroën *deux-chevaux* approaching from behind, out of the *garrigue*. As it neared me I moved aside, but to my surprise it stopped. Turning, I saw a round, rosy face with a neat, almost white moustache and blue eyes topped by a peaked cap looking at me through the open off-side window. '*Bonsoir*,' I said.

'*Bonsoir. Vous faîtes une bonne promenade?*'

Very good, I said. '*C'est un pays magnifique.*'

'*Ah oui!*' he agreed. '*Ici*' (with a slight movement of head and eyes he indicated the *garrigue* that surrounded us) '*Ici c'est un peu sauvage, mais c'est beau quand même.*' Where had I come from, he asked. 'But that's a long way!' he exclaimed, 'And where are you going?'

'Caunes-Minervois,' I replied. Then – though I knew the answer – 'How far's that?'

'Oh, it's all of another four or five kilometres. Here – !' Reaching over, he pushed open the off-side door, then tipped the passenger seat forward for me to put my pack and stick on the back seat. '*Vous êtes bien équipé,*' he commented, nodding towards my boots and gaiters as I got in and closed the door. Yes, I said. It was necessary if one was going to walk '*sérieusement*'. And up here in the *garrigue*, I added, by way of accounting for what I well knew to be the odd-looking gaiters, there could be thistles and thorns and things that could be a nuisance if one's ankles and lower legs weren't protected; especially if (as I was) one happened to be wearing shorts.

By now we were moving again along the track. 'Bertrand,' he announced, as if, decent preliminaries accomplished, a start might be made with proper formalities. '*Vigneron*.' The hand he offered entirely suited my idea of what a vigneron's hand ought to be: dry and rather rough, with a grasp that was full and firm.

'Buxton,' I answered. '*Journaliste*.'

'*Ah! Journaliste! Et en vacances?*' Not really, I said; I was making a sort of '*reportage*' on the wine areas of Languedoc.

'*Et pour quel journal?*' asked Monsieur Bertrand. Well, not for any paper, really, I said; I was working on a book.

The French tend to distinguish severely between journalists and writers, to the disadvantage of the former. Ah, a writer! exclaimed Monsieur Bertrand with evident satisfaction. And what sort of things was I going to write about in the wine areas of Languedoc, Monsieur Bertrand wanted to know. Oh, all kinds of things, I said. It all depended on what I saw and what sort of people I came across. He digested the reply, then, 'Are you in a hurry to get to Caunes?' No, I said; not at all, as long as I got there before they stopped serving dinner. Good, he said. In that case I should come and drink a glass of wine with him. I must be thirsty.

In a short while we reached the hard-top road and turned towards Caunes, then, when the town itself was in sight, turned off again down a dirt road that wound through vines and higher, *garrigue*-covered ground, under a disused railway line, across a stream ('L'Argent-Double,' explained

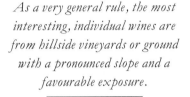

*As a very general rule, the most interesting, individual wines are from hillside vineyards or ground with a pronounced slope and a favourable exposure.*

Monsieur Bertrand) and through more vines until at last we reached an isolated huddle of stone buildings, occupying three sides of a dirt courtyard, which looked almost as though they had grown from the very earth itself. A small mongrel dog rushed up as we arrived and fawned on Monsieur Bertrand before turning its attention to me, then back to its master. In a kitchen that seemed dark after the sun, Monsieur Bertrand pulled a chair away from a table covered in blue oil-cloth and invited me to sit down. 'My wife's gone to Peyriac to see her mother. The old lady's eighty-three and not well. But sit down! Sit down. Or do you want to use the facilities?'

*A corner of Caunes-Minervois on the Argent-Double stream. The local* cave coopérative *is well reputed, and the Hôtel d'Alibert with its astonishing Renaissance architectural touches and its authentic cuisine du patron is a delight.*

When I returned there was an unlabelled, bordeaux-shaped bottle on the table and Monsieur Bertrand, still wearing his cap, was carefully slicing a piece of sausage. 'Sit down! Sit down!' Seating himself, he poured red wine into two squat tumblers, pushed one across the oil-cloth to me and raised the other in a gesture of greeting. '*A votre santé! Et bonne continuation de votre travail.*' The wine was a lovely ruby colour, cool, fruity and floral (I thought I caught the scent of acacia again).

'Delicious,' I said.

'Well I must say, it's not bad,' said my host. What grapes had gone into it, I asked.

'Carignan, Grenache, a little Cinsault.' An experiment in 1986, but a successful one, he thought, passing me the sausage. And the soil, I asked? Sandstone and schist (flaky rock), mostly, with some pockets of chalky clay, said Monsieur Bertrand. Not rich. Not well watered, either. The vines had to work to stay alive, which had a lot to do with the quality of the wine.

It was his only wine. Like the great majority of vignerons in Languedoc, Monsieur Bertrand takes all but a few of his grapes to the local *coopérative*. The few that he keeps are vinified by the most traditional of methods, to the extent of fermentation in a very old open vat and daily submerging of the 'cap' of solid matter that forms during the process, so as to keep it in contact with the juice. After fermentation, the wine spends a year or more in oak barrels ('I've only got four. They cost a lot.') before clarifying and bottling. Monsieur Bertrand supplies a brother who lives in Lyon, a married sister in Montpellier and a few friends with a few dozen bottles of his home brew, and he keeps the rest. 'It doesn't last long.'

He pressed me to take a bottle with me when I left. '*Allons!*' he said, 'I have business to attend to in Caunes this evening, so it's no trouble to get you to the d'Alibert in time to eat.'

'A pretty little town,' he commented proudly as we negotiated narrow streets to reach the hotel opposite the church and the *mairie*, 'and very interesting. You must visit the abbey.' I invited him to have a drink with me before going about his 'business', but he said no, another time.

Bernard Rigaudis had been right: the Hôtel d'Alibert was all that I might have hoped for and much more. I never did see the Benedictine abbey, for I started early next morning as soon as I had been to the *boulangerie*. And safely in my pack, well wrapped up so as to stay cool, was Monsieur Bertrand's wine.

# THE WINE

A few years ago I talked with a wine-maker near la Livinière, in the Haut Minervois. He was no ordinary wine-maker, and not a native of Languedoc. His father and grandfather had been in the wine business and he himself had created a highly successful wine marketing company before coming across the estate in the Minervois where he now spent most of his time. Languedoc, he believed, had enormous potential. It had the soil and the climate for producing wine every bit as good as any in Bordeaux; all it needed was the right grapes, the right technology, the know-how, of course, and the determination. He was employing all four, and with considerable success.

He gave me half a morning, showing me his vines and his cellars. Believe it or not, he told me, the two sides of the vineyard track we were standing on gave wines of different quality owing to a freak local condition which resulted in one side receiving more rainfall than the other. This rootstock, he said, was Carignan, the most traditional and most widely planted variety of grape in Languedoc. It gave quantity, but in his opinion not quality. The graft on it was Syrah, the 'noble' grape of Hermitage, in the Rhône valley. He liked Syrah very much and would give me a one hundred per cent Syrah wine to taste later. The new grafts were wrapped in a special plastic that came especially from California, where huge advances in wine technology had been made in the last decade or so. Such methods had to be

*Landscapes like this, looking south from the approaches to the Montagne Noire towards the Montagne d'Alaric, in the Corbières, are characteristic of the Minervois. They embrace many miles of paths easily followed with the aid of a 1:25,000 map. In April and May, when the* garrigue *on uncultivated ground is in flower, they are especially delightful.*

employed here in France.

And so on, in a fascinating flow of information and opinion. As well as Carignan and Syrah, he had Cinsault and Mourvèdre, which were permitted in an *appellation contrôlée* Minervois, and Cabernet Sauvignon and Merlot, which were not, but which he could use in a *vin de pays*. For white wines he had, among other things, Sauvignon, which he was experimenting with (we would taste a pure Sauvignon, oak-aged) and a small amount of Chardonnay, which was also the subject of current experiments. Neither is a traditional variety of the Midi. 'For Sainsbury's,' he remarked, as a large consignment of wine on a truck and trailer prepared to leave his yard.

It is a bold man who attempts to lay down any laws concerning the wines of the Minervois and its neighbours today. 'Almost exclusively reds', says a publication not five years old: not true when it was written and patently misleading now. There is much more red than white, and more white than rosé, but neither white nor rosé is a rarity. The best of the region's wines are probably still red, but experimentation and innovation are taking place all the time.

The emergence of estate-made and estate-bottled wines from individual wine-makers is both a cause and an effect of the great change that has occurred in the last two or three decades. Once, all but a very small part of the total grape production of the Midi went anywhere other than to *coopératives*, often to become grape spirit. Now, individual estate names are to be found in Harrods and Sainsbury's, and some of the *coopératives* are offering wines that are very good indeed.

Forget about '*le pays du gros rouge*'; welcome to '*la nouvelle Californie*'.

*Just south of Minerve, the village of Azillanet in the Haut Minervois looks out to the plain that reaches to Olonzac, the Canal du Midi and the River Aude.*

# CORBIÈRES

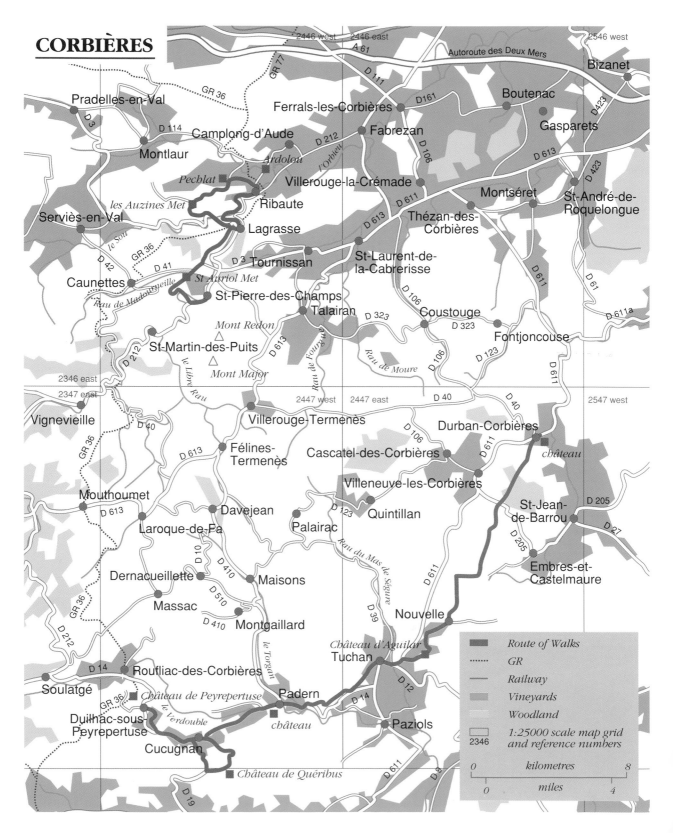

**CORBIÈRES**

2446 west | 2446 east | 2546 west
A 61
GR 77
Autoroute des Deux Mers
Bizanet
GR 36
D 111
Boutenac
Pradelles-en-Val
D 161
Gasparets
D 3
D 114
Camplong-d'Aude
D 212
Ferrals-les-Corbières
Fabrezan
D 423
Montlaur
l'Orbieu
D 106
D 613
Ardolou
Pechlat
Villerouge-la-Crémade
Montséret
St-André-de-Roquelongue
les Auzines Met
Ribaute
D 611
D 613
Serviès-en-Val
Lagrasse
Thézan-des-Corbières
D 611
le Sou
D 3
Tournissan
St-Laurent-de-la-Cabrerisse
D 61
GR 36
D 41
D 42
St Auriol Met
D 106
D 611a
Caunettes
Rau de Madourneille
St-Pierre-des-Champs
D 323
Coustouge
Fontjoncouse
Talairan
D 323
Mont Redon
D 613
D 106
D 123
D 611
St-Martin-des-Puits
Rau de Fours
D 212
Mont Major
le Libre Rau
Rau de Moure
2346 east
2347 east
2447 west | 2447 east
D 40
2547 west
Vignevieille
D 40
Villerouge-Termenès
D 106
Durban-Corbières
D 613
Félines-Termenès
château
GR 36
Cascatel-des-Corbières
D 611
Mouthoumet
Villeneuve-les-Corbières
D 205
D 613
Davejean
D 123
Quintillan
St-Jean-de-Barrou
Laroque-de-Fa
Palairac
D 611
D 27
D 10
D 205
Dernacueillette
D 410
Maisons
Rau du Mas de Ségure
Embres-et-Castelmaure
GR 36
D 510
Massac
D 410
Montgaillard
le Torgan
D 39
Nouvelle
D 212
Château d'Aguilar
D 14
Roufliac-des-Corbières
Tuchan
D 12
Soulatgé
GR 36
Château de Peyrepertuse
Padern
D 14
Paziols
Duilhac-sous-Peyrepertuse
le Verdouble
château
Cucugnan
D 611
Château de Quéribus
D 9
D 19

| | Route of Walks |
|---|---|
| | GR |
| | Railway |
| | Vineyards |
| | Woodland |
| 2346 | 1:25000 scale map grid and reference numbers |

0 _____ kilometres _____ 8
0 _____ miles _____ 4

# BRIEFING

## THE LIE OF THE LAND

Consider another imaginary quadrilateral, this time with its corners at Carcassonne, Narbonne, Salses (some 16 kilometres or 10 miles north of Perpignan) and Quillan (on the upper Aude). Within these boundaries lie the Corbières. Or imagine that, travelling southwards from the Massif Central and through the Minervois, you cross the Canal du Midi, the lower Aude (between Carcassonne and the Mediterranean) and the Autoroute des Deux Mers between Bordeaux and Narbonne, and continue towards the Pyrenees. South of the river and the *autoroute* you enter the least known, least populated and to many minds most beautiful wine country in the whole of France.

One revealing illustration of the nature of the region is to be found in any fairly detailed motoring map. Major roads are non-existent, secondary roads are few and far between, and almost all roads of whatever kind, surfaced or unpaved, are dauntingly sinuous. The all-important deduction to be made, especially by the would-be walker, is that there is precious little easy country in the Corbières far south of Lézignan-Corbières. It is all hills and valleys; all formidable, forbidding, harsh limestone heights; all ravines and gorges, not a few of them with clear-running streams in their depths. 'Spectacular, wild and mysterious', says an official tourist office brochure. So it is. There are castle ruins on improbable crags as at d'Aguilar, Quéribus, and Peyrepertuse; there are *garrigue*-covered uplands where goats roam over unmarked Moorish tombs and at evening it would be easy to suppose that one was alone in the world. There are picturesque villages with medieval backstreets, and watermills that were grinding grain at the time of Charlemagne. There are forests and meadows and some 25,000 hectares (61,775 acres) of vines.

The largest concentrations of vineyards are to be found occupying mostly the low ground of the valleys nearest the lower Aude, around the villages of Montlaur, Servis-en-Val, Fabrezan, Camplong, Tournissan, St Laurent, Ferrals, Thézan and Gasparets, among others; otherwise, vineyards tend to be widely distributed.

## WALKS

**Lagrasse to St Pierre-des-Champs, in the valley of the Orbieu, and back** About 12 kilometres/7.5 miles; allow 4 hours.

Take the bridge about 1.5 kilometres (1 mile) west of St Pierre to reach the north bank of the river; cross the high ground before descending to St Auriol, then continue to Lagrasse on the D 41 or tracks.

**Lagrasse to the Domaine de Pechlat, returning by Ribauté** Slightly longer than Lagrasse to St Pierre-des-Champs.

Take the D 3 west from Lagrasse and slightly north to a bridge over the stream, then west and north-east to the *métairie* or farm (*mét* on the map) of les Auzines, then north-east to Clamançou (*mét*) and Pechlat; from here head back south-eastwards to the Orbieu and Ribauté, then take a track east of the D 212, above the river, back to Lagrasse.

**Durban-Corbières to Tuchan on the Sentier Cathare** About 20 kilometres/12.5 miles; allow 6–7 hours.

Durban is the focal point of an important vine-growing area, but after about the first 2 kilometres (1.25 miles) of the walk the route seldom comes close to vineyards until some 4 kilometres (2.5 miles) before Tuchan – though small, astonishingly isolated ones are to be seen in unlikely places. Tuchan (Fitou) is the centre of another of the most important viticultural areas of the Corbières.

**Tuchan to Duilhac-sous-Peyrepertuse** by way of Padern, Cucugnan and the ruins of the Château of Quéribus. About 18 kilometres/11.25 miles; allow 7–8 hours.

Plenty of vines in the 7 or 8 kilometres (4.5 or 5 miles) between Tuchan and Padern, then the high road as taken in the narrative is looking down on the vineyards of the Cucugnan valley all the way to Duilhac. Cucugnan itself is virtually surrounded by vines. A visit to the ruins of Quéribus is not counted in the rough estimate of time.

| Maps | | | | |
|---|---|---|---|---|
| 1:25,000 | 2346 est | Cazilhac | | |
| | 2347 est | Arques | | |
| | 2347 ouest | Quillan | | |
| | 2348 est | St Paul-de-Fenouillet | includes south Galamus | |
| | 2446 ouest | Capendu | includes Lagrasse | |
| | 2446 est | Ferrals-les-Corbières | | |
| | 2447 est | Tuchan | Durban to Tuchan | |
| | 2447 ouest | Padern | beyond Tuchan to short of Galamus | |
| | 2546 est | Narbonne | Sentier Cathare to Quillan | |
| | 2546 ouest | Narbonne | | |
| 1:50,000 | 2446 | Capendu | includes Lagrasse | |
| 1:100,000 | 72 | Béziers to Perpignan | | |
| Guide | | *Le Sentier Cathare: de la Mer à Montségur* Editions Randonnées Pyrénéennes, C.I.M.E.S Pyrénées, BP 88, 09200 St Girons, France | | |
| Topo-Guide | 36 | | | |

# IN THE FOOTSTEPS OF PILGRIMS AND CATHARS

We began the walk in Padern, in the foothills of the Pyrenees north-west of Perpignan, not only because it was on the Sentier Cathare, but because we reckoned on its being able to supply our wants for a lunchtime picnic. It was not until I found myself outside the Café de la Paix that I remembered having been there before – which was odd, as the occasion had been memorable enough. I had spent the night in Tuchan, the next village to the north-east, where they had installed me as a member of the Mesnie des Chevaliers de Fitou, one of those jolly brotherhoods in which viticultural France abounds. Next morning, after a tasting at the admirable *cave coopérative*, and feeling generally over-wined and over-dined as a result of the events of the previous twenty-four hours, I had thought that the best corrective might be to walk the 16 kilometres (10 miles) or so from the nearby Château d'Aguilar, a ruin of considerable historical interest and romantic beauty, to the village of Cucugnan, which, apart from its associations with Alphonse Daudet and Occitan literature, was also said to be a pretty place in a remarkably beautiful setting. Moreover, I had been told that close to the village I would find the Domaine du Révérend, whose wines of fast-growing reputation I was eager to taste.

It was a delightful walk, at first through the vines, then some hundreds of feet above the valley of the Verdouble stream. At noon, having time to spare, I thought that instead of continuing by the route into Padern recommended by the Sentier Cathare, I would cross to the south side of the ravine, take a track up through the vines and picnic somewhere high above them. The morning's walk had dispelled the fog of the previous day's over-indulgences, the sky was blue, and the thought of a glass or two of Fitou d'Aguilar from Tuchan with lunch, followed perhaps by a siesta in the shade of an evergreen oak, proved a spur to the steepish climb that now followed.

I found my oak, and a view, and greatly enjoyed the wine, and lunched happily, and put insect repellent on ankles and elsewhere, and slept. An hour later I was woken by a clap of thunder. Lightning flashed in a sky now half as dark as night. At a jog trot I hurried back the way I had come, not so much seeking shelter from the coming storm as not wanting to let it catch me on the high ground. The sky grew darker. The thunder drew closer. Leaving the broad path for a track that dropped more steeply towards the ravine, I scrambled on down towards the Verdouble, reaching a bridge and the road as the heavens opened in tropical abandon, lightning turned early night into terrifying day, and great thunder claps slammed from wall to wall of the canyon, searching for me where I cowered in an illusion of shelter provided by an overhang.

Later, legs and feet sodden and no taxi being available in Padern, I had

*The River Orbieu rises in the Pyrenees and flows through the western Corbières to join the River Aude near Narbonne. Les Vignerons du Val d'Orbieu is one of the largest, most progressive wine businesses in Languedoc.*

*Few vineyards in the world are more romantically situated than those of Aguilar, near Tuchan in the Fitou country of the high Corbières. Guarding both the frontier with Spain and the approaches to Carcassonne, the twelfth-century château is a feature of the Sentier Cathare: hard walking country, but very rewarding.*

*Stony paths such as this, approaching the wine centre of Lagrasse in the valley of the Orbieu, are hard on the footwear and muscles of the walker in the Corbiéres. In the warm sun the air is scented with the pines and the shrubs of the* garrigue.

sat in that same Café de la Paix, drinking coffee and cognac while waiting for a rescuer to come from Tuchan. On the way back I saw that the Verdouble stream had become a torrent. But it was October, and the grapes were safely fermenting in the vats.

Now, on a July morning three years later, we climbed steeply up through the alleys and little passageways of Padern, between the houses and on up to the ruins of the castle and to the view and the path that we hoped would take us to Quéribus, Cucugnan and Duilhac-sous-Peyrepertuse. Some 13 kilometres (eight miles) on the map, it should take 4 hours 45 minutes according to the guidebook, not counting stops and deviations. One and a half hours from Padern we had reached the ruins of an ancient priory 489 metres (1605 feet) above sea level, with distant views (mentioned by the guidebook) and a clear, fast-flowing, deliciously cold spring (unaccountably not). We drank from the spring and replaced the already tepid contents of our bottles with cold water before toiling on up towards the ruin of the château of Quéribus on its pinnacle of rock at 729 metres (2600 feet) of altitude.

*Towards* Quéribus, but not *to* it: the sun was at its zenith, and an hour and a half after leaving the spring and some three hours in all from Padern, mostly uphill, we were hot again, thirsty again, hungry, and more than content to settle for a picnic with a view a few hundreds of feet inferior to that offered by the vertiginous ruin on the skyline above.

We found our ideal place where a few hardy evergreen oaks shaded a rare more or less level patch of earth made private by smooth boulders and outcroppings of rock. The view, though it might not have surveyed the plain of Roussillon and the Mediterranean as Quéribus does, nevertheless richly rewarded our so-far-moderate exertions. Steeply below was Cucugnan, fortress-like on its hill, commanding the vineyard valley eastwards down and back to Padern and westwards gently up to the Col du Tribi and Duilhac-sous-Peyrepertuse. Beyond the village, and stretching for 50 kilometres (30 miles) to the valley of the Aude, were the wild heights of the very heart of the Corbières: fold upon fold, ridge upon ridge fading into a blue haze of summer. And five kilometres (three miles) to our left, beyond Duilhac and 406 metres (2650 feet) up in the cloudless sky, we could just make out the ruins of Peyrepertuse, one of the great bastions of the medieval marches with Spain, and later a desperate refuge of the Albigensian heretics. Barely distinguishable from the towering wall of the rock itself, it amply deserved the name bestowed by one writer on these Cathar strongholds: *citadelles du vertige*.

We did not go down into Cucugnan. Keeping to the high ground at the southern limit of the vines for as long as possible, we descended at last to the valley road, then rejoined the prescribed route to the little village of Duilhac and the three-kilometre (two-mile) serpentine climb to Peyrepertuse. 'Worth every ounce of the effort,' we declared to one another, as from the gaping windows and wind-buffeted battlements of this most awe-inspiring fortress we contemplated some of the loveliest landscapes in

France. 'Worth walking any distance for,' we agreed, later, drinking very cold beer on the terrace of the Auberge du Vieux Moulin in Duilhac.

Later, as an evening breeze choreographed the long, slim branches of a willow in a slow dance above our heads, we drank a Corbières Blanc from Tuchan as an aperitif and marvelled at the stamina of a party of French walkers, women and men, who with formidably large rucksacks had come all the gruelling nine- or ten-hour way from Aguilar and were now off to pitch camp for the night. They would make the '*hors itinéraire*' excursion up to Peyrepertuse before continuing to Bugarach next day, they remarked casually. Bugarach – as we, and they, knew – is a nine-or ten-hour haul from Duilhac as even the moderately-laden walker goes.

Once beyond the northern end of the Gorges de Galamus, the walker is committed to all the additional 15 kilometres (nine miles) to Bugarach or nothing. Our own plans, therefore, were limited to a mere three and a half hours to the gorges, to be followed by an hour down into the valley and a night at St Paul-de-Fenouillet. Strictly speaking, by continuing thus on the GR 36 and the coincident Sentier Cathare, we would be leaving the wine-country of the Hautes Corbières behind us, Rouffiac-des-Corbières, less than three kilometres (two miles) from Duilhac, marking its extreme south-western limit. But the book said that the 11 kilometres (seven miles) of mountain path between Duilhac and the gorges represented '*certainement le parcours le plus pittoresque*' of the entire route: a recommendation that we could not resist.

The noisy departure of other walkers woke us next morning. Having followed our noses to the *boulangerie* soon after it opened, shopped more enthusiastically than sensibly at the village store, and filled our water-bottles at the shaded, cold, and bounteous spring (which used to supply the mill-race) hard by the *auberge*, we took the Peyrepertuse road again, before leaving it soon afterwards for the high *garrigue* under a morning sun that was hot on our backs long before noon.

*At Lagrasse, on the borders of les Corbières Centrales and les Corbières d'Alaric, the stone bridge spanning the River Orbieu closest to the fourteenth abbey was built two centuries earlier. Charlemagne is said to have named the valley for its richness; one of the meanings of grasse is 'luxuriant'.*

*There is precious little easy country in the Corbières. Vineyards tend to be widely separated by hills and valleys where path-finding may not be easy and careful map-reading is essential.*

On our left for some distance was the awesome, 243-metre (800-foot) deep ravine of the Riben stream. Soon we were standing at an altitude of 660 metres (2166 feet) on a wide, grassy plateau where the ruins of a *bergerie*, a familiar feature on the hills, stood as testament to the once-vital, centuries-old tradition of sheep-grazing in the high Corbières. We admired the views over Peyrepertuse and the eastern Corbières, and a little later, from the Col de Corbasse (419 metres or 1375 feet), the Pyrenees. And as well as these far prospects of mountains there were also the sun, and air as clear as one supposes it was in Eden, and the hot summer scents of the *garrigue* (box, juniper, wild thyme), and the god-given breeze. For once, 'on top of the world' seemed a permissible description of our feelings. 'Breathtaking', we said; 'glorious'; 'unbelievable', before falling silent as stout Cortez.

For a while we sat there on a rocky bench, just looking; then we drank a glass of Réserve du Révérend rosé from Cucugnan, kept cold in an insulated bag, and with a hyperbole bred of circumstance pronounced the agreeable wine 'sensational'.

'Un havre de fraîcheur' was the guidebook's description of the Sentier Cathare to the Gorges de Galamus: a haven of coolness. So it is, or so it was for us that noon in late July as we came to the end of an unavoidable mile uphill on the glaring D 7 under a tyrant sun. St John the Divine's image of the 'pure river of water of life, clear as crystal' could be interpreted quite literally here. Surely the medieval pilgrims on their arduous journey to Santiago de Compostela must have paused here to drink?

Deep down between the limestone cliffs, in the course it had cut for itself over time unimaginable, the Agly tumbled, cascaded, flowed smoothly and voluptuously from pool to limpid turquoise pool, bordered here and there by willows and pink oleanders under an empyrean sky. Descending somewhat perilously (as it seemed to me) to a beach of clean gravel, we dumped our rucksacks, eagerly rid ourselves of clothes and jumped, dived or ventured tentatively into the cold water. For us at that moment, no pool was ever better or more enchantingly situated, or cleaner, or conceivably more exhilarating. We explored a little up and down the gorge, climbing over water-worn slabs of grey rock, romping in other pools. 'Glorious!' we said again. 'Unbelievable!' we repeated. We dried in the sun and lunched there at the water's edge. Long before the sun set we were in shadow, but the rocks were storage heaters and there was no hurry to pack up and leave.

That evening, sitting with a jug of rosé in the *auberge* in St Paul-de-Fenouillet waiting for our first course to arrive, we read the guidebook's description of the Sentier Cathare from Galamus to Bugarach: 'the massif of the Hautes Corbières ... vast, semi-desert plateaus of great beauty ... hard climate. ...' How had the French fared that blazing day on the unshaded trail? No doubt they would have taken in their stride the 1230-metre (4000-foot) Pic de Bugarach and the view which according to the book embraced '*des horizons illimités*', but they could hardly have had time for the rock pools at the Agly, so we envied them not at all.

# THE WINE

A lot of what has been said about the wines of the Minervois is equally applicable to its neighbour on the other side of the Autoroute des Deux Mers. The vineyards of the Corbières are among the first whose origins we can be certain about, according to Hugh Johnson: they were planted by the Romans, and after the Romans came the monks. From such good beginnings the region had by the middle of the present century declined to the obscurity in which the Minervois also languished. Now quality, not quantity is the watchword. Notably poor-quality, high-yield vineyards in the least favourable locations have been grubbed up, and new plantings are to be seen on higher slopes that satisfy all theoretical conditions for the growing of excellent grapes, the prime requirement of excellent wine.

Already preoccupied with excellence, the Corbières area is now, like the Minervois, without doubt one of the most promising and interesting wine-growing regions of France; it has great character, huge variety and steadily improving quality. And as with the Minervois, most of the best Corbières are red, but there are good whites and better than passable rosés. That said, it is hard to think of a worthwhile generalization about the wine of the Corbières that can be considered entirely safe from revision a few years hence.

*Most of the grapes from the many thousands of hectares of vines grown in the plains of Languedoc are vinified by coopératives.*

# WALKING INFORMATION

It is much easier than it used to be to go for a casual walk in France. Encouraged by local pride, fashion or tourism, communities are increasingly making special provision for walkers. This most usually and usefully consists of identifying itineraries of varying distances, marking them with signposts or waymarks, and through tourist and other information offices – not infrequently at the *mairie* – providing some sort of documentation which in theory at least enables the visitor to do without conventional maps. Hotels and other places of accommodation almost always know of the existence of such marked paths and are often able to supply the supporting literature. *Balader* is a key word in this context. *Une balade* in French is a stroll or a ramble, but is used of more purposeful walking too. Increasingly also, walking tours of 'wine country' are being organized on a modest commercial basis by local individuals, some of them wine-makers. I predict a very significant growth in these sorts of enterprises as competition in the wine business obliges small proprietors to maximize exploitation of all their resources and larger organizations to seek new promotional devices.

In keeping with this whole recreational trend, many a 'Comité Départemental de la Randonnée Pédestre' is often to be found under the same roof as the Comité Départemental du Tourisme. Certainly the departmental tourist offices know the best authoritative sources of local walking information, including outdoor clubs of various kinds.

But when all is said and done, it may not be necessary to look much further than the local Syndicat d'Initiative: every town and many a village has one and as a general rule they live up to their name.

## REGIONAL TOURIST OFFICES

Tourism in France is organized by region, department and commune, in descending order of territorial and bureaucratic responsibility. For example, Provence as a whole is the responsibility of the Comité Régional de Tourisme Provence-Alpes-Côte d'Azur in Marseille; tourism in the Var comes under the Comité Départemental du Tourisme du Var in Draguignan; and the promotion of tourism in Grasse is a matter for the Office de Tourisme de Grasse, in Grasse itself. Each is more or less autonomous.

Generally speaking, the visitor seeking information about any particular wine district need look no further than the departmental organization, and very possibly no further than the Syndicat d'Initiative or Office de Tourisme. There follows a list of the departmental offices, together with those local tourist offices whose details were available as this book went to print. In theory at least, all departmental tourist offices are equipped to answer telephone enquiries in several languages, including English. When telephoning provincial France from the United Kingdom, dial 010–33, followed by the eight-digit number. For Paris, preface the eight-digit number with a 1.

### Alsace

Office Départemental du Tourisme du Bas-Rhin
Maison du Tourisme
9, rue du Dôme – BP 53
67061 Strasbourg Cedex
Tel. 88 22 01 02

Office de Tourisme
Palais des Congrès
Tel. 88 37 67 68

Association Départementale du Tourisme du Haut-Rhin
Hôtel du Département
68006 Colmar
Tel. 89 23 21 11;
89 22 68 00

Office de Tourisme
4, rue d'Unterlinden
Tel. 89 41 02 29

### Champagne

Office de Tourisme
2, rue Guillaume de Machault
51100 Reims
Tel. 26 47 25 69

Comité Départemental du Tourisme de la Marne
2 *bis*, boulevard Vaubécourt
51000 Chalons-sur-Marne
Tel. 26 68 37 52

Comité Départemental du Tourisme de l'Aube
Hôtel du Département –
BP 394
Quai du Comte Henri
10026 Troyes Cedex
Tel. 25 42 50 50

Office de Tourisme
16 Boulevard Carnot
Tel. 25 73 00 36

### Burgundy

Comité Départemental du Tourisme de l'Yonne
1/2, quai de la République
89000 Auxerre
Tel. 86 52 26 27

Comité Départemental du Tourisme de la Côte d'Or
Hôtel du Département –
BP 1601
21035 Dijon Cedex
Tel. 80 63 66 00

Office de Tourisme
Place d'Arcy
Tel. 80 43 42 12

Saône et Loire Tourisme
Maison de la Saône-et-Loire
389, avenue de Lattre-de-Tassigny
71000 Mâcon
Tel. 85 38 27 92

### Loire

Comité Départemental du Tourisme du Cher
10, rue de la Chappe
18000 Bourges
Tel. 48 65 31 01

Office de Tourisme
21, rue Victor Hugo
Tel. 48 24 75 33

Comité Départemental du Tourisme du Loiret
3, rue de la Bretonnerie
45000 Orléans
Tel. 38 54 83 83

Office de Tourisme
Place Albert 1er
Tel. 38 53 05 95

Comité Départemental du Tourisme de Loir-et-Cher
41, place du Château
41000 Blois
Tel. 54 78 55 50

Office de Tourisme
3, avenue Jean-Laigret
Tel. 54 74 06 49

Comité Départemental du Tourisme d'Indre-et-Loire
9, rue Buffon
37032 Tours Cedex
Tel. 47 31 47 12

Office de Tourisme
Boulevard Heurteloup
Tel. 47 05 58 08

Comité Départemental du Tourisme d'Anjou
Place Kennedy – BP 2147
49021 Angers
Tel. 41 88 23 85

Office de Tourisme
Place de la Bilange
49400 Saumur
Tel. 41 51 03 06

Comité Départemental du
Tourisme de Loire-
Atlantique
Maison du Tourisme
Place du Commerce
44000 Nantes
Tel. 40 89 50 77

Office de Tourisme
Place du Commerce
Tel. 40 47 04 51

**Bordeaux**

Comité Départemental du
Tourisme de la Gironde
21, cours de l'Intendance
33000 Bordeaux
Tel. 56 52 61 40

Office de Tourisme
12, cours du 30 Juillet
Tel. 56 44 28 41

Comité Départemental du
Tourisme de la Dordogne
16, rue Wilson
24000 Périgueux
Tel. 53 53 44 35

Mission Départementale de
Développement Touristique
22 *ter*, rue Jean-Jacques de
Monaix
64000 Pau
Tel. 59 30 01 30

**Savoy**

Association Départementale
du Tourisme de la Savoie
24, boulevard de la Colonne
73000 Chambéry
Tel. 79 85 12 45

**Rhône**

Comité Départemental du
Tourisme du Rhône
146, rue Pierre-Corneille
69426 Lyon Cedex 03
Tel. 72 61 78 90

Comité Départemental du
Tourisme de la Drôme
1, avenue de Romans
26000 Valence
Tel. 75 43 27 12

Chambre Départemental de
Tourisme – Vaucluse
Place Campana – BP 147
84008 Avignon
Tel. 90 86 43 42

Office de Tourisme
41, cours Jean-Jaurès
Tel. 90 82 65 11

Comité Départemental du
Tourisme de l'Ardèche
4, cours du Palais – BP 221
07002 Privas
Tel. 75 64 04 66

**Provence**

Comité Départemental du
Tourisme des Bouches-du-
Rhône
6, rue de jeune Anacharsis
13001 Marseille
Tel. 91 54 92 66

Comité Départemental du
Tourisme du Var
Conseil Général du Var
1, bd Foch – BP 99
83007 Draguignan Cedex
Tel. 94 68 58 33

Comité Départemental du
Tourisme du Var-Provence
5, avenue Vauban
83000 Toulon
Tel. 94 09 00 69

Office de Tourisme
8, avenue Colbert
Tel. 94 22 08 22

Office de Tourisme
avenue Thiers
06000 Nice
Tel. 93 87 07 07

**Languedoc**

Comité Départemental du
Tourisme du Gard
3, place des Arènes –
BP 122
30011 Nimes Cedex
Tel. 66 21 02 51

Office de Tourisme
6, rue Auguste
Tel. 66 67 29 11

Comité Départemental du
Tourisme de l'Hérault
Maison du Tourisme
Avenue des Moulins –
BP 3067
34034 Montpellier Cedex 1
Tel. 67 84 71 70

Comité Départemental du
Tourisme de l'Aude
39, bd Barbès – BP 862

11000 Carcassonne
Tel. 68 71 30 09

Office de Tourisme
15, boulevard Camille
Pelletan
Tel. 68 25 07 04

Comité Départemental du
Tourisme des Pyrénées-
Roussillon
Quai de Lattre-de-Tassigny –
BP 540
66005 Perpignan Cedex
Tel. 68 34 29 94

Office Municipal du
Tourisme
Place Armand Lanoux
Palais des Congrès
Tel. 68 66 30 30

**Paris**

Office du Tourisme et des
Congrès
127, Champs-Elysées
75008 Paris
Tel. 47 23 61 72

# MAPS AND MAP-READING

As stated at the beginning of the book, the directions accompanying suggestions for specific walks almost all derive from use of the 1:25,000 maps of the IGN. Let no would-be walker allow himself or herself to be persuaded that such maps may lightly be dispensed with (outside of local systems of paths that are unmistakably marked and signed); or that a good motoring map, or any other map of a scale smaller than 1:50,000, plus common sense, will do the job just as well. They will not, and attempts to prove otherwise are bound sooner or later to run into difficulties, or worse. Not a few walkers, myself included, have been in situations when the lack of an adequate map, or the inability to make use of it, could very easily have proved fatal.

The 1:50,000 scale is mentioned only because maps of that scale, though in the process of being taken out of publication by the IGN, are still obtainable in France. Whether the appropriate 1:50,000 IGN sheets are available or not, however, walkers are far better advised to obtain maps of the larger, 1:25,000 scale, and to learn how to use them. I am not suggesting that this should necessarily entail anything more advanced than simple direction-finding by visual observations, and in particular the simple identification on the ground of mapped paths of one sort or another. But in unfamiliar country even so basic a use can be more difficult than the novice might suppose. A more advanced use involves map-reading, that is the interpretation of the various devices and conventional signs used by the cartographer to convey on the printed map the actual physical nature of the ground: whether it is high or low; abruptly or gently rising or falling; normally firm or normally marshy; wooded or open; whether a slope is steep or precipitous, and so on and so forth. To the person who is fully capable of interpreting it, a 1:25,000 IGN map may reveal more than even an oblique aerial photograph.

Clearly, there are degrees of competence in map-reading, and it is not suggested that walkers in French wine country need to have the capabilities of an infantry patrol leader; nevertheless anything that they can do to increase their proficiency in the use of a map is certain to be worthwhile. *Follow the Map*, by John G. Wilson, published by A. & C. Black in association with the Ordinance Survey at £6.99 and available at Stanfords, is a good basic introduction to the subject.

To readers who, whether theoretically prepared or not, are unpractised in the use of the 1:25,000 map, I offer two pieces of very elementary advice born of hard experience. First, it is very easy in poor light, or in a hurry, or through giving way to wishful thinking, to mistake boundary lines of one sort or another on the map for minor footpaths and tracks. Second, it is a great handicap not to have a good idea of what measurements on the map represent in terms of actual distance on the ground. A worthwhile exercise, therefore, is to compare the map with a known distance. One might, for example, take two points not more than a kilometre apart and identifiable with certainty on the map, then pace out the distance between them on the ground.

## Books about walking

*Le Sentier Cathare: de la mer à Montségur.* Editions Randonnées Pyrénéennes, Comité des Randonnées de l'Aude, 115 francs. The story of the Cathars – the Pure Ones – and the Albigensian movement, which took its name from Albi, near Toulouse, reached its climax with the burning of some two hundred believers – men, women and children – at Montségur, near Carcassonne, in 1247. It is a story as colourful, as heroic and as terrible as any in all history. Its most impressive memorials are the ruined strongholds of Quéribus and Peyrepertuse in the Corbières, which feature in our walk in the Corbières, and Montségur itself.

This admirable book is organized partly on the lines of a *Topo-Guide* and includes sectionalized 1:50,000 maps; but it is also a brief account of the Cathars and a guide to the ruined castles of the region. Also deeply rewarding for its prose and its photographs is *Citadelles du Vertige* by Michel Roquebert and Christian Soula, published in 1987 by Editions Privat, 14, rue des Arts, 31068 Toulouse Cedex, 158 francs. Good bookshops in the Languedoc may have copies.

Rob Hunter, *Walking in France*, Oxford Illustrated Press 1982, revised edition 1986; £7.95. Wine country is only incidental to this work dealing with all France, but the book contains a lot of well presented, useful information about the author's favourite subject.

Adam Nicolson, *Long Walks in France*, Weidenfeld and Nicolson 1983. Eight long walks in France, including the Loire, Burgundy and Provence.

## GR paths and *Topo-Guides*

France is highly organized for walkers. The Fédération Française de Randonnée Pédestre (FFPR), an arm of the Comité National des Sentiers de Grande Randonnée (CNSGR) has established a country-wide network of long-distance paths (Grandes Randonnées or GRs), documented in a large collection of *Topo-Guides*. With the exception of a few that have been translated into English and published by Robertson McCarta, the *Topo-Guides* are available in French only. Each covers a substantial section of a path, some of which are very long, and represents several days of walking. Each includes appropriate extracts from the IGN 1:50,000 topographical maps, overprinted with the GR route, for which a detailed description is provided. There are also notes about tourist sights, possibilities of accommodation and refreshment, shopping for supplies, and so on. The special IGN map number 903 shows the whole network of GR routes, with their numbers, and thus serves as a catalogue for the *Topo-Guides*.

## Obtaining maps and *Topo-Guides* in Britain

**Stanfords 12–14 Long Acre, London WC2E 9LP**
**Tel. 071–836 1321; Fax 071–836 0189**
Stanfords is an institution held in high regard by travellers of

all kinds. Maps and guides are their speciality and there is no better source for either. It is not simply that their stock of material is large and maintained as comprehensive and up-to-date as possible; they understand their customers' needs and are prepared to go to sometimes embarrassingly conscientious efforts to satisfy them. No less important is their ability to advise upon other sources of information and material. A visit to the shop is a pleasure in its own right and many a journey of high adventure has started there.

The brief notes below concern material especially relevant to *Walking in Wine Country*. Other than *Topo-Guides*, no guidebooks are mentioned, but the availability of publications such as the Michelin green guides and many others may be taken for granted. Maps of France and *Topo-Guides* are the subject of special, remarkably extensive regional lists which are obtainable from Long Acre on request.

The following is taken from Stanfords' information sheets: General mapping – road atlases and road maps of the whole of France, specialist maps including physical and administrative wall maps, historical maps, wine maps, and raised relief maps.
Regional Lists:
1  North-west including Brittany, Normandy, the Loire valley and the Ile de France (excluding Paris and its suburbs).
2  North-east including the Jura, the Vosges and Burgundy.
3  South-west including the Atlantic Coast and the Dordogne.
4  Massif Central including the Auvergne, the Cévennes and Languedoc.
5  South-east including the Alps, Provence and the Riviera.
6  Pyrennes including the Spanish side.
7  Corsica
8  Paris including the town plans and touring maps of the area around the city.

IGN Blue Series: official 1:25,000 survey, £4.95 per half sheet
The largest-scale topographic survey maps published by the Institut Géographique National, the French national survey organization, in a new series begun in 1976. The contour interval is 5 metres, except in mountainous areas, where the maps have hill shading and contours at 10 metre intervals. Each map published in the Blue Series covers an area of 20 × 14 km (12.5 × 8.75 miles).

Didier Richard Series (1:50,000), £7.95 per map
A series of special tourist maps based on the 1:50,000 IGN topographic survey, overprinted with footpaths, including GR routes, ski routes, refuge huts and shelters. Each map is designed to show a popular tourist area, such as a national park, on one sheet. The Didier Richard maps are valuable primarily for their combination of topographic and tourist detail, rather than as conventional road maps. Each sheet covers approximately 60 × 50 km (37.5 × 31.25 miles).

IGN Green Series (1:100,000), £3.95 per map
This is a fully contoured topographical series, with an overprint showing long distance footpaths (GR routes). The maps cover a substantial area per sheet, approximately 90 × 110 km (56.25 × 62.5 miles).

Long Distance Footpaths: map and *Topo-Guides*
The entire network of the GR routes is shown on a special IGN map, no. 903: Long Distance Footpaths (1:100,000), price £3.95
A selection of *Topo-Guides* is held in stock, but the complete list is a very long one, so ordering in advance is likely to be necessary.

*Vignobles de Bourgogne en Côte-d'Or* (Provicart/Wine Maps),
1:35,700, size: 158.5 cm × 60 cm, (62.5 × 23.5 inches), £10.50
(flat)
Very detailed, contoured map of two of the major wine-
producing areas of Burgundy: 'Côte and Hautes-Côtes-de-
Beaune' and 'Côte and Hautes-Côtes-de-Nuits', extending from
Dijon through Beaune to Cheilly-lès-Maranges. An attractively
coloured map, illustrating the types of wines produced in each
specific area. Additional information panels list the major wine-
growing villages of this region.

*Vignobles de Bourgogne (Yonne) Chablis (Provicart)*, size:
99 cm × 88 cm (39 × 34.5 inches), £10.50 (flat)
A very attractive contoured map covering the Auxerre, Chablis
and Tonnerre area in great detail. The map indicates the
vineyards and the type and qualities of wines produced in each
one. Inserts give details of some of the Grands Crus.

*Beaujolais* (IGN), 1:100,000, £2.95
Folded map, with an extract from the IGN Green Series as a
base, showing the Beaujolais wine-growing areas (east of the
A6 motorway between Mâcon and Villefranche-sur-Saône). An
extensive overprint shows the GR routes and local footpaths
through the vineyards, camp sites, etc. *Coopératives* selling wine
or providing wine tasting facilities are also indicated.

*Bordeaux* (Provicart/Wine Maps), 1:256,000, size: 60 cm × 83 cm
(23.5 × 32.5 inches), £10.50 (flat)
Highly coloured map illustrating the principal wine-producing
areas of the Bordeaux, possibly the most prestigious of all wine-
growing regions. The map shows the different types of vines
grown in each area, with separate lists of the official
classifications of the great wines of Bordeaux.

## Obtaining maps abroad

IGN maps are very well distributed. *Librairies* – booksellers
and stationers, including the ubiquitous Maisons de la Presse –
almost invariably stock them. Where there is no *librairie* or
Maison de la Presse they are often found in *tabacs*. They are not
cheap – probably 35 to 40 francs per map – but to forego them
because of price could be a false economy.

In Paris, IGN has a shop at 107, rue la Boétie, 75008. Tel. (1)
42 25 87 90. This is on the north side of the Champs-Elysées,
not far from the Rond Point. Franklin Roosevelt and St
Philippe-du-Roule are the nearest Métro stations. Like
Stanfords in London, this is an Aladdin's cave for the serious
walker and map-lover. Apart from IGN maps, *Topo-Guides* and
other internationally well-known publications, many other
French books about walking in France are to be found here,
though I have not yet discovered any especially concerned with
the wine regions.

# EQUIPMENT

In addition to proper maps, the prudent walker will not go far
afield without a compass: not for taking bearings and
transferring them to the map, though the ability to do so can be
valuable, but simply for checks on general direction. In a
'white-out' in the Highlands of Scotland a compass once saved
me from a likely death by exposure. In the high Corbières, or in
one of France's great forests, a compass could save one from
hours of wasted time and effort, if not from something more
serious. The Silva 3NL, at £10, is admirable for basic direction-
finding. For more advanced work with compass and map, the

Silva type 4, at about £19, is to be recommended. Its mirror can
be handy for shaving or make-up. Most good camping shops,
including the Survival Shop, stock Silva.

As well as being more than vexed to leave base without a
compass when setting out for a serious walk, I would also be
irritated to find that I had forgotten to bring my powerful little
field glasses: twenty-year-old, much-prized Leica Trinovid,
though there are cheaper alternatives. These are useful for
verifying topographical and other detail as the need arises, as it
often does. If, for example, I would like to cross a stream at a
point I can discern some way ahead, but which is too far away
for me to have a good idea as to whether it ought to be
negotiable or not, with the binoculars I may be able to find out.
Or if, the map indicates 'ruins' on the edge of a wood on my
line of march, and I think the wood in question is the one that I
can see about half a mile away on the other side of a large
spread of vines, then the ruins ought to be visible. If a search
with the binoculars reveals them, I can continue with
confidence on what I had feared might be the wrong path.
There have been times when those field glasses have been
worth their weight in gold.

A few years ago, having tired of the inevitable and expensive
damage to my cameras if I kept them in a place where they were
easily accessible when I was walking, and of the inconvenience
if they were safely stowed, I sought and found the answer in the
shape of specially padded, Velcro-fastening carrying cases with
various kinds of quick-release straps and harness to match:
expensive, but a godsend. They come from Camera
Care Systems, Vale Lane, Headminster, Bristol B93 5RU;
tel. 0272 638362.

I also earnestly recommend a rucksack with good, balanced
side-pockets large enough to accommodate at least one well-
wrapped bottle apiece. The well-equipped walker's pocket
knife has a corkscrew among its other gadgets, naturally.

With the exception of the camera cases, virtually all my
equipment, including rucksack, camping gear and compasses (I
have broken two through misfortune allied to misuse) has been
obtained over the years at the Survival Shop, 11, Western
Colonnade, Euston Station, London NW1 2DY, tel. 071 388
8353. Headquarters are at Morland, Penrith, Cumbria CA10
3AZ; tel. 09314 444. Visits to this emporium of outdoor
clothing and equipment are no less inspiring and exciting than
visits to Stanfords. As at Stanfords, the staff of the Survival
Shop tend to know what they are talking about.

# CLOTHING

I doubt if readers require telling what to wear when they go
walking, so I shall confine myself here to a few special points.
Footwear: though some people, especially the young, seem
quite capable of scaling Everest or trekking to the South Pole
in trainers, I persist in advocating boots for serious walking.
Lightweight boots are perfectly adequate, and infinitely
preferable to shoes as they give support and protection to the
ankles, are less likely to admit foreign bodies such as stones,
usually have a deeper tread on the soles, and provide better
protection from wet. Somebody once told me that wearing a
thin pair of cotton socks inside thick woollen ones was a good
way of guarding against blisters, and it seems to be true.
Comical or not, gaiters are very useful indeed if one is walking
in rain or more than ankle-high vegetation, such as *garrigue*,
when shorts are inadvisable.

A piece of clothing I have come to regard as indispensable is
the 'bush vest' or 'safari vest', made of cotton, sleeveless, and

equipped with many pockets, several of which close with zips. Such a garment functions for me as a sort of extension of my rucksack, but with the contents (money, personal papers and credit cards, compass, Swiss Army knife, little Minox camera, film, light filters, miniature tape recorder, spare batteries, lip salve and so on) all conveniently accessible. I am also fond of my long, hooded, lightweight but weatherproof over-jacket, made of Gore-Tex with velcro and high-quality plastic zip fastenings.

My own safari vests have come from Travelling Light at Morland, Penrith, Cumbria (tel. 0931 714488) and have cost about £50.00. The firm also offers a 'Photo-Vest', intended not only for photographers, of more elaborate design and with no fewer than eight pockets, at about £75.

# WINE INFORMATION

Every significant wine region in France has its Comité Interprofessionnel, a promotional as well as regulatory body. Some, such as those of Burgundy and Bordeaux, are at least as well organized and as competent as the tourist authorities of the region, and complement their work with promotional initiatives of many kinds and by providing information in various forms. Ideally, the two work hand in hand. All are able to supply literature on request, some of it of excellent quality and much of it multi-lingual. This literature invariably includes directories of wine-makers accessible to the public, including indications as to hours of business and whether or not appointments are necessary, plus telephone numbers. A list of the appropriate organizations follows.

The Comités Interprofessionnels are not usually open to callers in person, but will respond to postal enquiries, and more often than not to sensible telephone ones. (They cannot, for example, be expected to give opinions as to the merits or otherwise of particular wine-makers.) Their information services are often accessible through 'Maisons des Vins' in the wine districts. Local Syndicats d'Initiative can nearly always advise where and how to get the sort of wine information needed for any particular purpose.

## COMITÉS INTERPROFESSIONNELS DES VINS

### Alsace
Comité Interprofessionnel des Vins d'Alsace
12 avenue de la Foire aux Vins – BP 1217
68012 Colmar Cedex
Tel. 89 41 06 21;
Fax 89 24 09 45

### Champagne
Comité Interprofessionnel du Vin de Champagne
5 rue Henri Martin – BP 115
51204 Epernay Cedex
Tel. 26 54 47 20;
Fax 26 55 19 39

### Burgundy
Bureau Interprofessionnel des Vins de Bourgogne
12 boulevard Bretonnière – BP 157
21200 Beaune
Tel. 80 24 70 20;
Fax 80 24 69 36

Délégation Régionale Chablis du B.I.V.B.
Le Petit Pontigny – BP 31
89800 Chablis
Tel. 86 42 42 22;
Fax 86 42 80 16

Délégation Régionale Beaune du B.I.V.B.
Rue Henri Dunant – BP 150
21204 Beaune Cedex
Tel. 80 22 21 35;
Fax 80 24 15 29

La Maison des Hautes-Côtes
Marey-les-Fussey
21700 Nuits-St Georges
Tel. 80 62 91 29

La Maison des Vins de la Côte Chalonnaise
Promenade Ste-Marie
71100 Chalon-sur-Saône
Tel. 85 41 64 00

Comité Interprofessionnel des Vins de Bourgogne et du Mâconnais
389, avenue Mal-de-Lattre-de-Tassigny
71000 Mâcon
Tel. 85 38 20 15

### Beaujolais
Union Interprofessionnelle des Vins du Beaujolais
210 boulevard Vermoril
69400 Villefranche-sur-Saône
Tel. 74 65 45 55;
Fax 74 60 02 32

Commission de Promotion des Vins de Pouilly
1, rue de Paris
58150 Pouilly-sur-Loire
Tel. 86 39 00 34

### The Loire
Comité Interprofessionnel des Vins de Touraine
19 Square Prosper Mérimée
37000 Tours
Tel. 47 05 40 01;
Fax 47 66 57 32

Comité Interprofessionnel des Vins d'Anjou et de Saumur
Hôtel Godeline
73 rue Plantagenet – BP 2327
49023 Angers Cedex 02
Tel. 41 87 62 57;
Fax 41 86 71 84

Maison du Vin de l'Anjou
5 bis Place Kennedy
49000 Angers
Tel. 41 88 81 13

Comité Interprofessionnel des Vins de Nantes
Maison des Vines
Bellevue
44690 La Haye Fouassière
Tel. 40 36 90 10;
Fax 40 36 95 87

### Bordeaux
Conseil Interprofessionnel du Vin de Bordeaux
1 Cours du xxx Juillet
33000 Bordeaux
Tel. 56 00 22 66;
Fax 56 00 22 82

### Médoc
Counseil des Vins du Médoc
1 Cours du xxx Juillet
33000 Bordeaux
Tel. 56 48 18 62;
Fax 56 79 11 05

### Savoy
Comité Interprofessionnel des Vins de Savoie
3 rue du Château
73000 Chambéry
Tel. 79 33 44 16

### The Rhône
Comité Interprofessionnel des Vins d'AOC Côtes du Rhône et de la Vallée du Rhône
Maison des Vins
6 rue des Trois Faucins
84000 Avignon
Tel. 90 27 24 00;
Fax 90 27 24 13

### Provence
Comité Interprofessionnel des Vins des Côtes de Provence
Maison des Vins
RN 7
83460 Les Arcs-sur-Argers
Tel. 94 73 33 38;
Fax 94 47 50 37

Coopérative des Vins de Bandol
Cave du Moulin de la Roque
83740 La Cadière d'Azur
Tel. 94 90 10 39

### Fitou – Corbières – Minervois
Conseil Interprofessionnel des Vins de Fitou, Corbières et Minervois
RN 113
11200 Lézignan-Corbières
Tel. 68 27 03 64;
Fax 68 27 31 66

## VISITING WINE-MAKERS

More grapes are grown by people who do not make their own wine than by people who do. Instead of vinifying his – or her – own crop, a grower may sell it to a wine-maker, or send it to a *coopérative*. Not all wine-makers market their own wines: many sell their products to someone else to use in several possible ways.

For those many thousands of vignerons – or vigneronnes – who do market their own products, direct sales at the wine-making property can be a vital part of their whole business; in many instances – though the makeshift quality of many a *vente directe* sign at the roadside might seem to belie the fact – such sales are the most significant of all.

So it is not a good idea to visit an individual wine domaine (as opposed to a *cave* where there are dozens of different wines on sale) without any intention of buying at least a bottle or two: wine-makers tend to enjoy what they do, but their time is usually precious. On the other hand, genuine interest and enthusiasm on the visitor's part can be an effective counterbalance to a trivial purchase.

Skill in wine-tasting need hardly concern the more or less casual visitor to a wine cellar. Usually there are at most two or three wines on offer and the question is simply whether one likes them or not. Of course, the more the visitor knows and the more skilled he or she is at tasting, the greater will be the opportunity to talk about the wine being offered and to gain the interest of the vendor. If the sampling of one or two wines and the buying of a bottle is all that the visit involves, language does not usually present much difficulty, even with the most unsophisticated of wine-makers. Beyond that, especially in the case of many small concerns, an inability to speak and to understand French can be limiting.

Lists of wine domaines that welcome visitors are seldom hard to find in the wine regions: the various wine-makers' organizations and local tourist information offices see to that. Most hotels in wine districts have such lists, too, and they are usually happy to give advice and make suggestions. Asked nicely, they may also be more than willing to telephone a wine-maker to ask about the convenience or otherwise of a possible visit. Nowadays, most of the firms whose labels represent household names, especially in the Bordeaux region (Margaux, Lafite, Mouton Rothschild and the like), are obliged to receive visitors by appointment only.

## THE FRENCH WINE CATEGORIES

The relationship between quality and quantity in French wine production is perhaps best expressed by a pyramid-shaped diagram:

Apellation d'Origine Contrôlé — A.O.C.

Vins délimités de Qualité supérieure — V.D.O.S

Vins De Pays

vins de table / table wines

V.Q.P.R.D.*

VINS DE TABLE TABLE WINES

*according to the E.E.C. regulation

## HARVEST TIMES

As a general rule, the grape harvest begins a hundred days after the flowering of the vines, which naturally tends to be earlier in the south of the country than in the north, but of course there are considerable variations from region to region and from year to year. In the Mediterranean areas, picking has been known to start at the end of August; in Alsace it can still be happening in November, though most of the crop will have been gathered by the end of October. Mid-September to mid-October is probably the period in which most of the *vendanges* in France normally take place. The regional wine committees ought to be able to forecast the date for their own areas to within a few days of accuracy a week or two in advance.

# STAYING IN WINE COUNTRY

For the walker in wine country, romantic fancy must surely envisage staying overnight in the perfect hotel or *chambre d'hôte*, in the prettiest of villages or the most hospitable of farmhouses among the vineyards; but how to translate fancy into reality? The most comprehensive attempt at relating of hotels (but only hotels) to wine country that I know of is in the 'Travel Information' section of the admirable Johnson and Duijker *Wine Atlas of France* (see wine books list). The entries are valuable, but they are inevitably vulnerable to dating.

The truth is that, short of a reliable, personal recommendation by word of mouth, there is no magic method of locating the ideal place to stay: it is a matter of studying the published sources of information about accommodation in conjunction with information about wine country itself. Below are some of the sources known to me. Every region of France also produces more or less excellent, comprehensive and free literature on accommodation, and the first place to seek it is the French Government Tourist Office, 178 Piccadilly, London W1V 9BD; tel. 071-499 6911 (recorded messages) or 071-491 7622. The best way to make use of this, in my view, is in conjunction with the guides listed below.

**Camping** can have much to recommend it and is by no means confined to those who do it for reasons of economy. 'Bed in the bush' in the Robert Louis Stevenson style – camping wild among the vineyards – is not to be encouraged, but in all regions there are camp sites close to or not far from the vineyards. Some of the municipal ones (I recall Fleurie in the Beaujolais and Rochecorbon, near Tours) are excellent, especially out of high season – Easter, holiday weekends in high summer and harvest time. Michelin publish an excellent annual guide to camping and caravanning in France, costing between £7 and £8 and available from good booksellers, including Stanfords. The French Government Tourist Office also supplies a publication called *The Camping Traveller in France*. All French regional tourist literature features camping, as does information produced by the motoring organizations. Camping is big business, and in France it is as highly developed as anywhere in the world.

**Chambres d'hôtes** and **gîtes** (respectively, bed and breakfast and self-catering accommodation of various kinds) may sometimes represent the best way of staying as close as possible to the vineyards; they are increasing in number and a few are even offered by the vignerons themselves. Again, information is available from regional tourist literature, the

Logis/Gîtes de France organization, and other sources known to the French Government Tourist Office.

The French organization Gîtes de France publishes an annual directory. The full guide to all properties, *gîtes* and *chambres d'hôtes* in France costs between £12 and £13, including postage, or it may be obtained by personal callers at the French Government Tourist Office. The telephone number of Gîtes de France is 071–493 3480. A guide to a much smaller selection of properties is available free.

**Hotels** close to the vineyards are another story: they may be fairly common in one wine region, but not in another. While they are not uncommon in the villages of Alsace and on the Côte d'Or in Burgundy, for example, they are comparatively and curiously hard to find in the Médoc amd elsewhere in the wine region of the Gironde (Bordeaux). Even wine towns, as opposed to mere villages, are often less well equipped with hotels than one might suppose.

Some of the best possibilities are represented by the **Logis de France**, an association consisting of more than 5,000 hotels and *auberges* of varying degrees of modesty and quality, some disappointing, the great majority very acceptable, and some very good indeed. For instance, the Hôtellerie du Val d'Or in Mercurey, Côte Chalonnaise, a few minutes walk from the vines, has the highest Logis rating, a 'comfortable' rating in the Michelin red guide, and a single Michelin star for its food. Almost exactly the same description fits the Hostellerie des Clos in Chablis. The Relais Fleurie at Pouilly-sur-Loire, near Sancerre, in Pouilly-Fumé country, temporarily lacks only the Michelin star. Again, at la Croix-Blanche, near Cluny in the Mâconnais, the Relais du Mâconnais has Logis '2-chimney' rating and a 'quite comfortable' rating in Michelin, with a good table. Chez Jeannette in Fixin, at the northern end of the Côte de Nuits in Burgundy, comes into much the same class. The full annual guide costs about £10, also by post or from the French Government Tourist Office.

### Michelin France:

The famous red guide to hotels and restaurants is an institution in its own right, and in my view is still incomparably the most useful general guide to accommodation, wining and dining in France. Its town plans alone can be invaluable. The guide is usually available in Britain at about the end of March and costs between £12 and £13.

### Relais & Châteaux:

The Relais & Châteaux association of hotels and restaurants is now also something of an institution. The annual guide lists some 150 hotels throughout France, ranging from the very comfortable to the opulently luxurious. Some are admirably located in wine country and are outstanding sources of information and introductions to wine producers. The Château de Rochegude, in the Rhône Valley near Orange, for example, has as its director André Chabert, who has an encyclopaedic knowledge of wines of the Rhône, and also has a Michelin star for its food. The Hôtel Royal Champagne at Champillon, owned by Moët et Chandon, is also exceptional, as are the Relais de Margaux (what a name for claret country!) some 26 kilometres (16 miles) from Bordeaux in the Médoc, and the Château de Marçay, near Tours in the Loire, virtually surrounded by its vines. Near Carcassonne, Bernard Rigaudis, the *chef-patron* of the Michelin-starred Domaine d'Auriac, is passionately fond of the wines of the Corbières and probably knows everything about them worth knowing. He is also a living *Who's Who* for those parts.

The substantial annual guide is available free to personal callers from the Relais & Châteaux office at 7, Cork Street, London W1X 1PB; tel. 071–491 2516, or from the French Government Tourist office, or at a cost of £4.00 by post.

### Château Accueil:

A well established association of privately owned properties offering a considerable range of accommodation, from nineteenth-century small and snug but elegant, to huge and inclined-to-be-draughty seventeenth-century with parkland to match. Some of them are either in or close to wine country. The guide costs 30 francs for postage and is available from Pyrène Voyage, 5, rue de Metz, 31000 Toulouse, France; tel. 62 15 02 90.

### La Vie de Château:

Similar to Château Accueil, very well organized, and able to handle reservations in France: tel. 48 58 42 73; fax 48 58 42 09. Perhaps a dozen of the members of this association of decidedly superior properties (one of which is the Château de la Verrerie mentioned in the chapter about Sancerre) are either in wine country or very conveniently placed for country walkers. The well illustrated guide is a pleasure in its own right, evoking as it does the supreme richness of rural France. At a cursory glance I have noted likely addresses in the Loire valley, the Beaujolais, the heart of the Médoc (where hotels are few) and Languedoc. Just as good hotels can give extremely useful advice regarding wine producers in their localities, so the resident owners of these often enchanting private properties can provide the walker in wine country with invaluable intelligence, both about the wine and about the countryside itself.

### Châteaux-Hotels Indépendants et Hostelleries de l'Atmosphère:

At Morey-St Denis, near Dijon, the Pinot Noir vines grow to the very garden walls of the Castel de Très Girard, a former eighteenth-century manor with 15 guest rooms, six of which have four-poster beds. At Condrieu, near Vienne in the Rhône valley, the Viognier vines of the Côte Rôtie are a stone's throw from the famed riverside Hôtel Beau Rivage, which now has one Michelin star for its table. At Peyriac-Minervois, in Languedoc, the Château de Violet is itself a wine-making domaine where I once started a walk. And in inimitable Aix-en-Provence the Hôtel Villa Gallici and the Restaurant Clos de la Violette (one Michelin star) are a joint property of high distinction where I recently lunched wondrously after a walk the day before in the appellation of Coteaux d'Aix. All are among the more than 200 members of the association, whose guide may be obtained from 15 rue Malbranche, 75005 Paris; tel. (1) 43 54 74 99, in return for a Eurocheque for 25 francs or an ordinary cheque for £2.50.

### Loisirs Accueil and Accueil de France:

Most departments in France have set up officially-backed booking services under the name Loisirs Accueil. As the name implies, their function is to make bookings not only for all forms of accommodation, but also for 'activity' holidays of all kinds, a list of which should be available from the French Government Tourist Office in London. Additionally, a number of cities and large towns have hotel booking offices under the name of Accueil de France, available to personal callers seeking bookings for the same day or up to eight days in advance. Information can be obtained from the organization's headquarters in Paris, tel. (1) 47 23 61 72.

## The French Government Tourist Office

A great deal of literature and information on all aspects of tourism in France is available here, though it is strongly advisable to make enquiries in person, rather than by telephone if possible. 178 Piccadilly, London W1V 0AL; tel. 071 491 7622.

# BOOKS ABOUT WINE

The more one knows about wine, the greater the pleasures one derives from it, so that good books about wine seem to me to represent a wise investment. In labouring the point that *Walking in Wine Country* itself has no pretensions to being yet another wine book, and in offering at some length the following selection of titles, I am motivated by what seem to me the dangers and undesirability of so-called 'useful' summaries of subjects that do not lend themselves to simplification. Wine is a subject about which many of us are glad, if not eager, to learn all we can: hence the proliferation of consumer wine columns in newspapers and magazines; but hence also our vulnerability to misleading information from what might appear to be authoritative sources. Myths or half-truths such as 'Beaujolais is a wine to be drunk cool and young', or absurdities such as 'champagne does not improve with age' (both statements to be found in a best-selling guide to France) can gravely impair enjoyment, if nothing worse. Imagine presenting a good friend with a Duboeuf-bottled Morgon (a 'keeping' *cru* of the Beaujolais) from an excellent but very recent vintage, then having him draw the cork there and then before putting the wine in an ice-bucket for a salad lunch on the patio.

Here, then, are suggestions for a few books about wine, written in English and with the overall accent on France, though several of the works listed embrace the subject of wines in general. I have included only titles which are reported to be currently in print and available (the great majority), or which, though out of print, may still occasionally appear in bookshops. There are, of course, many works which are not mentioned here, some of them classics of their subjects, which are to be found in libraries. A notably extensive bibliography is a feature of Hugh Johnson's *The Story of Wine*.

In one or two of the regional selections (the Languedoc is an obvious example) there may be few if any alternatives. Where I know of no monograph on a particular region, or none that I would recommend, I have referred to what seems to me the most convenient source of information. My choice does not imply any disparagement whatever of other titles that may be available. It is possible that I am simply unaware of their existence.

## WINE IN GENERAL

Hugh Johnson, *The Story of Wine*, Mitchell Beazley 1989; £25.00
With scrupulous honesty, the author disclaims any pretensions to being a historian: 'That is why I have called this book *The Story of Wine*: it is my interpretation of its history, my attempt to place it in the context of its times, and to deduce why it is that we have the vast variety of wines that we do – and why we don't have others.' Nevertheless, aided by Helen Bettinson, a Cambridge historian, a history of wine is what Hugh Johnson has produced, and a fascinating and thoroughly readable one at that.

Though *The Story of Wine* knows no national boundaries, far more space is devoted to Europe in one way or another than to any other part of the world, and the wines of France feature more prominently than those of any other country. What emerges clearly from the whole story is France's supremacy in the making of quality wines; a supremacy that has been challenged but never yet surpassed. In France today, says Johnson, quantity is rapidly giving way to quality. In supermarkets 'anonymous *vin ordinaire* is steadily being replaced by *vins de pays*; wines of local character from specific, if obscure, grapes and regions – some of them, perhaps, the Appellations of the future'.

Johnson concludes with a message which I hope *Walking in Wine Country* may reinforce: 'No critic should forget, as he dallies with epithets, ... that wine is one of the miracles of nature, and that its 10,000 years of partnership with man has not removed that element of mystery. ... Farmer and artist, drudge and dreamer, hedonist and masochist, alchemist and accountant – the wine-grower is all these things, and has been since the Flood.'

Hugh Johnson, *Wine*, Mitchell Beazley, first published 1966, new edition 1992; £14.99
Essentially, this is the book first published in 1966 which launched the author's prodigiously successful career as the world's leading writer about wine. A revised edition was published in 1974 and the 1992 edition includes updated vintage charts.

So why is Hugh Johnson's *Wine* still worth reading? Because although much has changed in the world of wine, much abides, and Johnson writes about it in a particularly lucid and readable way. The principles of wine-making are the same as they have always been, and Johnson explains them to us. The places where wine has traditionally been made have not altered fundamentally, and we are given informative, sometimes evocative introductions to them. Not least, the pleasures of wine, far from diminishing, may be greater today than ever they were by reason of the huge increase in variety that has occurred with the development of wine-making in the New World. Certainly, far more people are able to appreciate wine today than was the case in 1966. The pleasure that Hugh Johnson himself derives from wine comes through on almost every page of his work, and is infectious. The book is worth having for that alone.

Jancis Robinson, *Vines, Grapes and Wines*, Mitchell Beazley 1986, reprinted 1987; £14.99
The title sounds rather academic, but while the contents might certainly be called scholarly they do not even begin to be dry. This is partly because the author – a Master of Wine – writes without a trace of pomposity or ponderousness, and partly because the more one knows about vines and grape varieties in particular, the more one also learns about wine in general.

Take champagne: as we know, conventional champagne is made from three grape varieties, Pinot Noir, Chardonnay and Pinot Meunier, the last being the least 'noble' of the three. Yet surprisingly, says Jancis Robinson, about 50% of all vineyards in the heartland of Champagne are planted with Pinot Meunier, with the other two varieties accounting respectively for only about 24% and 26%. Why? The explanation, according to the book, is that Pinot Meunier, though a lowly variety of grape by comparison with Pinot Noir, is far easier to grow. Its comparative invulnerability to spring frosts, for example, is the reason why it is the only grape planted in the low-lying areas of the Vallée de la Marne, while the much harder to grow Pinot

Noir occupies the higher slopes there and on the Montagne de Reims, where it has the best chance of escaping frost and enjoying sun. Thus if ever we had any doubts as to the crucial importance to wine of the *terroir* (which includes the local climate), this book will dispel them.

Or again, knowing more about a particular grape variety may significantly enhance one's appreciation of a particular wine-maker's capabilities. The Silvaner (as Jancis Robinson spells it), lacking in particular the 'nose' of – say – Riesling or Sauvignon Blanc, commands scant respect anywhere. But I remember with delight the Silvaner made by Domaine Weinbach (Colette Faller) of Kaysersberg in Alsace, and note with pleasure that Jancis Robinson cites it as an example of what can be done with the lowly grape. Such things are surely part of the whole fascination of wine.

Keen amateurs of any particular subject are always ready to convince themselves that an especially good book about it is 'indispensable'. Jancis Robinson's study can hardly be said to be essential to a good general knowledge and understanding of the wines of France, but anyone aiming to assemble a wine library that will be comprehensive and compact ought to be sure to include it.

# FRENCH WINES IN GENERAL

Rosemary George, *French Country Wines*, Faber and Faber 1990; £8.99
A fair description of the subject matter of *French Country Wines* might be 'all those wines and wine areas of France about which you may know little or of which you may never have heard'. It is no good looking for Beaujolais in the extensive index and hoping to find the subject dealt with in detail in the main text, for example, as it is mentioned only in reference to other wines. Neither Sancerre nor Muscadet is mentioned at all. Saussignac, a sweet wine from near Bergerac, is listed, however, as is Serrière, a village in the appellation of Chautagne, Savoy. Again, Chablis receives only an incidental mention, whereas the treatment of la Clape, a wine district near Narbonne, runs to five pages.

*French Country Wines* runs to 395 pages and includes a number of good maps. The author says the research took two years, but I would not have been surprised if it had taken twice as long. Many a worthwhile wine that other equally admirable works acknowledge only in passing, or not at all, is described and discussed in detail here. Without doubt, some such wines will one day be as familiar to us as Beaujolais Nouveau, which twenty or thirty years ago was not known far beyond the bistros of France itself.

Hugh Johnson and Hubrecht Duijker, *The Wine Atlas of France and Traveller's Guide to the Vineyards*, Mitchell Beazley 1987, revised and reprinted 1988; £17.95
This is a work that delivers more than the title might suggest. Certainly, the excellent maps are a major feature. They are of two kinds: wine maps and touring maps. The former enable the reader to locate not only the territories of all the important French wine appellations and many lesser ones, but also in some instances individual vineyards. The touring maps assume that the mode of travel is by car.

But the maps are incidental to a text which might almost justly claim to be 'all you need to know about the wines of France'. In addition to descriptions of the various viticultural regions and their wines, there are notes about 'Producers of

special interest', together with selected guidebook information under the heading of 'Places of interest' and 'Travel information'. This includes suggestions about hotels and restaurants, which considering the changes that may occur in the space of a year or two ought probably to be treated with circumspection.

Robert Joseph, consultant editor Joanna Simon, *The White Wines of France*, Salamander Books 1987; £8.95
A comprehensive, well-presented, very well illustrated, explicit, factual treatment of the subject by a well-known wine journalist and author with a consultant editor of similar credentials.

*The Red Wines of France* by Margaret Rand (£9.95) is a companion volume with much the same general virtues, but perhaps conveying not quite the authority of the other, and rather less well written.

Alexis Lichine, in collaboration with Samuel Perkins, *A Guide to the Wines and Vineyards of France*, Alfred A. Knopf, New York, revised edition 1984; Papermac 1986; £9.95
The late Alexis Lichine was at once wine merchant, vineyard owner and wine-maker. This revised edition of his work is a very companionable volume which I have often found to contain useful and interesting facts and observations lacking in many other works. It is far better than the majority of wine books at conveying the topographical character of the wine regions, for example, and much better informed about the wine trade as it affects the ordinary *amateur* (in the French sense) of wine.

The book has plenty of good maps and the usual sort of chapters on tasting, food and wine, vintages and so on: altogether, a work worth having on one's shelves no matter what other titles may be there already.

P. Morton Shand, *A Book of French Wines*, Jonathan Cape 1928, revised and edited by Cyril Ray, Penguin 1964
A classic of wine literature.

Steven Spurrier, *Guide to French Wines*, Mitchell Beazley 1991; £14.99
Steven Spurrier spent a number of years in the wine trade and is now an eminent wine consultant and wine writer. Especially knowledgeable about France, he founded a wine shop and school in Paris.

Most of his *Guide to French Wines* consists of a gazetteer of the main wine-producing regions, with introductory sections in each case dealing with climate, soil and vinification. All the main appellations – AC, VDQS, Vin de Pays – are then listed with appropriate details. If asked what Steven Spurrier's book offers as a general guide to French wines that the admirable Johnson-Duijker *Wine Atlas* does not do, I would say that it gives significantly more information about the wine regions, the wines themselves and the producers, and that much of it is more up-to-date. The Spurrier guide has far fewer maps and illustrations than the *Wine Atlas*, but what there are are very good. On the other hand, certain of Spurrier's subsidiary sections, such as 'How to Buy Wines' and 'How to Read a Wine Label', are useful additions. Though there is inevitably a certain amount of duplication of information between the two, it seems reasonable to regard Spurrier as a very useful complement to the *Wine Atlas*.

Roger Voss, *Guide to the Wines of the Loire, Alsace, the Rhône and other French Regional Wines*, Mitchell Beazley 1992; £7.99

This is Roger Voss's original pocket guide, revised, updated, expanded and presented in conventional paperback format.

His guide, says Voss, 'is about the rest of France'. More precisely, it is 'a region-by-region guide to Appellation Contrôlée (AC) wines and Vins Délimités de Qualité Supérieure (VDQS), and the people who produce them, in all the wine-growing regions of France, apart from Bordeaux, Burgundy and Champagne (which are dealt with in companion volumes).'

Here, then, is a fundamental difference between *French Country Wines* and this guide. Like Roger Voss, Rosemary George excludes Bordeaux, Burgundy and Champagne, but thereafter her book is exclusively about 'unknown', or less-well-known wines. Voss on the other hand, to take one example, while including Domaine de Galoupet, arguably an 'unknown' though well-respected producer in the Côtes de Provence, also includes Guigal in the Côte Rôtie appellation of the northern Rhône, one of the biggest wine names in the business. The larger part of the text consists of descriptions and brief assessments of individual wine-makers and their wines. Addresses of wine-makers are given, together in each case with advice as to whether visits require appointments or not. The enterprising reader ought to have no difficulty in obtaining telephone numbers from directory enquiries.

# FRENCH WINES BY REGION

### Alsace

Pamela Vandyke Price with Christopher Fielden, *Alsace Wines and Spirits*, Sotheby's Publications 1984, reprinted with additions 1986; £16.95
A comprehensive, down-to-earth account by the doyenne of wine writers of a subject which has had far less attention in print than it deserves.

### Champagne

Patrick Forbes, *Champagne: the wine, the land and the people*, Victor Gollancz 1967; £15.00
For many years the late Patrick Forbes's monumental work was the definitive treatment of the subject, and in all essentials it remains so. The author was a well-known member of the champagne trade for most of his working life, knew his subject intimately, loved it and covers every aspect of it, including appraising, choosing, buying, serving and drinking champagne.

Serena Sutcliffe, *A Celebration of Champagne*, Mitchell Beazley 1988; £20.00
Serena Sutcliffe says that throughout her life champagne has been 'a constant companion and permanent delight'. The result is that she writes of it with evident enthusiasm allied to genuinely expert knowledge, the one making a powerful vehicle for conveying the other to the reader.

The reader could start at the first page knowing nothing whatever about champagne except that they liked it, and arrive at the last educated enough in the entire champagne story to engage in lively discussions as to the 'styles' of all the well-known brands of champagne and the merits or otherwise of several lifetimes of vintages. Anyone tempted to answer the question 'What's your favourite champagne?' with a single name, or even, more circumspectly, with two or three names, might do well to pay particular attention to the sections on the great champagne houses and vintages past and present. An

expert's favourite for the 1982 vintage might have been, say, Krug; for the 1984 vintage it might be Bollinger; for 1986 (a 'difficult' year in Champagne) perhaps Ayala or Billecart-Salmon, or one of half a dozen other thoroughly good 'house' names. In other words, the true expert will not answer the question without a great deal of qualification, if at all.

The book is thus a celebration and a treasury. More than anything else, perhaps, it is the availability of works such as this which has persuaded me that to attempt anything but the briefest of wine notes in *Walking in Wine Country* would be little short of ridiculous. 'Above all,' says Serena Sutcliffe, 'I have wanted to describe the *tastes* of champagne and how they are achieved.' She has succeeded brilliantly.

### Burgundy

Simon Loftus, *Puligny-Montrachet*, Ebury Press 1992; £19.99
Simon Loftus, say his publishers, 'is a wine merchant, hotelier, restaurateur and writer'. Passionately fond of the wines of Montrachet and the village that is the subject of his monograph, he has provided us with an intimate, entertaining study of both, in the course of which he imparts a wealth of knowledge concerning the making of all Burgundy wines. More than that, he gives wine-lovers an insight into viticultural Burgundy in general, and into life on the Côte d'Or in particular, which can hardly fail to inform and greatly enhance their own experience of the region and the delectable best of its products.

Robert Parker, *Burgundy*, Dorling Kindersley 1991; £25.00
True to the Parker style, a remarkably searching, detailed study of individual producers and their wines, vintage by vintage, intended very much for the serious consumer.

Serena Sutcliffe, *Guide to the Wines of Burgundy*, revised and updated with Michael Schuster, Mitchell Beazley 1993; £7.99
The original pocket guide, revised, updated, expanded and presented in conventional paperback format. My copy of the original guide is the worse for wear, for it has accompanied me on numerous journeys in Burgundy. Serena Sutcliffe is not only a Master of Wine, but is also in the wine business. 'Her day-to-day dealings with Burgundy and Burgundians give her an up-to-date insight such as none before her has tried to pack into the convenient compass of a pocket book,' says Hugh Johnson in an introduction. The wines of Burgundy constitute a formidable subject, yet in terms of what the vast majority of wine-lovers would be likely to want to know about Chablis, the Côte d'Or, the Côte Chalonnaise, the Mâconnais and Beaujolais it is hard to find an aspect of the subject that is not adequately covered in the work.

Not least of the virtues of Serena Sutcliffe's work is her 'personal selection' of producers for each appellation. Time passes, circumstances alter, and all such 'selections' ought to be regarded with circumspection; but her readers may feel that if they cannot put a good deal of trust in Serena Sutcliffe's choice they cannot trust any.

### Bordeaux

Edmund Penning-Rowsell, *The Wines of Bordeaux*, first published 1969, Penguin, sixth edition 1989; £17.99
The classic, definitive work by one of the most respected authorities on the subject.

David Peppercorn, *Guide to the Wines of Bordeaux*, Mitchell Beazley 1992; £7.99

The original pocket guide revised, updated, expanded and presented in conventional paperback format. Like its companion on the wines of Burgundy, it is a triumphant example of *multum in parvo*. Not only is it concentrated information, it is also information of a very high order. The author, says Hugh Johnson in his introduction, 'is one of the most perceptive and respected of that ancient aristocracy of Anglo-Saxon merchants whose speciality is the wine of Bordeaux'. He combines two essential elements: 'a background of experience and a fund of knowledge constantly kept up to date'.

Geography, historical background, technical progress and innovation, the appellations, grape varieties, the château system and classifications, *négociants*, the work of the vineyards, the making of wine, vintages: all these and more are dealt with. Very useful indeed are the 'A to Z of châteaux' and 'Château profiles' for all the major appellations (Médoc, Graves, Sauternes and Barsac, St Emilion and the St Emilion satellites, Pomerol and Lalande-de-Pomerol), plus the minor ones such as Côtes de Blaye and Premières Côtes de Bordeaux.

For anyone not already expert in the matter who would like to find his or her way, figuratively or literally, round the far-from-simple subject of the wines of the Bordeaux region, this seems to me an indispensable accessory to reading or travels.

### The Rhône and Provence

John Livingstone Learmonth and Melvyn C. H. Master, *The Wines of the Rhône*, Faber and Faber, first published 1978, third revised edition 1992; £6.95

*The Wines of the Rhône* has been acclaimed as the most detailed and intimate account of any wine region ever published in the English language. The Côte Rôtie, for example, is given 50 pages; Hermitage 66; Gigondas 34; Châteauneuf-du-Pape 168; and Côtes du Rhône and Côtes du Rhône-Villages 102. Such thoroughness could be tedious, but as it is the author's expertise sits so comfortably with him and is conveyed so readably that it never tires the reader. For the reader of *Walking in Wine Country*, a feature likely to be of special interest is the detail devoted to the properties, methods, wines, opinions and personalities of so many individual wine-makers. Given the appropriate appointments and the information that *The Wines of the Rhône* provides, would-be visitors would be as well prepared to profit from their explorations as they could reasonably ever hope to be.

Robert M. Parker Jnr, *The Wines of the Rhône Valley and Provence*, Simon and Schuster, 1987; Dorling Kindersley, 1988; £14.95
Robert M. Parker is an American who has come comparatively lately to international prominence in the field of wine criticism and who exercises enormous influence, not least commercially. By virtue of his reputation for integrity, industry and expertise as a wine taster he also commands wide professional respect.

The American publishers of *The Wines of the Rhône Valley and Provence* are justified in claiming that it 'presents consumer-oriented, independent reviews and commentaries of the wines' of the two regions, with the growers in each appellation 'listed and ranked according to the overall quality of their wines'. It also offers 'extensive vintage charts assessing the quality of the different appellations' and 'recommendations for visiting the Rhône Valley and Provence, including notes on the best hotels and restaurants, and those vineyards most worth a call'.

In spite of a maddeningly inadequate index, his book seems to me required reading for anyone who is concerned more than casually with buying wines from the regions concerned, and

very useful indeed for anyone wishing to visit the wine-makers. Parker's hotel and restaurant recommendations seem to be very largely what travellers might well arrive at for themselves by way of a perusal of the Michelin *Red Guide* for France, with additional help from the Guide Relais et Châteaux; all the same, it is very convenient to have them assembled in this context and on the whole they survive the test of time.

### Languedoc

Liz Berry, *The Wines of Languedoc-Roussillon*, Ebury Press 1992; £19.99
Liz Berry is a Master of Wine and is in the wine business. Languedoc-Roussillon, she says, 'is not a region that calls for much detailed discussion of rare old vintages around the dinner table, nor a region that will delight the classic wine snob'. There are, however, 'perhaps more discoveries to be made here than in the great wine regions of France'.

As far as I know, this is the first study of these wines to appear as an original work in English. This, combined with the fact that the author is herself in the wine trade, seems to me to have tempted her to write as much for her professional peers as for a far wider, amateur readership, with the result that the book contains a great deal of information which few except members of the wine trade will be likely to find enthralling. But a detailed account of the wines of Languedoc-Roussillon emerges, and the keen amateur who is interested in 'the California of France' cannot fail to profit from Liz Berry's considerable researches and experience 'in the field'. This included finding the incomparably delightful restaurant Le Mimosa at St Guiraud in the Hérault, a discovery which has inspired a two-page description in the book, but not a line too much.

# WINE–TASTING

Michael Broadbent, *Pocket Guide to Wine Tasting*, Mitchell Beazley, new edition 1988; £5.99
If breadth and length of experience are taken into account along with sensitivity of palate and all the other attributes required of a capable practitioner in the business, Michael Broadbent – Master of Wine, head of Christie's wine department – is probably the most expert wine taster in the world. Added to this, he has an engaging style of writing, with simplicity and clarity. And last – though in writing and talking about wine it is an especially valuable characteristic – he despises humbug.

The information and advice it contains go far beyond mere technicalities. For example, one of the difficulties facing the wine lover, says Broadbent, is finding out what a wine ought to taste like, and few of the otherwise excellent books on wine actually help with this. 'Nevertheless, if you read widely, an impression of the characteristics of the wines of various areas and districts will eventually be conveyed. A combination of reading, and visits (with tastings, of course) to wine areas is the best way of learning the salient characteristics.'

He has a gift for stating truths simply, for example: 'Quality is always relative. Even the best Yugoslav Riesling will be on a lower quality plane than a good classic Rheingau; the best sparkling Loire wine rates lower than a good *grande marque* champagne; and the best unblended beaujolais is below the peak of a *grand cru* Côte de Nuits.' That strikes me as a truth with implications much beyond its application to the techniques of wine-tasting.

Finally, here is Michael Broadbent on the subject of the wine snob: 'If there is such a thing as a wine snob, he or she will have all the attributes of any other sort of snob: affectation and pretentiousness covering up the lack of everything that makes a person worthy of serious attention. . . . Those who are knowledgeable about wine should merely be careful on what occasion and in whose company they air their opinions and display their scholarship.'

## OTHER SOURCES

The Travel Bookshop, 13 Blenheim Crescent, London W11 2EE, tel. 071-229 5260, has a large collection of titles about France, both new and second-hand. Nearest Underground stations are Ladbroke Grove on the Metropolitan line, or Notting Hill Gate on the Central line.

*Decanter* magazine, published monthly, price £2.40, is the leading wine magazine in Britain and always contains substantial features about French wines. An annual subscription costs £33 from Decanter Subscriptions, Stephenson House, Brunel Centre, Bletchley, Milton Keynes MK2 2EW.

*France* magazine. An admirable quarterly glossy devoted to France and things French, including regular features on wine and wine country. From good newsagents, £3.00. Annual subscription UK £14.00. Freepost, Stow-on-the-Wold, Glos GL54 1BN. Tel. (0451) 870871

The Guildhall Library, at the Guildhall, City of London, EC2P 2EJ, has one of the best collections of publications about wine in the country; perhaps the best. It is open to the public from 9.30 am to 5 pm, Monday to Saturday inclusive.

# TRAVEL INFORMATION

## AIR

Destinations most convenient for the wine regions and served direct from the UK are as follows:

ALSACE – Strasbourg or Basle/Mulhouse. British Airways from London, Heathrow.

CHAMPAGNE – Paris, Charles de Gaulle: BA from London, Heathrow; London, City; London, Gatwick; Bristol; Birmingham; Manchester; Glasgow; Edinburgh. Air France from London, Heathrow.

BURGUNDY – Chablis: Paris, as above, or Dijon by Air Proteus from Stanstead. Côte d'Or: Lyon, BA and AF from London, Heathrow. Or Dijon, as above.

LOIRE – Paris, by BA and AF, as above; or Nantes by Air France from London. Or Tours, or Poitiers by TAT from Gatwick, June–September.

BORDEAUX – Bordeaux: BA and AF from London, Gatwick. Or Toulouse: BA from Heathrow or Gatwick; AF from Heathrow.

SAVOY – Geneva: BA from London, Heathrow. Or Lyon, as above.

RHÔNE – Lyon, as above. Or Marseille: BA and AF from London, Heathrow. Or Montpellier: BA from London, Gatwick.

PROVENCE – Marseille: BA and AF, as above. Or Nice: BA and AF from London, Heathrow; BA from London, Gatwick, and from Birmingham and Manchester. Or Montpellier: BA from Gatwick.

LANGUEDOC – Toulouse or Montpellier, as above. Or Perpignan: BA from London, Gatwick.

### Information and enquiries

#### British Airways

| Reservations, fares and advance travel information: | |
| --- | --- |
| Calls within the Greater London area | 081 897 4000 |
| Club class Europe | 0345 222747 |
| Rest of UK & Eire | 0345 222111 |

#### Air France

| Reservations, fares | 081 742 6600 |
| --- | --- |
| Air Proteus, handled by Air France | |

## RAIL

### Mainline destinations

| Alsace | Colmar, Strasbourg |
| --- | --- |
| Champagne | Epernay, Reims |
| Chablis | Auxerre |
| Côte d'Or | Dijon, Beaune |
| Chalonnais | Chalon-sur-Saône, Tournus |
| Mâconnais | Macon, Tournus |
| Beaujolais | Macon, Villefranche, Lyon |
| Sancerre | Bourges, Nevers |
| Saumur-Touraine | Blois, Tours, Saumur |
| Muscadet | Nantes |
| Médoc | Bordeaux |
| St Emilion | Libourne |
| Entre-Deux-Mers | Bordeaux, Langon, Marmande |
| Savoy | Chambéry |
| S. Rhone | Orange, Avignon |
| Provence | Aix-en-Provence, Marseille, Toulon, Nice |
| Minervois | Béziers, Narbonne, Carcassonne |
| Corbières | Narbonne, Carcassonne, Perpignan |

The above are no more than the most obvious and best-served destinations likely to be most convenient for the various wine areas featured in this book. About half of them are served by TGV (Trains de Grande Vitesse). Many regional bus services are operated in conjunction with French Rail (SNCF). As well as ordinary passenger services, including sleeper and couchette facilities to most of the places named, French Rail offers various Motorail services. From Calais, for example, Bordeaux, Biarritz, Brive, Toulouse, Narbonne, Avignon, St Raphäel and Nice are all served. There are other Motorail services from Dieppe, Lille and Paris.

There is a variety of very attractive special fares and rail passes, including 'senior citizens' and under-26 discounts. Certain special packages include accommodation as well as rail travel. Car and bicycle hire can be arranged; so can cross-Channel ferry bookings. Additionally, the two national carriers, French Rail and Air France offer an advantageously priced combined air-rail ticket enabling the traveller to fly from one of a number of airports in Britain to any SNCF station in France.

With the arrival of the 1990s, French Rail has made very significant advances in customer services. A telephone sales service in London is linked directly to the SNCF main computer in France, so that information can be given and bookings made with impressive speed and efficiency.

The SNCF 'Rail Shop' is at 179 Piccadilly, London W1V oBA (close to the French Government Tourist Office) and is open Monday to Friday 8.30 am to 6.30 pm, and on Saturday from 10.00 am to 4.00 pm. Telephone: information only 0891-515 477; bookings 071-495 4433.

# CROSS-CHANNEL FERRIES

### Brittany Ferries

| | | Crossing Times |
|---|---|---|
| Wharf Road | Portsmouth – Caen | 6 hours |
| Portsmouth PO2 8RW | Portsmouth – St Malo | 9 hours |
| Tel. 0705 827702 | | |
| | Plymouth – Roscoff | 6 hours |
| Millbay Docks | Poole – Cherbourg | 4 hrs 30 mins |
| Plymouth PL1 3EW | | |
| Tel. 0752 221321 | | |

### Hoverspeed

| | | |
|---|---|---|
| Eastern Docks | Dover – Calais | 35 mins |
| Dover CT17 9TG | Dover – Boulogne | 35 mins |
| Tel. 0304 240241 | | |

### P&O European Ferries

| | | |
|---|---|---|
| Channel House | Dover – Calais | 1 hr 15 mins |
| Channel View Road | Portsmouth – Le Havre | 5 hrs 45 mins |
| Dover CT16 3BR | | |
| Tel. 0304 203388 | Portsmouth – Cherbourg | 4 hrs 45 mins |

### Sally Line

| | | |
|---|---|---|
| 81 Piccadilly | Ramsgate – Dunkirk | 2 hrs 30 mins |
| London W1V 9HF | | |
| Tel. 071-409 2240 | | |

### Sealink Stena Line

| | | |
|---|---|---|
| Charter House | Dover – Calais | 1 hr 30 mins |
| Park Street | S/hampton – Cherbourg | 5 hours |
| Ashford TN24 8EX | | |
| Tel. 0233 647047 | Newhaven – Dieppe | 4 hours |